McGraw-Hill's

SPANISH

–*for*–

EDUCATORS

McGraw-Hill's
SPANISH
-for-
EDUCATORS

José M. Díaz and María F. Nadel

New York Chicago San Francisco Lisbon London Madrid Mexico City
Milan New Delhi San Juan Seoul Singapore Sydney Toronto

Library of Congress Cataloging-in-Publication Data

Díaz, José M.
    McGraw-Hill's Spanish for educators / José M. Díaz, María F. Nadel.
      p.   cm.
    ISBN 0-07-146490-5
    1. Spanish language—Conversation and phrase books (for school employees)   I. Title:
Spanish for educators.   II. Nadel, María F.   III. Title.

    PC4120.S34D53   2006
    468.3'421024371201—dc22   2006044421

     5 6 7 8 9 10 11 12 13 14 15 16 17 18 19 20 21 22 23   FGR/FGR   0 9   (0-07-146490-5)
3 4 5 6 7 8 9 10 11 12 13 14 15 16 17 18 19 20 21 22 23   FGR/FGR   0 9 8 (0-07-148842-1)

ISBN 978-0-07-146490-1 (book alone)
MHID   0-07-146490-5 (book alone)

ISBN 978-0-07-146491-8 (book and CD set)
MHID   0-07-146491-3 (book and CD set)

ISBN 978-0-07-148842-6 (book for set)
MHID   0-07-148842-1 (book for set)

McGraw-Hill books are available at special quantity discounts to use as premiums and sales promotions
or for use in corporate training programs. To contact a representative, please visit the Contact Us pages
at www.mhprofessional.com.

This book is printed on acid-free paper.

To Mark Nadel and Sonya Mosco

Contents

1 Information Parents Need to Enroll Their Children in School 31

2 The School Building 65

3 The Primary Grades 95

5 Success in School: Enlisting Parental Support 187

6 Health, Medical Problems, and Emergencies 225

7 In the Counselor's Office 249

Preface

McGraw-Hill's *Spanish for Educators* is a comprehensive, easy-to-follow book that offers the essential tools for communicating with Spanish-speaking students, parents, and school personnel. The book focuses on the aspects of school life and education about which you will most likely have to communicate with Spanish-speaking students and their parents.

Communicating in Spanish will help you establish a partnership with parents in the education of their children by demonstrating respect for and appreciation of their language and culture. It will also be a satisfying experience for you, and you can use this book as a point of departure for increasing your knowledge of the Spanish language. As your ability to understand and speak Spanish improves, you can use your knowledge to help your students improve their knowledge of English.

McGraw-Hill's *Spanish for Educators* uses standard Spanish that can be understood by any native speaker of the language. It would be impossible to cover all the regionalisms found in Spanish-speaking countries and in the United States, but once you become familiar with the vocabulary that appears in this book, you will be able to learn more from the Spanish speakers you encounter.

The book begins with an introduction to Spanish pronunciation, greetings, and grammar. Each of the seven chapters that follow includes lists of useful vocabulary and sample sentences that you will be able to start using immediately, plus relevant grammatical explanations and practice exercises.

How to Use This Book

McGraw-Hill's *Spanish for Educators* emphasizes two main skills: listening and speaking. Although you can set to work on Chapter 1 with very little (or no) preparation, we suggest that you begin by reading the Introduction, which covers basic guidelines for Spanish pronunciation, important "grammar basics," and vocabulary and expressions essential to social interchange.

Beyond the Introduction, you can choose any topic or chapter that interests you or that is pertinent to your school situation, or you can begin with Chapter 1 and proceed through the rest of the book.

How you use this book depends on your particular situation. Are you an administrator? A counselor? A teacher? What grades do you teach? Do many students in your school work after school? Go to college? Have special needs? The answer to these and other questions—that is to say, your needs at any given time—will determine where you begin and which chapters you concentrate on.

Throughout the book, we have incorporated cultural notes, which will help you to understand salient differences between the educational system in the United States and that in many Spanish-speaking countries.

Vocabulary

Building a large storehouse of words is important for spoken language. *McGraw-Hill's Spanish for Educators* is full of everyday words, phrases, and expressions that are useful in a school environment, and it provides an opportunity to learn words and sentences without worrying about grammar. Each chapter includes lists of useful vocabulary related to the theme of the chapter. We have used the most generic words and expressions wherever possible, since it would be impossible to include all words and expressions found in the Spanish-speaking world. Generally, we have chosen the word that is most commonly used in America. As you read through a section, it is not necessary to learn all the words presented there, but obviously the more you commit to memory, the more confident and fluent your Spanish will be. The following tips will be very helpful.

- Use the knowledge that you already have. For example, take advantage of the fact that English and Spanish share many cognates.
- Create your own personalized vocabulary by listing the words you find most useful and practicing them aloud regularly. Keep separate lists for nouns, adjectives, and verbs, and even sublists such as the following.
  - Nouns—feminine/masculine
  - Verbs—ending in **-ar**, **-er**, or **-ir**, regular verbs, irregular verbs, stem-changing verbs

  Creating such lists will not only help you to remember the words, it will help you to use them.
- Do the practice exercises carefully, check your answers, and learn the vocabulary used in them. The vocabulary practiced in the exercises was chosen for its usefulness in communicating in a school setting.
- Practice with and learn from the Spanish speakers you encounter. They can expand your knowledge and are a great source of regionalisms from their country of origin. Take advantage of their expertise.

Chapter 4 provides an extensive list of school subjects that a typical student encounters, as well as useful vocabulary in each subject area.

The English-Spanish Glossary focuses on the Spanish used in school and school-related activities. Use it for quick reference to answer the question "How do you say that in Spanish?" (**¿Cómo se dice en español?** [KOH-moh seh DEE-seh ehn ehs-pah-NYOHL]).

Grammar

While the Introduction covers what we consider "grammar basics," other grammar points are gradually introduced as needed in the chapters. When using the grammar sections, be sure to carefully read the examples, which not only illustrate the grammar point but also show you the differences between English and Spanish, differences that don't allow word-for-word translation of sentences. Essential grammar and vocabulary are repeated throughout the book and reinforced in the examples and practice exercises.

In the Appendix, rules for conjugating regular verbs are summarized, and several important stem-changing and irregular verbs are conjugated.

Even though essential grammar points are covered in these pages, *McGraw-Hill's Spanish for Educators* is not a grammar book. It is not necessary to become confident with all the topics discussed in any grammar section before proceeding to another section of the book. It is up to you how thoroughly you want to explore a given topic; you may want to consider using a basic Spanish grammar book to supplement your knowledge.

Pronunciation

The Introduction begins with basic guidelines for Spanish pronunciation. In addition to knowing the sounds of the letters, authentic pronunciation requires some knowledge of stress—the loudness of a syllable. To make communication easier, *McGraw-Hill's Spanish for Educators* incorporates the phonetic pronunciation of every word and phrase used in it, with the stressed syllable in CAPITAL letters.

Remember that your best source for pronunciation is the Spanish speaker with whom you are communicating. Don't hesitate to ask him or her to pronounce any word or phrase in this book. Spanish speakers are always willing to help those who try to communicate with them in Spanish. Listen to and imitate the sounds they make.

It also helps to listen to spoken Spanish every chance you get. Spanish TV newscasters are excellent models. You may want to tape sections of a program (sports, weather, or soap operas) and listen to the tape over and over. Initially, you may understand only a few words, but don't give up. Limit the time you spend listening at first, then—as you get more comfortable—increase the length of the session. You can also tape-record your own speech, then listen to the tape as a way to check your pronunciation.

In conclusion, the only way to learn a language is to use it. Take every opportunity you are given to practice, practice, and practice some more. If you wait until you can say something perfectly, you will never speak Spanish. Take chances! You will not only learn to communicate in Spanish—you will establish new relationships, cement old ones, and learn more about the world around you, here in the United States and in the Spanish-speaking world.

Introduction to Spanish Pronunciation, Greetings, and Grammar

Spanish Pronunciation

You will find that Spanish pronunciation is much more uniform than the pronunciation of English. With very few exceptions, Spanish consonants and vowels have one sound and one length. Learning the correct pronunciation of each letter in Spanish will help you to form syllables and, in turn, to form words. If you are not sure of the correct pronunciation, be sure to use body language when you are speaking. This will help you get the message across.

Some basic pronunciation guidelines follow to help you get started.

- Spanish vowel sounds are clipped and short. To help you mimic authentic pronunciation, we have added "h" (not pronounced) after the vowels *a, e,* and *o* ("ah," "eh," "oh"). The vowels *i* and *u* are represented by "ee" and "oo" in the pronunciation.
- Spanish consonants are not pronounced as strongly as English consonants and are never followed by the "h" sound that often follows English consonants.
- Each Spanish word of more than one syllable has a syllable that is stressed. The stressed syllable appears in CAPITALS in the pronunciation.
- Spanish *b* and *v* are both pronounced like a weak English "b."
- Spanish *c* (before *a, o,* or *u*) and *qu* (before *e* or *i*) are pronounced like English "k."
- Spanish *c* (before *e* or *i*) and *z* (in all positions) are pronounced like English "s."
- Spanish *ch* is pronounced like the "ch" in "church."
- Spanish *g* (before *e* or *i*) and *j* (in all positions) are pronounced like a very strong English "h."
- When Spanish *h* appears at the beginning of a syllable, it is silent.
- Spanish *ll* is pronounced like the "y" in "yes."
- Spanish *ñ* is pronounced like the "ny" in "canyon."
- Spanish *rr* and *r* (at the beginning of a word or after l, *n,* or *s*) are strongly trilled.

In this book, Spanish words, expressions, and sentences in text are followed by their pronunciation in square brackets, as shown here: **yo** [yoh].

Greetings, Introductions, and Leave-Taking Expressions

As you begin to learn Spanish, there are some expressions that are key to greeting, introducing yourself, and getting to know the Spanish-speaking parents, students, and support staff in your school.

While you are studying these expressions, note that Spanish has both a formal and an informal way to address a person. If you are talking to someone older, someone you are meeting for the first time, or someone in a position of leadership, you should use **usted (Ud.)** [OOS-TEHD]. After knowing the person for a while, or after they ask you to address them informally, you may use the **tú** [too] form. Keep in mind that in some Spanish-speaking countries, parents and children use **usted** [OOS-TEHD] to address each other. In some countries, parents use the **usted** [OOS-TEHD] form to make a statement more forceful. When you address a student, you will normally use the **tú** [too] form, but at times—such as to emphasize the serious nature of what you are saying—you may use the **usted** [OOS-TEHD] form when addressing him/her.

Practice the following expressions by saying them aloud.

Good morning.	**Buenos días.**
	BWEH-nohs DEE-ahs
Good afternoon.	**Buenas tardes.**
	BWEH-nahs TAHR-dehs
Good evening. / Good night.	**Buenas noches.**
	BWEH-nahs NOH-chehs
Hi. / Hello.	**Hola.**
	OH-lah

If you want to introduce yourself, there are a couple of ways to do this in Spanish.

My name is _____.	**Me llamo _____.**
	meh YAH-moh
I am Mr. _____.	**Soy el señor _____.**
	SOH-ee ehl seh-NYOHR
I am Mrs. _____.	**Soy la señora _____.**
	SOH-ee lah seh-NYOH-rah
I am Miss/Ms. _____.	**Soy la señorita _____.**
	SOH-ee lah seh-nyoh-REE-tah
I am the (English) teacher. (*male*)	**Soy el maestro de (inglés).**
	SOH-ee ehl mah-EHS-troh deh (een-GLEHS)
I am the (Spanish) teacher. (*female*)	**Soy la maestra de (español).**
	SOH-ee lah mah-EHS-trah deh (ehs-pah-NYOHL)

If you want to introduce someone in Spanish, you may use the following pattern.

This is (Pablo). (*male*)	**Este es (Pablo).** EHS-teh ehs (PAH-bloh)
This is (Ana). (*female*)	**Esta es (Ana).** EHS-tah ehs (AH-nah)
May I introduce (Pepe).	**Quisiera presentarle a (Pepe).** kee-SYEH-rah preh-sehn-TAHR-leh ah (PEH-peh) **Le presento a (Pepe).** leh preh-SEHN-toh ah (PEH-peh)

If you are the person being introduced, you may respond with any of the following expressions.

A pleasure.	**Mucho gusto.** MOO-choh GOOS-toh
The pleasure is mine.	**El gusto es mío.** ehl GOOS-toh ehs MEE-oh
It is a pleasure meeting you (*male*).	**Es un placer conocerlo.** ehs oon plah-SEHR koh-noh-SEHR-loh
It is a pleasure meeting you (*female*).	**Es un placer conocerla.** ehs oon plah-SEHR koh-noh-SEHR-lah

In Spanish, when you are talking *about* a teacher or other person with a title, you use the definite article (**el, la, los, las** [ehl, lah, lohs, lahs]) with the title, for example, **señor** [seh-NYOHR], **profesor** [proh-feh-SOHR], **doctor** [dohk-TOHR], followed by the person's last name.

Mr./Mrs. Pérez	**el señor / la señora Pérez** ehl seh-NYOHR / lah seh-NYOH-rah PEH-rehs
Doctor Wahl	**el doctor / la doctora Wahl** ehl dohk-TOHR / lah dohk-TOH-rah Wahl
Professor Smith	**el profesor / la profesora Smith** ehl proh-feh-SOHR / lah proh-feh-SOH-rah Smith
Mrs. Moore is the math teacher.	**La señora Moore es la maestra de matemáticas.** lah seh-NYOH-rah Moore ehs lah mah-EHS-trah deh mah-teh-MAH-tee-kahs

When you are addressing someone *directly*, do not use the definite article with the title.

Mr. Pérez, where is your daughter today?	**Señor Pérez, ¿dónde está su hija hoy?** seh-NYOHR PEH-rehs, DOHN-deh ehs-TAH soo EE-hah OH-ee

There are several ways to express "good-bye" in Spanish. Here are some of the most common ones.

Good-bye.	**Adiós.** ah-DYOHS
Have a nice day!	**¡Qué te vaya bien!** (*informal*) keh teh BAH-yah byehn
	¡Qué le vaya bien! (*formal*) keh leh BAH-yah byehn
See you (on) Monday.	**Hasta el lunes.** AHS-tah ehl LOO-nehs
See you (on) Tuesday.	**Hasta el martes.** AHS-tah ehl MAHR-tehs
See you (on) Wednesday.	**Hasta el miércoles.** AHS-tah ehl MYEHR-koh-lehs
See you (on) Thursday.	**Hasta el jueves.** AHS-tah ehl HWEH-behs
See you (on) Friday.	**Hasta el viernes.** AHS-tah ehl BYEHR-nehs
See you (on) Saturday.	**Hasta el sábado.** AHS-tah ehl SAH-bah-doh
See you (on) Sunday.	**Hasta el domingo.** AHS-tah ehl doh-MEEN-goh

As you can see, you can use **hasta** [AHS-tah], meaning "until," with a time expression to indicate when you will see that person. Here are a few other common expressions.

See you later.	**Hasta luego.** AHS-tah LWEH-goh
See you soon.	**Hasta pronto.** AHS-tah PROHN-toh
See you tomorrow.	**Hasta mañana.** AHS-tah mah-NYAH-nah

See you next week.	**Hasta la semana próxima.** AHS-tah lah seh-MAH-nah PROHK-see-mah
See you next month.	**Hasta el mes próximo.** AHS-tah ehl mehs PROHK-see-moh
See you next year.	**Hasta el año próximo.** AHS-tah ehl AH-nyoh PROHK-see-moh

To ask about someone's well-being, you may use the following questions.

How are you?	**¿Cómo estás tú?** KOH-moh ehs-TAHS too
	¿Cómo está usted? KOH-moh ehs-TAH OOS-TEHD
How is it going?	**¿Cómo te va?** KOH-moh teh bah

Here are some typical responses.

I am fine, thanks. And you?	**Estoy bien, gracias. ¿Y tú? /¿Y Ud.?** ehs-TOH-ee byehn, GRAH-syahs. ee too / ee OOS-TEHD
Very well.	**Muy bien.** MOO-ee byehn
So-so.	**Regular.** rreh-goo-LAHR
	Así, así. ah-SEE, ah-SEE

¿Qué tal? [keh tahl] is a more informal way to find out how someone is doing. It is perhaps equivalent to the English "What's up?" You may respond to it with the expressions you have already learned.

Many Spanish speakers use two last names. The first name is usually followed by the paternal last name, then by the maternal last name, for example, **Diego Orozco Velásquez** [DYEH-goh oh-ROHS-koh beh-LAHS-kehs]. Some women take their husband's last name, but retain their maiden name. In this case they use **de** [deh] before the husband's last name, for example, **Ana Loyola de Rivero** [AH-nah loh-YOH-lah deh rree-BEH-roh]. This custom is beginning to disappear, but it is still common.

Practice I-1

Write in Spanish what you would say in each of the following situations.

1. You have just met the parents of one of your students, and you want them to meet your student teacher. Introduce him/her.

   _____

2. You have met the mother of one of your students. During Parents' Night you are introduced to the father. What do you say?

   _____

3. At the end of Parents' Night, you want to say good-bye to the parents. What do you say?

   _____

4. Introduce yourself to the mother of one of your students.

   _____

5. It is Friday, and one of your students is leaving the classroom. Tell him/her that you will see him/her on Monday.

   _____

6. You have made an appointment with the parents of one of your students. They are supposed to come back next week. Tell them that you will see them then.

   _____

7. Find out how one of your students is doing.

   _____

8. You are not feeling well and one of your students asks you how you are. How do you respond?

   _____

9. While walking down the hall, one of your students says **"¿Qué tal?"** to you. How do you respond?

   _____

10. Tell one of your students to have a nice day.

    _____

Grammar Basics

Subject Pronouns

When you hear Spanish being spoken, you will be able to know about whom the person is speaking if you pay attention to the ending of the Spanish verb. You will find that Spanish speakers often leave out the subject pronouns. If you are a beginner, however, you should use the subject pronouns until you become familiar with the different endings. Then if by any chance you make a mistake on a particular verb ending, the listener will know about whom you are talking.

The subject pronouns are as follows.

I	**yo**	yoh
you (*informal*)	**tú**	too
he	**él**	ehl
she	**ella**	EH-yah
you (*formal*)	**usted (Ud.)**	OOS-TEHD
we	**nosotros**	noh-SOH-trohs
we (*all females*)	**nosotras**	noh-SOH-trahs
they	**ellos**	EH-yohs
they (*all females*)	**ellas**	EH-yahs
you (*plural*)	**ustedes (Uds.)**	OOS-TEH-dehs

In this book we will be using both the **tú** [too] and the **usted (Ud.)** [OOS-TEHD] forms, depending on whom you are addressing. When you are talking to more than one person, use the formal **ustedes (Uds.)** [OOS-TEH-dehs] form. The plural familiar form (**vosotros/vosotras** [boh-SOH-trohs/boh-SOH-trahs]), is not included here because it is rarely used in Latin America.

Verbs

Information about the conjugation of present tense verbs is included here to provide familiarity with basic verb forms as you begin your study, as is a short explanation of command forms. Discussion of the different categories of irregular verbs appears throughout the text, with the conjugations of the most common irregular verbs—identified as (*irreg.*) in verb lists—included in the Appendix.

Present Tense

Meanings and Uses of the Present Tense   The present tense in Spanish can have more than one translation in English.

ENGLISH MEANINGS	SPANISH
I walk very little.	
I am walking very little.	**Yo camino muy poco.**
I do walk very little.	yoh kah-MEE-noh MOO-ee POH-koh

It can also be used in the following ways.

- To ask for instructions

  Shall I buy the book?   **¿Compro el libro?**
                               KOHM-proh ehl LEE-broh

- To refer to what will happen in the near future

  I'll go out tomorrow.   **Salgo mañana.**
                               SAHL-goh mah-NYAH-nah

  I'm running tomorrow.   **Corro mañana.**
                               KOH-rroh mah-NYAH-nah

In the set of examples above, the word "tomorrow" (**mañana** [mah-NYAH-nah]) makes it clear that the verb expresses a future action. In Chapter 5, pages 197–198, you will find a list of words and expressions that are useful when talking about the future.

When talking about what you do, are doing, or will do in the near future, use the present tense.

We arrive at school early.	**Nosotros llegamos a la escuela temprano.**
	noh-SOH-trohs yeh-GAH-mohs ah lah ehs-KWEH-lah tehm-PRAH-noh
I am reading a novel.	**Yo leo una novela.**
	yoh LEH-oh OO-nah noh-BEH-lah
She will erase the chalkboard later.	**Ella borra la pizarra más tarde.**
	EH-yah BOH-rrah lah pee-SAH-rrah mahs TAHR-deh

Regular Verbs English infinitives include the word "to" with the verb. Spanish infinitives have one of three endings: **-ar**, **-er**, or **-ir**. To form the present tense of a regular Spanish verb, drop the infinitive ending (**-ar**, **-er**, **-ir**) and add the following endings to the verb's stem (the part that remains when you remove the infinitive ending).

- Verbs ending in **-ar**

PRONOUN	VERB ENDING
yo	-o
tú	-as
él	-a
ella	-a
Ud.	-a
nosotros	-amos
nosotras	-amos
ellos	-an
ellas	-an
Uds.	-an

estudiar [ehs-too-DYAHR] to study

I study	**yo estudio**	yoh ehs-TOO-dyoh
you study	**tú estudias**	too ehs-TOO-dyahs
he studies	**él estudia**	ehl ehs-TOO-dyah
she studies	**ella estudia**	EH-yah ehs-TOO-dyah
you study	**Ud. estudia**	oos-TEHD ehs-TOO-dyah
we study	**nosotros estudiamos**	noh-SOH-trohs ehs-too-DYAH-mohs
we study	**nosotras estudiamos**	noh-SOH-trahs ehs-too-DYAH-mohs
they study	**ellos estudian**	EH-yohs ehs-TOO-dyahn
they study	**ellas estudian**	EH-yahs ehs-TOO-dyahn
you (*plural*) study	**Uds. estudian**	oos-TEH-dehs ehs-TOO-dyahn

- Verbs ending in **-er**

PRONOUN	VERB ENDING
yo	-o
tú	-es
él	-e
ella	-e
Ud.	-e
nosotros	-emos
nosotras	-emos
ellos	-en
ellas	-en
Uds.	-en

correr [koh-RREHR] to run

I run	**yo corro**	yoh KOH-rroh
you run	**tú corres**	too KOH-rrehs
he runs	**él corre**	ehl KOH-rreh
she runs	**ella corre**	EH-yah KOH-rreh
you run	**Ud. corre**	oos-TEHD KOH-rreh
we run	**nosotros corremos**	noh-SOH-trohs koh-RREH-mohs
we run	**nosotras corremos**	noh-SOH-trahs koh-RREH-mohs
they run	**ellos corren**	EH-yohs KOH-rrehn
they run	**ellas corren**	EH-yahs KOH-rrehn
you (*plural*) run	**Uds. corren**	oos-TEH-dehs KOH-rrehn

- Verbs ending in **-ir**

PRONOUN	VERB ENDING
yo	**-o**
tú	**-es**
él	**-e**
ella	**-e**
Ud.	**-e**
nosotros	**-imos**
nosotras	**-imos**
ellos	**-en**
ellas	**-en**
Uds.	**-en**

escribir [ehs-kree-BEER] to write

I write	**yo escribo**	yoh ehs-KREE-boh
you write	**tú escribes**	too ehs-KREE-behs
he writes	**él escribe**	ehl ehs-KREE-beh
she writes	**ella escribe**	EH-yah ehs-KREE-beh
you write	**Ud. escribe**	oos-TEHD ehs-KREE-beh
we write	**nosotros escribimos**	noh-SOH-trohs ehs-kree-BEE-mohs
we write	**nosotras escribimos**	noh-SOH-trahs ehs-kree-BEE-mohs
they write	**ellos escriben**	EH-yohs ehs-KREE-behn
they write	**ellas escriben**	EH-yahs ehs-KREE-behn
you (*plural*) write	**Uds. escriben**	oos-TEH-dehs ehs-KREE-behn

Practice I-2

A *Determine all possible subjects of each verb below and write them in Spanish on the lines provided. There may be more than one answer for some items.*

1. estudiamos   _____

2. corre   _____

3. escriben _____

4. estudias   _____

5. escribo   _____

6. corren   _____

B *Conjugate each of the following regular verbs according to the subject given. These verbs may be new to you, so you will need to pay attention to the verb endings.*

1. comprender

    ellos _____

    yo _____

    nosotros _____

2. recibir

    tú _____

    Uds. _____

    ella _____

3. terminar

    yo _____

    Ud. _____

    nosotras _____

C *Translate the conjugated verbs from Exercise B.*

1. _____

    _____

    _____

2. _____

    _____

    _____

3. _____

_____

_____

D *Write all of the possible translations for the following sentences.*

1. Escribo una novela.

_____

2. ¿Estudias muy poco?

_____

3. Corremos en el parque mañana.

_____

Verbs with Special Changes   In this section you will learn about changes that need to be made to the stem of some verbs in order to conjugate them in the present tense. In the present tense, changes to the stem of these verbs occur in all persons except the **nosotros** [noh-SOH-trohs] and **nosotras** [noh-SOH-trahs] form. The three patterns of stem changes are shown below.

- e > ie
- o > ue
- e > i

In this book, the infinitive form in vocabulary lists will be followed by **(ie)**, **(ue)**, or **(i)** to indicate which stem change is needed, as shown here.

to close	**cerrar (ie)**	seh-RRAHR
to sleep	**dormir (ue)**	dohr-MEER
to serve	**servir (i)**	sehr-BEER

cerrar (ie) [seh-RRAHR] to close

I close	**yo cierro**	yoh SYEH-rroh
you close	**tú cierras**	too SYEH-rrahs
he closes	**él cierra**	ehl SYEH-rrah
she closes	**ella cierra**	EH-yah SYEH-rrah
you close	**Ud. cierra**	oos-TEHD SYEH-rrah
we close	**nosotros cerramos**	noh-SOH-trohs seh-RRAH-mohs
we close	**nosotras cerramos**	noh-SOH-trahs seh-RRAH-mohs
they close	**ellos cierran**	EH-yohs SYEH-rrahn
they close	**ellas cierran**	EH-yahs SYEH-rrahn
you (*plural*) close	**Uds. cierran**	oos-TEH-dehs SYEH-rrahn

dormir (ue) [dohr-MEER] to sleep

I sleep	**yo duermo**	yoh DWEHR-moh
you sleep	**tú duermes**	too DWEHR-mehs
he sleeps	**él duerme**	ehl DWEHR-meh
she sleeps	**ella duerme**	EH-yah DWEHR-meh
you sleep	**Ud. duerme**	OOS-TEHD DWEHR-meh
we sleep	**nosotros dormimos**	noh-SOH-trohs dohr-MEE-mohs
we sleep	**nosotras dormimos**	noh-SOH-trahs dohr-MEE-mohs
they sleep	**ellos duermen**	EH-yohs DWEHR-mehn
they sleep	**ellas duermen**	EH-yahs DWEHR-mehn
you (*plural*) sleep	**Uds. duermen**	OOS-TEH-dehs DWEHR-mehn

servir (i) [sehr-BEER] to serve

I serve	**yo sirvo**	yoh SEER-boh
you serve	**tú sirves**	too SEER-behs
he serves	**él sirve**	ehl SEER-beh
she serves	**ella sirve**	EH-yah SEER-beh
you serve	**Ud. sirve**	OOS-TEHD SEER-beh
we serve	**nosotros servimos**	noh-SOH-trohs sehr-BEE-mohs
we serve	**nosotras servimos**	noh-SOH-trahs sehr-BEE-mohs
they serve	**ellos sirven**	EH-yohs SEER-behn
they serve	**ellas sirven**	EH-yahs SEER-behn
you (*plural*) serve	**Uds. sirven**	OOS-TEH-dehs SEER-behn

Some of the most common verbs in each category are listed below.

e > ie

to begin	**comenzar**	koh-mehn-SAHR
to begin	**empezar**	ehm-peh-SAHR
to lose	**perder**	pehr-DEHR
to recommend	**recomendar**	rreh-koh-mehn-DAHR
to think	**pensar**	pehn-SAHR
to understand	**entender**	ehn-tehn-DEHR

o > ue

to be able	**poder**	poh-DEHR
to cost	**costar**	kohs-TAHR
to count, tell	**contar**	kohn-TAHR
to die	**morir**	moh-REER
to eat lunch	**almorzar**	ahl-mohr-SAHR
to find	**encontrar**	ehn-kohn-TRAHR
to play	**jugar (u>ue)**	hoo-GAHR
to remember	**recordar**	rreh-kohr-DAHR
to return, give back	**devolver**	deh-bohl-BEHR

| to return, go back | **volver** | bohl-BEHR |
| to show | **demostrar** | deh-mohs-TRAHR |

e > i

to dress	**vestir**	behs-TEER
to repeat	**repetir**	rreh-peh-TEER
to request, ask for	**pedir**	peh-DEER

Practice I-3

A *Write the correct form of each of the following verbs according to the subject given.*

1. (cerrar)   ellos _____

2. (volver)   nosotros _____

3. (vestir)   tú _____

4. (servir)   yo _____

5. (dormir)   nosotras _____

6. (pensar)   ella _____

7. (encontrar) Uds. _____

8. (jugar)   él _____

9. (pedir)   nosotros _____

10. (comenzar) yo _____

B *Study the verbs with special changes, then complete the translation of each of the following sentences with the correct form of the appropriate verb.*

1. *You close the door.*

   Tú _____ la puerta.

2. *They do not sleep much.*

   Ellos no _____ mucho.

3. *We serve lunch early.*

   Nosotros _____ el almuerzo temprano.

4. *She repeats the words.*

   Ella _____ las palabras.

5. *I don't understand anything.*

   Yo no _____ nada.

6. *We return all the books.*

   Nosotros _____ todos los libros.

7. *The notebook costs a lot.*

   El cuaderno _____ mucho.

8. *We start at nine.*

   Nosotros _____ a las nueve.

9. *Do you play in the park?*

   ¿_____ Uds. en el parque?

10. *I return tomorrow.*

    Yo _____ mañana.

Commands

Telling Someone to Do Something (Ud./Uds.)   Spanish has only a few irregular formal command forms. Therefore, it will be easier for you to become familiar with giving commands in Spanish if you use only the **Ud./Uds.** [oos-TEHD/oos-TEH-dehs] form for commands at first.

For all verbs that end in **-o** in the **yo** form of the present tense, the **Ud./Uds.** command is formed by removing the **-o** ending from the **yo** form of the present tense and adding endings as follows.

- For **-ar** verbs

  Add **-e** if the command is given to one person.
  Add **-en** if the command is given to more than one person.

Walk slowly. (*to one person*)	**Camine Ud. despacio.**
	kah-MEE-neh oos-TEHD dehs-PAH-syoh
Walk slowly. (*to more than one person*)	**Caminen Uds. despacio.**
	kah-MEE-nehn oos-TEH-dehs dehs-PAH-syoh

- For **-er** verbs

  Add **-a** if the command is given to one person.
  Add **-an** if the command is given to more than one person.

Run fast. (*to one person*)	**Corra Ud. rápido.**
	KOH-rrah oos-TEHD RRAH-pee-doh
Run fast. (*to more than one person*)	**Corran Uds. rápido.**
	KOH-rrahn oos-TEH-dehs RRAH-pee-doh

- For **-ir** verbs

  Add **-a** if the command is given to one person.
  Add **-an** if the command is given to more than one person.

Write on the chalkboard. (*to one person*)	**Escriba Ud. en la pizarra.** ehs-KREE-bah oos-TEHD ehn lah pee-SAH-rrah
Write on the chalkboard. (*to more than one person*)	**Escriban Uds. en la pizarra.** ehs-KREE-bahn oos-TEH-dehs ehn lah pee-SAH-rrah

In summary, the rules above can be used to form the formal (**Ud./Uds.** [oos-TEHD/oos-TEH-dehs]) command forms for any verb for which the **yo** [yoh] form of the present tense ends in **-o.**

yo FORM	**Ud.** COMMAND	**Uds.** COMMAND
caminar (to walk)		
camino kah-MEE-noh	**camine** kah-MEE-neh	**caminen** kah-MEE-nehn
correr (to run)		
corro KOH-rroh	**corra** KOH-rrah	**corran** KOH-rrahn
escribir (to write)		
escribo ehs-KREE-boh	**escriba** ehs-KREE-bah	**escriban** ehs-KREE-bahn
hacer (to do, make)		
hago AH-goh	**haga** AH-gah	**hagan** AH-gahn
poner (to put)		
pongo POHN-goh	**ponga** POHN-gah	**pongan** POHN-gahn
salir (to leave, go out)		
salgo SAHL-goh	**salga** SAHL-gah	**salgan** SAHL-gahn
traducir (to translate)		
traduzco trah-DOOS-koh	**traduzca** trah-DOOS-kah	**traduzcan** trah-DOOS-kahn
traer (to bring)		
traigo TRAH-ee-goh	**traiga** TRAH-ee-gah	**traigan** TRAH-ee-gahn
ver (to see)		
veo BEH-oh	**vea** BEH-ah	**vean** BEH-ahn

If the **yo** form of the present tense does not end in **-o**, the command form will be irregular. The following verbs have irregular command forms.

yo FORM	Ud. COMMAND	Uds. COMMAND
dar (to give)		
doy	**dé**	**den**
DOH-ee	deh	dehn
estar (to be)		
estoy	**esté**	**estén**
ehs-TOH-ee	ehs-TEH	ehs-TEHN
ir (to go)		
voy	**vaya**	**vayan**
BOH-ee	BAH-yah	BAH-yahn
saber (to know)		
sé	**sepa**	**sepan**
seh	SEH-pah	SEH-pahn
ser (to be)		
soy	**sea**	**sean**
SOH-ee	SEH-ah	SEH-ahn

Telling Someone Not to Do Something (Ud./Uds.)   When you want to tell someone *not* to do something, you use a negative formal (**Ud./Uds.** [oos-TEHD/oos-TEH-dehs]) command, which is formed by adding **no** before the affirmative formal (**Ud./Uds.**) command. The conjugated verb does not change.

Don't sign the form.	**No firme Ud. el formulario.**
	noh FEER-meh oos-TEHD ehl fohr-moo-LAH-ryoh
Don't read the book now.	**No lea Ud. el libro ahora.**
	noh LEH-ah oos-TEHD ehl LEE-broh ah-OH-rah
Don't open the door.	**No abran Uds. la puerta.**
	noh AH-brahn oos-TEH-dehs lah PWEHR-tah

Practice I-4

A *Write the* **Ud.** *and* **Uds.** *command forms of the following verbs.*

	Usted	Ustedes
1. caminar (*to walk*)	_____	_____
2. leer (*to read*)	_____	_____

	Usted	Ustedes
3. ir *(to go)*	_____	_____
4. asistir *(to attend)*	_____	_____
5. dar *(to give)*	_____	_____
6. saber *(to know)*	_____	_____
7. estar *(to be)*	_____	_____
8. escuchar *(to listen)*	_____	_____
9. ser *(to be)*	_____	_____
10. beber *(to drink)*	_____	_____
11. traducir *(to translate)*	_____	_____
12. traer *(to bring)*	_____	_____

B Explain how you would make the commands in Exercise A negative. What changes would you need to make to the verb?

_____

_____

C *Complete the following commands. Try to remember the new words that appear in the sentences.*

1. *Walk quickly.*

   _____ Ud. rápido.

2. *Be good.*

   _____ (Ser) Uds. buenos.

3. *Give the homework to the teacher.*

   _____ Ud. la tarea al maestro.

4. *Go to the office.*

   _____ Uds. a la oficina.

5. *Attend the meeting.*

   _____ Ud. a la reunión.

6. *Listen to the announcements.*

   _____ Uds. los anuncios.

7. *Read the book.*

   _____ Uds. el libro.

8. *Erase the chalkboard.*

   _____ Ud. la pizarra.

9. *Run carefully.*

   _____ Ud. con cuidado.

10. *Be here on time.*

   _____ (Estar) Uds. aquí temprano.

D *Although you would not want to give some of the commands in Exercise C to your students, practice changing them to the negative form here.*

1. _____

2. _____

3. _____

4. _____

5. _____

6. _____

7. _____

8. _____

9. _____

10. _____

Telling Someone to Do Something (tú) To tell someone to do something with the informal **tú** [too] command, you use the **él** [ehl] form of the present tense (but without including the word **él** [ehl]).

Review the sentences.	**Repasa las oraciones.**
	rreh-PAH-sah lahs oh-rah-SYOH-nehs
Understand my situation.	**Comprende mi situación.**
	kohm-PREHN-deh mee see-twah-SYOHN

Several important verbs have irregular **tú** commands.

ser (to be)	**sé** [seh]
venir (to come)	**ven** [behn]
hacer (to do)	**haz** [ahs]
ir (to go)	**ve** [beh]
salir (to leave, go out)	**sal** [sahl]
poner (to put)	**pon** [pohn]
decir (to tell)	**di** [dee]

Practice I-5

Complete the following sentences using the informal **tú** *command.*

1. *Do the homework.*

    _____ la tarea.

2. *Leave now.*

    _____ ahora.

3. *Be good.*

    _____ bueno.

4. *Put the books on the shelf.*

    _____ los libros en el estante.

5. *Come early.*

    _____ temprano.

6. *Tell the truth.*

    _____ la verdad.

7. *Go with me.*

    _____ conmigo.

Telling Someone Not to Do Something (tú) If you want to use the informal (**tú** [too]) command to tell someone *not* to do something, use the negative **tú** [too] command, which is formed by adding **-s** to the negative **Ud.** [oos-TEHD] command.

ENGLISH COMMAND	NEGATIVE Ud. COMMAND	NEGATIVE tú COMMAND
Don't eat in the hallway.	**No coma en el pasillo.** noh KOH-mah ehn ehl pah-SEE-yoh	**No comas en el pasillo.** noh KOH-mahs ehn ehl pah-SEE-yoh
Don't walk in the street.	**No camine en la calle.** noh kah-MEE-neh ehn lah KAH-yeh	**No camines en la calle.** noh kah-MEE-nehs ehn lah KAH-yeh

Practice I-6

A *Review the affirmative and negative* **tú** *commands, then write the correct command form in each column. Focus on their meanings, since some of them may be new to you.*

	Affirmative **tú**	Negative **tú**
1. escuchar (*to listen*)	_____	_____
2. salir (*to leave*)	_____	_____
3. hacer (*to do*)	_____	_____
4. escribir (*to write*)	_____	_____
5. ser (*to be*)	_____	_____
6. comer (*to eat*)	_____	_____
7. poner (*to put*)	_____	_____
8. ir (*to go*)	_____	_____

B *Complete the following sentences with the correct* **tú** *command form of the verb.*

1. *Eat slowly.*

   _____ despacio.

2. *Speak louder.*

   _____ más alto.

3. *Don't run in the hallway.*

   No _____ en el pasillo.

4. *Come at three.*

   _____ a las tres.

5. *Don't listen to that program.*

   No _____ ese programa.

6. *Copy the instructions.*

   _____ las instrucciones.

7. *Learn all the words.*

   _____ todas las palabras.

8. *Bring the computer.*

   _____ la computadora.

9. *Don't erase the chalkboard.*

   No _____ la pizarra.

10. *Don't open the books.*

    No _____ los libros.

11. *Repeat the answers.*

    _____ las respuestas.

12. *Don't be absent.*

    No _____ (estar) ausente.

Asking Questions

Questions Asking for a Yes or No Answer The simplest way to ask yes/no questions in Spanish is to raise the pitch of your voice at the end of the sentence.

Do you run in the park?	**¿Corres en el parque?** KOH-rrehs ehn ehl PAHR-keh

You can also use the questions **¿verdad?** [behr-DAHD] or **¿no?** [noh] at the end of a statement, meaning "right?", when you want confirmation or rejection of what you have said. Again, raise the pitch of your voice when saying **¿verdad?** [behr-DAHD] or **¿no?** [noh].

You run in the park, right?	**Corres en el parque, ¿verdad?** KOH-rrehs ehn ehl PAHR-keh, behr-DAHD

When answering yes/no questions, follow the patterns below.

Yes, I run in the park.	**Sí, corro en el parque.** see, KOH-rroh ehn ehl PAHR-keh
No, I do not run in the park.	**No, no corro en el parque.** noh, noh KOH-rroh ehn ehl PAHR-keh
No, I walk in the park.	**No, camino en el parque.** noh, kah-MEE-noh ehn ehl PAHR-keh

Note that negative sentences in Spanish are formed by placing **no** in front of the conjugated verb.

I do not speak much in class.	**No hablo mucho en la clase.** noh AH-bloh MOO-choh ehn lah KLAH-seh

Other negative words that can be used to express negative sentences are found in Chapter 7, page 260.

Practice I-7

A *Form a question from each of the following strings of words. Remember to change the infinitive to a conjugated form of the verb that agrees with the subject. The words are not given in any particular order.*

1. español / hablar / verdad / tú

   _____

2. asistir a / Uds. / la clase de física

   _____

3. en el parque / ellos / correr

   _____

4. nosotros / la tarea / terminar

   _____

5. en la clase / ella / mucho / aprender / no

   _____

B *Answer the questions you wrote in Exercise A as if you are the person to whom the question is addressed. Answer at least two of the questions with the negative form.*

1. _____
2. _____
3. _____
4. _____
5. _____

Questions Asking for a Specific Piece of Information   Use the following question words to obtain specific information.

Where?	**¿Dónde?**
	DOHN-deh
From where?	**¿De dónde?**
	deh DOHN-deh
To where?	**¿Adónde?**
	ah-DOHN-deh

When?	**¿Cuándo?** KWAHN-doh
For when?	**¿Para cuándo?** PAH-rah KWAHN-doh
What?	**¿Qué?** keh
With what?	**¿Con qué?** kohn keh
For what?	**¿Para qué?** PAH-rah keh
Who?	**¿Quién?** (*singular*) kyehn
	¿Quiénes? (*plural*) KYEH-nehs
Whose?	**¿De quién?** (*singular*) deh kyehn
	¿De quiénes? (*plural*) deh KYEH-nehs
With whom?	**¿Con quién?** (*singular*) kohn kyehn
	¿Con quiénes? (*plural*) kohn KYEH-nehs
For whom?	**¿Para quién?** (*singular*) PAH-rah kyehn
	¿Para quiénes? (*plural*) PAH-rah KYEH-nehs
Why?	**¿Por qué?** pohr keh
How?	**¿Cómo?** KOH-moh
How many?	**¿Cuántos? / ¿Cuántas?** KWAHN-tohs / KWAHN-tahs
How much?	**¿Cuánto? / ¿Cuánta?** KWAHN-toh / KWAHN-tah
Where is the principal's office?	**¿Dónde está la oficina del director / de la directora?** DOHN-deh ehs-TAH lah oh-fee-SEE-nah dehl dee-rehk-TOHR / deh lah dee-rehk-TOH-rah

Where is the new student from?	**¿De dónde es el nuevo estudiante?** deh DOHN-deh ehs ehl NWEH-boh ehs-too-DYAHN-teh
(To) where are you going?	**¿Adónde va Ud.?** ah-DOHN-deh bah oos-TEHD
When does the class begin?	**¿Cuándo empieza la clase?** KWAHN-doh ehm-PYEH-sah lah KLAH-seh
Whose is the notebook?	**¿De quién es el cuaderno?** deh kyehn ehs ehl kwah-DEHR-noh
Whose is the office?	**¿De quiénes es la oficina?** deh KYEH-nehs ehs lah oh-fee-SEE-nah

Note that to answer a question asking "Why?" (**¿Por qué?** [pohr keh]), you use **porque** [POHR-keh], meaning "because."

Why don't you go to the meeting?	**¿Por qué no vas a la reunión?** por keh noh bahs ah lah rreh-oo-NYOHN
Because I don't have time.	**Porque no tengo tiempo.** POHR-keh noh TEHN-goh TYEHM-poh
With whom are you going to the party?	**¿Con quién vas a la fiesta?** kohn kyehn bahs ah lah FYEHS-tah
I am going with you.	**Voy contigo.** BOH-ee kohn-TEE-goh

Note that in Spanish "with me" is **conmigo** [kohn-MEE-goh] and "with you" is **contigo** [kohn-TEE-goh]. Pronouns used with **con** [kohn] are listed below.

conmigo	kohn-MEE-goh
contigo	kohn-TEE-goh
con él	kohn ehl
con ella	kohn EH-yah
con Ud.	kohn oos-TEHD
con nosotros	kohn noh-SOH-trohs
con nosotras	kohn noh-SOH-trahs
con ellos	kohn EH-yohs
con ellas	kohn EH-yahs
con Uds.	kohn oos-TEH-dehs

Practice I-8

A *Complete the following crossword puzzle.*

Across
1. when
4. how much
5. how many (*fem.*)
6. who
8. from where
10. why
12. to where

Down
1. with whom
2. for when
3. for whom
4. with what
6. what
7. how
9. whose
11. where

B *Read each of the following pairs of questions and answers carefully, paying particular attention to the underlined part of the answer, which identifies the information being requested. Then write the question word needed to complete each question.*

1. ¿_____ estudian?

   <u>Elena y Juan</u> estudian.

2. ¿_____ estudias?

   Yo estudio <u>matemáticas</u>.

3. ¿_____ no vas a la fiesta?

   Porque <u>tengo un examen</u>.

4. ¿_____ está la oficina?

   La oficina está <u>en la calle Victoria</u>.

5. ¿_____ es Juan?

   Juan es <u>de Bolivia</u>.

6. ¿_____ cuesta el libro?

   El libro cuesta <u>cinco dólares</u>.

7. ¿_____ es tu amigo?

   Mi amigo es <u>Alfonso</u>.

8. ¿_____ es la clase de inglés?

   La clase de inglés es <u>ahora</u>.

9. ¿_____ estás tú?

   Yo estoy <u>bien</u>, gracias.

10. ¿_____ vas al concierto?

    Yo voy <u>con mis amigas</u>.

Summary Practice

Each of the following sentences illustrates a situation that brings together much of what has been taught in this chapter. This summary should help you identify areas you may want to practice further. Write what you would say in Spanish in the following situations.

1. You need to introduce your principal to a new parent.

   _____

2. You want to wish a parent a nice day.

   _____

3. Tell a student that you will see him/her next week.

   _____

4. You need to tell a parent to sign a form. [*Use the* **Ud.** *command.*]

   _____

5. Tell a student to write on the chalkboard.

   _____

6. Tell a student not to run in the hallways.

   _____

7. Ask a student where Mr. Smith is.

   _____

8. Ask a student whose book it is.

   _____

Information Parents Need to Enroll Their Children in School

La información que los padres necesitan para matricular a sus niños en la escuela

General Information Form

El formulario de información

General Information
Información general

Last name of the child _____ Name _____
Apellido del niño/de la niña   *Nombre*

Date of birth _____ Sex _____
Fecha de nacimiento   *Sexo*

Street address _____
Dirección

City _____ State _____ Zip Code _____
Ciudad   *Estado*   *Código postal*

Last name of the father/mother/guardian _____
Apellido del padre/de la madre/del tutor

Name _____
Nombre

Home telephone _____ Work telephone _____
Teléfono de la casa   *Teléfono del trabajo*

Person responsible in case of emergency _____
Persona responsable en caso de emergencia

Telephone number _____
Número de teléfono

General Questions

Las preguntas generales

You can get almost all of the information above by asking general questions
(**las preguntas generales** [lahs preh-GOON-tahs heh-neh-RAH-lehs]) using the following pattern.

What is _____?   **¿Cuál es _____?**
                                      kwahl ehs

What is the child's date of   **¿Cuál es la fecha de nacimiento**
birth?   **del niño?**
                                      kwahl ehs lah FEH-chah deh
                                      nah-see-MYEHN-toh dehl NEE-nyoh

What is the phone number at work?	¿Cuál es el número de teléfono del trabajo? kwahl ehs ehl NOO-meh-roh deh teh-LEH-foh-noh dehl trah-BAH-hoh
What is your address?	¿Cuál es su dirección? kwahl ehs soo dee-rehk-SYOHN
In what city / state / zip code do you live?	¿En qué ciudad / estado / código postal vive Ud.? ehn keh see-oo-DAHD / ehs-TAH-doh / KOH-dee-goh pohs-TAHL BEE-beh OOS-TEHD

GRAMMAR · Talking About Age

You can find out the age of a child by using the following idiomatic expression in Spanish.

How old is he/she?	¿Cuántos años tiene él/ella? KWAHN-tohs AH-nyohs TYEH-neh ehl/EH-yah

The response, stating the age of someone, uses the following pattern.

He/She is (six) years old.	Él/Ella tiene (seis) años. ehl/EH-yah TYEH-neh (SEH-ees) AH-nyohs

If a child is just one year old, you would express it as follows.

He/She is one year old.	Él/Ella tiene un año. ehl/EH-yah TYEH-neh oon AH-nyoh

The idiomatic expression used to express age is one of several with the verb **tener** [teh-NEHR], meaning "to have." You will soon be introduced to more of these expressions, so it is a good idea for you to become familiar with the conjugation of the present tense of **tener**.

tener (*irreg.*) [teh-NEHR] to have

I have	yo tengo	yoh TEHN-goh
you have	tú tienes	too TYEH-nehs
he has	él tiene	ehl TYEH-neh
she has	ella tiene	EH-yah TYEH-neh
you have	Ud. tiene	OOS-TEHD TYEH-neh
we have	nosotros tenemos	noh-SOH-trohs teh-NEH-mohs
we have	nosotras tenemos	noh-SOH-trahs teh-NEH-mohs
they have	ellos tienen	EH-yohs TYEH-nehn
they have	ellas tienen	EH-yahs TYEH-nehn
you (*plural*) have	Uds. tienen	OOS-TEH-dehs TYEH-nehn

Some of the other important expressions with the verb **tener** [teh-NEHR] follow. The English translation is sometimes "to feel" instead of "to be."

to be (very) hungry	**tener (mucha) hambre**
	teh-NEHR (MOO-chah) AHM-breh
to be (very) thirsty	**tener (mucha) sed**
	teh-NEHR (MOO-chah) sehd
to be (very) cold	**tener (mucho) frío**
	teh-NEHR (MOO-choh) FREE-oh
to be (very) sleepy	**tener (mucho) sueño**
	teh-NEHR (MOO-choh) SWEH-nyoh
to be (very) afraid	**tener (mucho) miedo**
	teh-NEHR (MOO-choh) MYEH-doh
to be in a (big) hurry	**tener (mucha) prisa**
	teh-NEHR (MOO-chah) PREE-sah
to be (very) lucky	**tener (mucha) suerte**
	teh-NEHR (MOO-chah) SWEHR-teh
I am hungry.	**Yo tengo hambre.**
	yoh TEHN-goh AHM-breh
She feels very cold.	**Ella tiene mucho frío.**
	EH-yah TYEH-neh MOO-choh FREE-oh

Practice 1-1

Using the English phrase in parentheses as a clue, fill in the blanks from the strings of scrambled letters below.

1. tfnoems
   (*we are cold*)

	e		o		r	í	

2. tsuieenñoe
   (*you [pl.] are sleepy*)

			n				

3. tuertngoe
   (*I am lucky*)

	e			s			

4. tpiisenaes
   (*you are in a hurry*)

					r		

5. tamiebrne
   (*she is hungry*)

			e	h			

6. tedees
   (*we are thirsty*)

		n		m	o		s		

7. teidno
   (*I am afraid*)

			g	o		m		e		

8. tinaeñdozs
   (*he is ten years old*)

		e				i	e				

Asking for More Information

Para pedir más información

You may also want to familiarize yourself with the following questions in order to ask for more information (**para pedir más información** [PAH-rah peh-DEER mahs een-fohr-mah-SYOHN]).

How many people live in your house?
¿Cuántas personas viven en su casa?
KWAHN-tahs pehr-SOH-nahs BEE-behn ehn soo KAH-sah

Do both parents live with the child?
¿Viven ambos padres con el niño / la niña?
BEE-behn AHM-bohs PAH-drehs kohn ehl NEE-nyoh / lah NEE-nyah

Who is the person responsible for your child?
¿Quién está a cargo de su hijo/hija?
kyehn ehs-TAH ah KAHR-goh deh soo EE-hoh/EE-hah

Does your child have brothers and sisters (siblings)?
¿Tiene su hijo/hija hermanos?
TYEH-neh soo EE-hoh/EE-hah ehr-MAH-nohs

How many brothers and sisters (siblings) does your child have?
¿Cuántos hermanos tiene su hijo/hija?
KWAHN-tohs ehr-MAH-nohs TYEH-neh soo EE-hoh/EE-hah

What language(s) do you speak at home?
¿Qué lengua(s) hablan en casa?
keh LEHN-gwah(s) AH-blahn ehn KAH-sah

Is your child attending / Has your child attended a preschool program?
¿Asiste / Ha asistido su hijo/hija a un programa preescolar?
ah-SEES-teh / ah ah-sees-TEE-doh soo EE-hoh/EE-hah ah oon proh-GRAH-mah preh-ehs-koh-LAHR

Practice 1-2

Study the questions in the General Questions section (pages 32–33) and the Asking for More Information *section (page 35). Then write the appropriate question in Spanish to request the following information directly from a Spanish-speaking adult.*

1. the age of one of the students

    _____

2. a parent's address

    _____

3. if the child has any brothers and sisters

    _____

4. the child's date of birth

    _____

5. who the person responsible for the child is

    _____

6. the phone number at work

    _____

GRAMMAR · Possessive Adjectives: my, your

You may have noticed the possessive adjective **su** [soo], meaning "your," in some of the example questions. Each subject pronoun has its equivalent possessive adjective. For now, you need only become familiar with **mi** [mee] ("my"), **tu** [too] ("your" familiar), and **su** [soo] ("your" formal). Later you will learn all the others. The plural of **mi** is **mis** [mees] ("my"), the plural of **tu** is **tus** [toos] ("your" familiar), and the plural of **su** is **sus** [soos] ("your" formal). The plural forms have nothing to do with the person or persons who possess something. Instead, you will need to use the plural form when what is possessed is plural.

Who lives in your house?

¿Quiénes viven en su casa?
KYEH-nehs BEE-behn ehn soo KAH-sah

My husband, my children, and I live in my house.

Mi esposo, mis hijos y yo vivimos en mi casa.
mee ehs-POH-soh, mees EE-hohs ee yoh bee-BEE-mohs ehn mee KAH-sah

For more information about possessive adjectives, see Chapter 3, page 113.

Family Members and Relatives

Los miembros de la familia y los parientes

So far, you have learned how to request certain information about the child and his/her parents. Nowadays, however, a child's caretaker might be someone other than a parent—any of many family members and relatives (**los miembros de la familia y los parientes** [lohs MYEHM-brohs deh lah fah-MEE-lyah ee lohs pah-RYEHN-tehs]). Always remember the importance of family for Hispanics. In Spanish-speaking countries, there are many relatives who are considered close members of the family whom you might not consider to be part of your own immediate family.

Here is a list of family members and relatives that you will find very useful as you get to know the families with whom you work.

aunt	**la tía**	lah TEE-ah
boyfriend	**el novio**	ehl NOH-byoh
brother	**el hermano**	ehl ehr-MAH-noh
brother-in-law	**el cuñado**	ehl koo-NYAH-doh
cousin	**el primo / la prima**	ehl PREE-moh / lah PREE-mah
daughter	**la hija**	lah EE-hah
daughter-in-law	**la nuera**	lah NWEH-rah
father	**el padre**	ehl PAH-dreh
father-in-law	**el suegro**	ehl SWEH-groh
girlfriend	**la novia**	lah NOH-byah
goddaughter	**la ahijada**	lah ah-ee-HAH-dah
godfather	**el padrino / el compadre**	ehl pah-DREE-noh / ehl kohm-PAH-dreh
godmother	**la madrina / la comadre**	lah mah-DREE-nah / lah koh-MAH-dreh
godson	**el ahijado**	ehl ah-ee-HAH-doh
granddaughter	**la nieta**	lah NYEH-tah
grandfather	**el abuelo**	ehl ah-BWEH-loh
grandmother	**la abuela**	lah ah-BWEH-lah
grandson	**el nieto**	ehl NYEH-toh
husband	**el esposo**	ehl ehs-POH-soh
mother	**la madre**	lah MAH-dreh
mother-in-law	**la suegra**	lah SWEH-grah
nephew	**el sobrino**	ehl soh-BREE-noh
niece	**la sobrina**	lah soh-BREE-nah

relative	el pariente	ehl pah-RYEHN-teh
sister	la hermana	lah ehr-MAH-nah
sister-in-law	la cuñada	lah koo-NYAH-dah
son	el hijo	ehl EE-hoh
son-in-law	el yerno	ehl YEHR-noh
stepbrother	el hermanastro	ehl ehr-mah-NAHS-troh
stepdaughter	la hijastra	lah ee-HAHS-trah
stepfather	el padrastro	ehl pah-DRAHS-troh
stepmother	la madrastra	lah mah-DRAHS-trah
stepsister	la hermanastra	lah ehr-mah-NAHS-trah
stepson	el hijastro	ehl ee-HAHS-troh
uncle	el tío	ehl TEE-oh
wife	la esposa	lah ehs-POH-sah

Sometimes a masculine plural noun refers to both male and female persons.

| the parents | los padres | lohs PAH-drehs |
| the grandparents | los abuelos | lohs ah-BWEH-lohs |

Practice 1-3

A *Find the words in the list below within the grid of letters. Words can appear horizontally, vertically, diagonally, and backwards.*

abuelo
hermanastra
madrina
padrino
suegra
ahijada
esposa
hijo
novio
pariente
compadre
hermana
madre
padrastro
prima
yerno

```
T B H E R M A N A S T R A X V
M A V G O R M G N O V I O W P
L Z E V O L E U B A E V F S A
W Y E R M O D O N I R D A P D
S E U V D D V T A U D S U O R
U R N F F A A O A O A B V M A
E N F M I U P M J H M J Z C S
G O T L A C K M I I D M E E T
R T A T H D A U O R H G S T R
A P T I D I R N H C P L P N O
R G X Y Y I Q I A L R W O E S
T W W L B J Y C N M L L S I Q
B V J E J E O B H A R Q A R R
A D A J I H A A L D U E M A K
D L X T C U Y K C W D K H P B
```

B *¿Quién es?* Complete the following sentences with the missing word.

1. El hermano de mi madre es mi _____.

2. La esposa de mi hermano es mi _____.

3. La madre de mi padre es mi _____.

4. El hijo de mi hermana es mi _____.

5. El _____ de mi madre es mi hermano.

6. Mi _____ es la hija de mi tío.

7. La hija de mi tío es la _____ de mi abuela.

8. Mi futura esposa es mi _____ ahora.

GRAMMAR · Gender of Nouns and Articles

Unlike English nouns, all Spanish nouns are either masculine or feminine. In most cases, the gender of a noun has to be memorized, but here are some helpful guidelines.

- Nouns that refer to males are masculine. Example: **el hombre** [ehl OHM-breh] "the man."
- Nouns that refer to females are feminine. Example: **la mujer** [lah moo-HEHR] "the woman."
- Nouns ending in **-ista** can be either masculine or feminine. Examples: **el artista** (*male*) / **la artista** (*female*) [ehl ahr-TEES-tah / lah ahr-TEES-tah] "the artist."
- Nouns ending in **-dad, -tad, -tud, -ción**, and **-sión** are feminine. Examples: **la ciudad** [lah see-oo-DAHD] "the city," **la imaginación** [lah ee-mah-hee-nah-SYOHN] "the imagination."
- Nouns ending in **-o** are usually masculine. Example: **el cuaderno** [ehl kwah-DEHR-noh] "the notebook."
- Nouns ending in **-a** are usually feminine. Example: **la pluma** [lah PLOO-mah] "the pen."

In order to more easily remember the gender of a noun, it is helpful to learn it with its definite article. In Spanish, the article also has a masculine or feminine form, determined by the gender of the noun to which it is related. Vocabulary lists in this book always list each noun with its definite article.

GRAMMAR · The Definite Article

The definite article has four forms in Spanish, all of which mean "the."

- Two singular forms: **el** (*masculine*) and **la** (*feminine*)
- Two plural forms: **los** (*masculine*) and **las** (*feminine*)

MASCULINE SINGULAR	**el lápiz** ("the pencil")
	ehl LAH-pees
FEMININE SINGULAR	**la pizarra** ("the chalkboard")
	lah pee-SAH-rrah
MASCULINE PLURAL	**los lápices** ("the pencils")
	lohs LAH-pee-sehs
FEMININE PLURAL	**las pizarras** ("the chalkboards")
	lahs pee-SAH-rrahs

In Spanish, there are two contractions formed with the definite article **el**.

- **a + el = al**

  I'm going to the gym.   **Voy al gimnasio.**
                                 BOH-ee ahl heem-NAH-syoh

- **de + el = del**

  It's the principal's wallet.   **Es la cartera del director.**
                                 ehs lah kahr-TEH-rah dehl dee-rehk-TOHR

GRAMMAR · The Indefinite Article

The indefinite article has four forms in Spanish.

- Two singular forms: **un** (*masculine*) and **una** (*feminine*), meaning "a" or "an"
- Two plural forms: **unos** (*masculine*) and **unas** (*feminine*), meaning "some"

MASCULINE SINGULAR	**un lápiz** ("a pencil")
	oon LAH-pees
FEMININE SINGULAR	**una pizarra** ("a chalkboard")
	oo-nah pee-SAH-rrah
MASCULINE PLURAL	**unos lápices** ("some pencils")
	oo-nohs LAH-pee-sehs
FEMININE PLURAL	**unas pizarras** ("some chalkboards")
	oo-nahs pee-SAH-rrahs

Nationalities

Las nacionalidades

Although parents are not usually asked to identify their native country, if you express an interest in knowing this information, it will show your interest in them and it can be a point of departure for a pleasant conversation.

A Hispanic family can come from any of the countries in the Spanish-speaking world. Remember that it is always a good idea to use the **usted (Ud.)** [OOS-TEHD] form to address the parents; with students you may use the familiar **tú** [too] form. A conversation about nationality (**la nacionalidad** [lah nah-syoh-nah-lee-DAHD]) might include the following questions and responses.

Where are you from?	**¿De dónde eres tú / es Ud.?** deh DOHN-deh EH-rehs too / ehs OOS-TEHD
I am from _____.	**Soy de _____.** SOH-ee deh
What is your nationality?	**¿Cuál es tu/su nacionalidad?** kwahl ehs too/soo nah-syoh-nah-lee-DAHD
I am Panamanian.	**Soy panameño/panameña.** SOH-ee pah-nah-MEH-nyoh/ pah-nah-MEH-nyah
What nationality is he/she?	**¿De qué nacionalidad es él/ella?** deh keh nah-syoh-nah-lee-DAHD ehs ehl/EH-yah
He is Cuban.	**Él es cubano.** ehl ehs koo-BAH-noh
She is Cuban.	**Ella es cubana.** EH-yah ehs koo-BAH-nah

GRAMMAR · Using the Verb "To Be" to Express Origin

To ask about or to state the nationality of someone (or something), use the verb **ser** [sehr], meaning "to be."

The present tense of the verb **ser** [sehr] follows.

ser (*irreg.*) [sehr] to be

I am	**yo soy**	yoh SOH-ee
you are	**tú eres**	too EH-rehs
he is	**él es**	ehl ehs
she is	**ella es**	EH-yah ehs
you are	**Ud. es**	oos-TEHD ehs
we are	**nosotros somos**	noh-SOH-trohs SOH-mohs
we are	**nosotras somos**	noh-SOH-trahs SOH-mohs
they are	**ellos son**	EH-yohs sohn
they are	**ellas son**	EH-yahs sohn
you (*plural*) are	**Uds. son**	oos-TEH-dehs sohn

If you have an idea about where a person is from and would like to verify the information, you can also use the question that follows.

Are you from (Chile)?	**¿Eres tú de (Chile)? / ¿Es Ud. de (Chile)?**
	EH-rehs too deh (CHEE-leh) /
	ehs oos-TEHD deh (CHEE-leh)

Possible responses include the following.

Yes, I am from (Chile).	**Sí, soy de (Chile).**
	see, SOH-ee deh (CHEE-leh)
No, I am not from (Chile).	**No, no soy de (Chile).**
	noh, noh SOH-ee deh (CHEE-leh)
I am from (Mexico).	**Soy de (México).**
	SOH-ee de (MEH-hee-koh)
I am (Mexican). (*male*)	**Soy (mexicano).**
	SOH-ee (meh-hee-KAH-noh)
I am (Mexican). (*female*)	**Soy (mexicana).**
	SOH-ee (meh-hee-KAH-nah)

Spanish-Speaking Countries and Nationalities

Los países de habla hispana y las nacionalidades

A list of Spanish-speaking countries and nationalities (**los países de habla hispana y las nacionalidades** [lohs pah-EE-sehs deh AH-blah ees-PAH-nah ee lahs nah-syoh-nah-lee-DAH-dehs]) follows. In most cases, if you change the final **-o** of the masculine adjective denoting nationality to an **-a**, you will have the feminine form of the nationality. However, note that the adjective for someone from Costa Rica or from Nicaragua is the same in both the masculine and feminine forms. Also pay particular attention to the masculine and feminine forms of nationality for someone who comes from Spain.

Argentina
ahr-hehn-TEE-nah

argentino / argentina
ahr-hehn-TEE-noh / ahr-hehn-TEE-nah

Bolivia
boh-LEE-byah

boliviano / boliviana
boh-lee-BYAH-noh / boh-lee-BYAH-nah

Chile
CHEE-leh

chileno / chilena
chee-LEH-noh / chee-LEH-nah

Colombia
koh-LOHM-byah

colombiano / colombiana
koh-lohm-BYAH-noh / koh-lohm-BYAH-nah

Costa Rica
KOHS-tah RREE-kah

costarricense
kohs-tah-rree-SEHN-seh

Cuba
KOO-bah

cubano / cubana
koo-BAH-noh / koo-BAH-nah

Ecuador
eh-kwah-DOHR

ecuatoriano / ecuatoriana
eh-kwah-toh-RYAH-noh / eh-kwah-toh-RYAH-nah

El Salvador
ehl sahl-bah-DOHR

salvadoreño / salvadoreña
sahl-bah-doh-REH-nyoh / sahl-bah-doh-REH-nyah

España
ehs-PAH-nyah

español / española
ehs-pah-NYOHL / ehs-pah-NYOH-lah

Guatemala
gwah-teh-MAH-lah

guatemalteco / guatemalteca
gwah-teh-mahl-TEH-koh /
gwah-teh-mahl-TEH-kah

Honduras
ohn-DOO-rahs

hondureño / hondureña
ohn-doo-REH-nyoh / ohn-doo-REH-nyah

México
MEH-hee-koh

mexicano / mexicana
meh-hee-KAH-noh / meh-hee-KAH-nah

Nicaragua
nee-kah-RAH-gwah

nicaragüense
nee-kah-rah-GWEHN-seh

Panamá
pah-nah-MAH

panameño / panameña
pah-nah-MEH-nyoh / pah-nah-MEH-nyah

Paraguay
pah-rah-GWAH-ee

paraguayo / paraguaya
pah-rah-GWAH-yoh / pah-rah-GWAH-yah

Perú
peh-ROO

peruano / peruana
peh-RWAH-noh / peh-RWAH-nah

Puerto Rico
PWEHR-toh RREE-koh

puertorriqueño / puertorriqueña
pwehr-toh-rree-KEH-nyoh /
pwehr-toh-rree-KEH-nyah

República Dominicana
rreh-POO-blee-kah
doh-mee-nee-KAH-nah

dominicano / dominicana
doh-mee-nee-KAH-noh / doh-mee-nee-KAH-nah

Uruguay	**uruguayo / uruguaya**
oo-roo-GWAH-ee	oo-roo-GWAH-yoh / oo-roo-GWAH-yah
Venezuela	**venezolano / venezolana**
beh-neh-SWEH-lah	beh-neh-soh-LAH-noh / beh-neh-soh-LAH-nah

Unlike English, nationalities are not capitalized in Spanish.

Practice 1-4

A Find the words in the list below within the grid of letters. Words can appear horizontally, vertically, and backwards, but not diagonally. Then fill in the blanks below with the first 20 unused letters from the grid, beginning at the top left. What sentence is spelled out?

argentina
chilena
colombiana
cubano
dominicana
ecuatoriano
guatemalteco
mexicano
panameño
peruano
puertorriqueña
venezolano

```
T O D O P A N A M E Ñ O S S O
M D O M I N I C A N A O S A M
O C E T L A M E T A U G E R I
O C A N O S E W D K A G Q N P
N F A N A I B M O L O C C A E
A R S C E E M W X D R X C Z R
L F O N A C I X E M X I H A U
O X F H B W N K N W D Y I N A
Z X F Q X Q R P V L H R L I N
E V O N A I R O T A U C E T O
N Z V V T Z G H E K L M N N S
E A O Y H C U B A N O X A E N
V X K Q B E P Y L W G D D G Y
H P B J R B E B D L T O K R B
P U E R T O R R I Q U E Ñ A P
```

__ __ __ __   __ __ __ __   __ __ __ __ __ __ __ __ __

B Decode the message below by determining the correct letter substitutions. Here's a hint: In the decoded message, every L becomes S and every R becomes D, as shown in the grid below.

A	B	C	D	E	F	G	H	I	J	K	L	M	N	O	P	Q	R	S	T	U	V	W	X	Y	Z
											S						D								

¿_ _   _ _ _ _ _   _ _ _ _ ?   _ _ _   _ _   _ _ _
 R F   R J A R F   F E F L   L J I   R F   D J L

_ _ _ _ _ _ _   _ _ _ _ _ _ .
F L K W R J L   X A V R J L

C *Form a sentence from each of the following strings of words. Remember to conjugate the verb and to change the ending of the nationality for gender agreement, if necessary.*

1. ¿? / Ud. / ser / dónde / de

   _____

2. ¿? / ser / de / tú / Colombia

   _____

3. ¿? / él / nacionalidad / de / ser / qué

   _____

4. ser / nosotras / español

   _____

5. Nicaragua / yo / ser / de

   _____

GRAMMAR · Position and Gender of Adjectives

Unlike English adjectives, Spanish adjectives usually follow the noun, as is shown here.

the Peruvian president   **el presidente peruano**
                                    ehl preh-see-DEHN-teh peh-RWAH-noh

Another important difference is that in Spanish, adjectives also have masculine and feminine forms, determined by the gender of the noun to which they are related. Here are some general guidelines for adjectives.

- Adjectives ending in **-o** in the masculine singular change the **-o** to **-a** in the feminine singular.

  the Mexican man   **el hombre mexicano**
                                      ehl OHM-breh meh-hee-KAH-noh

  the Mexican woman   **la mujer mexicana**
                                      lah moo-HEHR meh-hee-KAH-nah

- Most other adjectives have the same form for the masculine and the feminine.

  the intelligent man   **el hombre inteligente**
                                      ehl OHM-breh een-teh-lee-HEHN-teh

  the intelligent woman   **la mujer inteligente**
                                      lah moo-HEHR een-teh-lee-HEHN-teh

GRAMMAR · Plural of Nouns and Adjectives

For Spanish nouns, the concept of number (that is, whether the word is singular or plural) works just like it does in English. The singular form is used when referring to one person, place, or thing, and the plural form is used when referring to two or more. Unlike English, however, in Spanish the article and the adjective are also number sensitive (singular or plural).

The plurals of nouns and adjectives are formed in the following ways.

• Add **-s** to nouns and adjectives ending in a vowel.

the black bag   **la bolsa negra**
                    lah BOHL-sah NEH-grah

the black bags   **las bolsas negras**
                    lahs BOHL-sahs NEH-grahs

• Add **-es** to nouns and adjectives ending in a consonant.

the easy exam   **la prueba fácil**
                    lah PRWEH-bah FAH-seel

the easy exams   **las pruebas fáciles**
                    lahs PRWEH-bahs FAH-see-lehs

Practice 1-5

A *Express the following phrases in Spanish.*

1. the Mexican girl   _____

2. the white papers   _____

3. the intelligent students _____

4. the (*female*) Guatemalan _____
   doctor

5. the big chalkboards   _____

6. the Cuban man   _____

B *Change the phrases in Exercise A to the plural if the phrase is singular and to the singular if it is plural.*

1. _____

2. _____

3. _____

4. _____

5. _____

6. _____

Family Income

Los ingresos de la familia

Knowing the economic situation of a family is an important key to providing the right help to both the child and the parents. Among other things, information about family income (**los ingresos de la familia** [lohs een-GREH-sohs deh lah fah-MEE-lyah]) is necessary in order for many schools to decide if the child will receive discounted or free breakfast and/or lunch.

Here are some questions that will help you find out this information.

How much money do you earn a week / a month / a year?	**¿Cuánto dinero gana Ud. a la semana / al mes / al año?** KWAHN-toh dee-NEH-roh GAH-nah oos-TEHD ah lah seh-MAH-nah / ahl mehs / ahl AH-nyoh
Do you have any other income?	**¿Tiene Ud. otros ingresos?** TYEH-neh oos-TEHD OH-trohs een-GREH-sohs
Do you receive food stamps?	**¿Recibe Ud. cupones para alimentos?** rreh-SEE-beh oos-TEHD koo-POH-nehs PAH-rah ah-lee-MEHN-tohs

Communication with Parents and Health Information

La comunicación con los padres y la información sobre la salud

The well-being of the students is crucial to their academic and social success while in school. School personnel must be familiar with any situation that may require special attention. Thus good communication with parents (**la comunicación con los padres** [lah koh-moo-nee-kah-SYOHN kohn lohs PAH-drehs]) is essential. Although the following list is not exhaustive, it includes questions about health information (**la información sobre la salud** [lah een-fohr-mah-SYOHN SOH-breh lah sah-LOOD]) that you may need to ask the students' parents.

Does your child have any condition that requires special attention?	**¿Tiene su hijo/hija alguna condición que requiere atención especial?** TYEH-neh soo EE-hoh/EE-hah ahl-GOO-nah kohn-dee-SYOHN keh rreh-KYEH-reh ah-tehn-SYOHN ehs-peh-SYAHL

Does he/she have problems with …?	**¿Tiene problemas con…?** TYEH-neh proh-BLEH-mahs kohn
eyesight	**la vista** lah BEES-tah
hearing	**el oído** ehl oh-EE-doh
speaking	**el habla** ehl AH-blah
Does he/she have … problems?	**¿Tiene problemas…?** TYEH-neh proh-BLEH-mahs
developmental	**de desarrollo** deh deh-sah-RROH-yoh
emotional	**emocionales** eh-moh-syoh-NAH-lehs
physical	**físicos** FEE-see-kohs
Does your child have any illness?	**¿Tiene su hijo/hija alguna enfermedad?** TYEH-neh soo EE-hoh/EE-hah ahl-GOO-nah ehn-fehr-meh-DAHD
Is your child taking any medication?	**¿Está tomando su hijo/hija alguna medicina?** ehs-TAH toh-MAHN-doh soo EE-hoh/EE-hah ahl-GOO-nah meh-dee-SEE-nah
Does your child have any allergies?	**¿Tiene su hijo/hija alguna alergia?** TYEH-neh soo EE-hoh/EE-hah ahl-GOO-nah ah-LEHR-hyah
Is he/she allergic …?	**¿Es alérgico/alérgica…?** ehs ah-LEHR-hee-koh/ah-LEHR-hee-kah
to antibiotics	**a los antibióticos** ah lohs ahn-tee-BYOH-tee-kohs
to aspirin	**a la aspirina** ah lah ahs-pee-REE-nah
to bee stings	**a la mordedura de las abejas** ah lah mohr-deh-DOO-rah deh lahs ah-BEH-hahs
to dust	**al polvo** ahl POHL-boh
to grass	**a la hierba** ah la YEHR-bah
to peanuts	**al maní / a los cacahuetes** ahl mah-NEE / ah lohs kah-kah-WEH-tehs

to pollen	**al polen** ahl POH-lehn
to shellfish	**a los mariscos** ah lohs mah-REES-kohs
Is your (*male*) child allergic to anything else?	**¿Es su hijo alérgico a otra cosa?** ehs soo EE-hoh ah-LEHR-hee-koh ah OH-trah KOH-sah
Is your (*female*) child allergic to anything else?	**¿Es su hija alérgica a otra cosa?** ehs soo EE-hah ah-LEHR-hee-kah ah OH-trah KOH-sah

The Physical Examination

El reconocimiento médico

All children who attend school need to have a comprehensive physical examination (**el reconocimiento médico** [ehl rreh-koh-noh-see-MYEHN-toh MEH-dee-koh]). If complete information is not turned in to the school, the admission of the child to school may be delayed. Here are some items that must be included in the medical examination.

height	**la estatura** lah ehs-tah-TOO-rah
weight	**el peso** ehl PEH-soh
blood pressure	**la tensión arterial** lah tehn-SYOHN ahr-teh-RYAHL
medical history	**la historia médica** lah ees-TOH-ryah MEH-dee-kah
nutritional evaluation	**la evaluación nutritiva** lah eh-bah-lwah-SYOHN noo-tree-TEE-bah
anemia screening	**el examen de anemia** ehl ehk-SAH-mehn deh ah-NEH-myah
dental screening	**el examen dental** ehl ehk-SAH-mehn dehn-TAHL
hearing screening	**el examen del oído** ehl ehk-SAH-mehn dehl oh-EE-doh
vision screening	**el examen de la vista** ehl ehk-SAH-mehn deh lah BEES-tah
developmental assessment	**la evaluación del desarrollo** lah eh-bah-lwah-SYOHN dehl deh-sah-RROH-yoh

lead poisoning assessment	**la evaluación de envenenamiento de plomo**
	lah eh-bah-lwah-SYOHN deh ehn-beh-neh-nah-MYEHN-toh deh PLOH-moh
tuberculosis test	**el examen de tuberculosis**
	ehl ehk-SAH-mehn deh too-behr-koo-LOH-sees

In Case of Emergency or Illness

En caso de emergencia o enfermedad

The following questions will be helpful if you need to ask whom to contact in case of emergency or illness (**en caso de emergencia o enfermedad** [ehn KAH-soh deh eh-mehr-HEHN-syah oh ehn-fehr-meh-DAHD]).

In case of an emergency, whom should we call?	**En caso de emergencia, ¿a quién debemos llamar?**
	ehn KAH-soh deh eh-mehr-HEHN-syah, ah kyehn deh-BEH-mohs yah-MAHR
What is his/her phone number at home / at work?	**¿Cuál es su número de teléfono en casa / en el trabajo?**
	kwahl ehs soo NOO-meh-roh deh teh-LEH-foh-noh ehn KAH-sah / ehn ehl trah-BAH-hoh

Health Insurance

El seguro de enfermedad

In many instances it is important to know if the child has health insurance (**el seguro de enfermedad** [ehl seh-GOO-roh deh ehn-fehr-meh-DAHD]).

Do you have health insurance?	**¿Tiene Ud. seguro de enfermedad?**
	TYEH-neh OOS-TEHD seh-GOO-roh deh ehn-fehr-meh-DAHD

Is your (*male*) child included in the health insurance?	**¿Está incluido su hijo en su seguro de enfermedad?** ehs-TAH een-kloo-EE-doh soo EE-hoh ehn soo seh-GOO-roh deh ehn-fehr-meh-DAHD
Is your (*female*) child included in the health insurance?	**¿Está incluida su hija en su seguro de enfermedad?** ehs-TAH een-kloo-EE-dah soo EE-hah ehn soo seh-GOO-roh deh ehn-fehr-meh-DAHD
Do you have Medicaid?	**¿Tiene Ud. seguro de enfermedad del estado (Medicaid)?** TYEH-neh OOS-TEHD seh-GOO-roh deh ehn-fehr-meh-DAHD dehl ehs-TAH-doh (meh-dee-KEH-eed)

There may be times when it is necessary to use an English word, for example, "Medicaid," since it may be the only way that parents will know what program you're asking about. For more information related to health issues, see Chapter 6.

Proof of Residency

Para comprobar el domicilio

Most schools require parents to provide proof of residency (**para comprobar el domicilio** [PAH-rah kohm-proh-BAHR ehl doh-mee-SEE-lyoh]). This would include proof of the family's address, proof of the child's previous schooling, and/or proof of his/her age. You must tell the parents which documents are acceptable as proof. The following will help you express these ideas.

To verify your address, you can bring ...	**Para comprobar su dirección puede traer...** PAH-rah kohm-proh-BAHR soo dee-rehk-SYOHN PWEH-deh trah-EHR
the electricity/gas/telephone bill	**la cuenta de la electricidad / del gas / del teléfono** lah KWEHN-tah deh lah eh-lehk-tree-see-DAHD / dehl gahs / dehl teh-LEH-foh-noh
the health insurance card	**la tarjeta de su seguro de enfermedad** lah tahr-HEH-tah deh soo seh-GOO-roh deh ehn-fehr-meh-DAHD

To verify your address, you can bring ...	**Para comprobar su dirección puede traer...** PAH-rah kohm-proh-BAHR soo dee-rehk-SYOHN PWEH-deh trah-EHR
the last income tax form	**el último formulario de declaración de impuestos** ehl OOL-tee-moh fohr-moo-LAH-ryoh deh deh-klah-rah-SYOHN deh eem-PWEHS-tohs
the driver's license	**la licencia de conducir** lah lee-SEHN-syah deh kohn-doo-SEER
To verify your child's previous schooling, you can bring a school transcript.	**Para comprobar la enseñanza previa de su hijo/hija puede traer la relación de notas de la escuela.** PAH-rah kohm-proh-BAHR lah ehn-seh-NYAHN-sah PREH-byah deh soo EE-hoh/EE-hah PWEH-deh trah-EHR lah rreh-lah-SYOHN deh NOH-tahs deh lah ehs-KWEH-lah
To verify your child's age, you can bring ...	**Para comprobar la edad de su hijo/hija puede traer...** PAH-rah kohm-proh-BAHR lah eh-DAHD deh soo EE-hoh/EE-hah PWEH-deh trah-EHR
the child's birth certificate	**el certificado de nacimiento del niño / de la niña** ehl sehr-tee-fee-KAH-doh deh nah-see-MYEHN-toh dehl NEE-nyoh / deh lah NEE-nyah
the child's baptismal certificate	**el certificado de bautismo del niño / de la niña** ehl sehr-tee-fee-KAH-doh deh bah-oo-TEES-moh dehl NEE-nyoh / deh lah NEE-nyah
the child's passport	**el pasaporte del niño / de la niña** ehl pah-sah-POHR-teh dehl NEE-nyoh / deh lah NEE-nyah

Vaccinations

Las vacunas

Students who are ready to enroll in any school must have a physical exam and proof of immunizations or vaccinations (**las vacunas** [lahs bah-KOO-nahs]) before they will be allowed to enroll in school.

You need to bring ...	**Necesita traer...**
	neh-seh-SEE-tah trah-EHR
the last physical exam report	**el reporte del último examen físico**
	ehl rreh-POHR-teh dehl OOL-tee-moh
	ehk-SAH-mehn FEE-see-koh
the report showing all vaccinations	**el reporte de todas las vacunas**
	ehl rreh-POHR-teh deh TOH-dahs lahs
	bah-KOO-nahs

Practice 1-6

A *Complete each of the following sentences with the missing Spanish words, using the English cues in parentheses.*

1. ¿Tiene Ud. _____ (other income)?

2. ¿Tiene problemas con _____ (hearing)?

3. ¿Está tomando su hijo _____ (any medicine)?

4. En caso de emergencia, ¿_____
   (whom should we call)?

5. ¿Tiene Ud. _____ (health insurance)?

6. Para comprobar su dirección, _____ (you can bring) la licencia de conducir.

7. Necesita traer _____
   (the report showing all vaccinations).

B Using the English cues in parentheses, unscramble each string of letters to form a Spanish word or expression, including its definite article. Then use the numbered letters to fill in the blanks below. What does the question ask?

vilasta (*eyesight*)

			19		1

mearendfaeld (*illness*)

		4									

eolpolv (*dust*)

5						

rososscialm (*shellfish*)

		6			9					

lihaebra (*grass*)

13	12	8	2	17	18		14

poelse (*weight*)

			11		

jmarebdouerladeaads (*bee sting*)

16	15				3		7		20							10		

¿ __ __ __ __ __   __ __   __ __ __ __   __ __ g u n __   __ __ __ __ g __ __ ?
  1 2 3 4 5   6 7   8 9 10 11   12 13   14   15 16 17 18   19 20

Traveling to School by Bus or by Car

Para viajar a la escuela en autobús o en coche/carro

Children often travel to school by school bus (**viajar a la escuela en autobús** [byah-HAHR ah lah ehs-KWEH-lah ehn ah-oo-toh-BOOS]) or are driven to school by car (**en coche/carro** [ehn KOH-cheh/KAH-rroh]) by their parents. The following will be helpful when communicating with parents about travel to and from school.

How does your child get to school?	**¿Cómo llega su hijo/hija a la escuela?** KOH-moh YEH-gah soo EE-hoh/EE-hah ah lah ehs-KWEH-lah
Who brings / picks up your child?	**¿Quién trae/recoge a su hijo/hija?** kyehn TRAH-eh/rreh-KOH-heh ah soo EE-hoh/EE-hah

A parent may have questions about travel to and from school, and may ask you questions similar to those that follow.

At what time should I bring / pick up my child?	**¿A qué hora debo traer/recoger a mi hijo/hija?** ah keh OH-rah DEH-boh trah-EHR/ rreh-koh-HEHR ah mee EE-hoh/EE-hah
Where do I drop off / pick up my child at school?	**¿Dónde dejo/recojo a mi hijo/hija en la escuela?** DOHN-deh DEH-hoh/rreh-KOH-hoh ah mee EE-hoh/EE-hah ehn lah ehs-KWEH-lah
At what time does the bus leave for school / for home?	**¿A qué hora sale el autobús para la escuela / para casa?** ah keh OH-rah SAH-leh ehl ah-oo-toh-BOOS PAH-rah lah ehs-KWEH-lah / PAH-rah KAH-sah
How long does it take to get to school?	**¿Cuánto tiempo dura el viaje a la escuela?** KWAHN-toh TYEHM-poh DOO-rah ehl BYAH-heh ah lah ehs-KWEH-lah
Where does the bus pick up the children?	**¿Dónde recoge el autobús a los niños?** DOHN-deh rreh-KOH-heh ehl ah-oo-toh-BOOS ah lohs NEE-nyohs
Where does he/she get off the bus?	**¿Dónde se baja del autobús?** DOHN-deh seh BAH-hah dehl ah-oo-toh-BOOS

Verbs

to arrive	**llegar**	yeh-GAHR
to get off	**bajar de**	bah-HAHR deh
to get on	**subir a**	soo-BEER ah
to leave	**salir** (*irreg.*)	sah-LEER
to pick up	**recoger** (*irreg.*)	rreh-koh-HEHR
to return	**regresar**	rreh-greh-SAHR
to return	**volver (ue)**	bohl-BEHR

Older children may either take public transportation or walk to school. Here is some important advice for students when they are traveling to school.

Get to the bus stop on time.	**Llega a tiempo a la parada.** YEH-gah ah TYEHM-poh ah lah pah-RAH-dah
Wait for the bus at the designated stop.	**Espera la llegada del autobús en la parada indicada.** ehs-PEH-rah lah yeh-GAH-dah dehl ah-oo-toh-BOOS ehn lah pah-RAH-dah een-dee-KAH-dah
Walk—don't run—when getting to or getting off the bus.	**Camina, no corras, para llegar al autobús ni tampoco al salir.** kah-MEE-nah, noh KOH-rrahs, PAH-rah yeh-GAHR ahl ah-oo-toh-BOOS nee tahm-POH-koh ahl sah-LEER
Don't stand near the curb.	**No te pares cerca del contén.** noh teh PAH-rehs SEHR-kah dehl kohn-TEHN
Don't push.	**No empujes.** noh ehm-POO-hehs
Stay seated.	**Manténte sentado.** mahn-TEHN-teh sehn-TAH-doh
Always obey the driver.	**Obedece siempre al chofer.** oh-beh-DEH-seh SYEHM-preh ahl choh-FEHR
Cross at the corner.	**Cruza en la esquina.** KROO-sah ehn lah ehs-KEE-nah
Wait for the green light.	**Espera la luz verde.** ehs-PEH-rah lah loos BEHR-deh

Wait for a signal from the driver before crossing.	**Espera la señal del chofer antes de cruzar.** ehs-PEH-rah lah seh-NYAHL dehl choh-FEHR AHN-tehs deh kroo-SAHR
Cross at least ten feet in front of the bus.	**Cruza siempre al menos diez pies delante del autobús.** KROO-sah SYEHM-preh ahl MEH-nohs dyehs pyehs deh-LAHN-teh dehl ah-oo-toh-BOOS

Some useful words for places and things around the neighborhood (**el barrio** [ehl BAH-rryoh]) follow.

alley	**el callejón** ehl kah-yeh-HOHN
apartment building	**el edificio de apartamentos** ehl eh-dee-FEE-syoh deh ah-pahr-tah-MEHN-tohs
avenue	**la avenida** lah ah-beh-NEE-dah
block	**la cuadra** lah KWAH-drah
bridge	**el puente** ehl PWEHN-teh
building	**el edificio** ehl eh-dee-FEE-syoh
bus stop	**la parada de autobuses** lah pah-RAH-dah deh ah-oo-toh-BOO-sehs
corner (outside)	**la esquina** lah ehs-KEE-nah
fence	**la cerca** lah SEHR-kah
intersection	**la bocacalle** lah boh-kah-KAH-yeh
sidewalk	**la acera** lah ah-SEH-rah
sign	**el letrero** ehl leh-TREH-roh

street	**la calle**
	lah KAH-yeh
street light	**el farol**
	ehl fah-ROHL
subway station	**la estación de metro**
	lah ehs-tah-SYOHN deh MEH-troh
traffic	**el tránsito**
	ehl TRAHN-see-toh
traffic sign	**la señal de tráfico**
	lah seh-NYAHL deh TRAH-fee-koh

Traffic Signs

Las señales de tráfico

one-way street	**la calle de dirección única**
	lah KAH-yeh deh dee-rehk-SYOHN oo-nee-kah
two-way street	**la calle de doble sentido**
	lah KAH-yeh deh DOH-bleh sehn-TEE-doh
pedestrian crossing	**el paso de peatones**
	ehl PAH-soh deh peh-ah-TOH-nehs
railroad crossing	**el cruce de ferrocarril**
	ehl KROO-seh deh feh-rroh-kah-RREEL
school crossing sign	**la señal de cruce escolar**
	lah seh-NYAHL deh KROO-seh ehs-koh-LAHR
stop sign	**la señal de parar**
	lah seh-NYAHL deh pah-RAHR
traffic light	**el semáforo**
	ehl seh-MAH-foh-roh
Do not cross!	**¡Prohibido cruzar!**
	proh-ee-BEE-doh kroo-SAHR
Do not enter!	**¡Paso prohibido!**
	PAH-soh proh-ee-BEE-doh
School crossing!	**¡Cruce escolar!**
	KROO-seh ehs-koh-LAHR
Stop!	**¡Pare!**
	PAH-reh
Yield!	**¡Ceda!**
	SEH-dah

At times, a parent may ask for directions or for help getting to school or to some other place. Following are some of the things that a parent may ask or say.

I am lost.	**Estoy perdido/perdida.** ehs-TOH-ee pehr-DEE-doh/pehr-DEE-dah
Would you tell me where _____ is?	**¿Podría decirme dónde está _____?** poh-DREE-ah deh-SEER-meh DOHN-deh ehs-TAH
Would you explain to me how to get to _____?	**Podría explicarme cómo llegar/ir a _____?** poh-DREE-ah ehs-plee-KAHR-meh KOH-moh yeh-GAHR/eer ah

GRAMMAR · Using the Verb "To Be" to Express Location

estar (*irreg.*) [ehs-TAHR] to be

I am	**yo estoy**	yoh ehs-TOH-ee
you are	**tú estás**	too ehs-TAHS
he is	**él está**	ehl ehs-TAH
she is	**ella está**	EH-yah ehs-TAH
you are	**Ud. está**	OOS-TEHD ehs-TAH
we are	**nosotros estamos**	noh-SOH-trohs ehs-TAH-mohs
we are	**nosotras estamos**	noh-SOH-trahs ehs-TAH-mohs
they are	**ellos están**	EH-yohs ehs-TAHN
they are	**ellas están**	EH-yahs ehs-TAHN
you (*plural*) are	**Uds. están**	OOS-TEH-dehs ehs-TAHN

To tell where something (or someone) is located, use the verb **estar** [ehs-TAHR], meaning "to be," + the location.

It is …	**Está…** ehs-TAH
at the intersection of	**en el cruce de** ehn ehl KROO-seh deh
down the street	**calle abajo** KAH-yeh ah-BAH-hoh
facing	**frente a** FREHN-teh ah
far away	**lejos (de aquí)** LEH-hohs (deh ah-KEE)
nearby	**cerca (de aquí)** SEHR-kah (deh ah-KEE)

It is …	**Está…**
	ehs-TAH
(four) minutes away	**a (cuatro) minutos**
	ah (KWAH-troh) mee-NOO-tohs
(five) blocks away	**a (cinco) cuadras**
	ah (SEEN-koh) KWAH-drahs
in the next block	**en la próxima cuadra**
	ehn lah PROHK-see-mah KWAH-drah
on the corner	**en la esquina**
	ehn lah ehs-KEE-nah
to the east	**al este**
	ahl EHS-teh
to the north	**al norte**
	ahl NOHR-teh
to the south	**al sur**
	ahl soor
to the west	**al oeste**
	ahl oh-EHS-teh
up the street	**calle arriba**
	KAH-yeh ah-RREE-bah

For more expressions indicating location, see Chapter 2, pages 77–78.

Practice 1-7

A *Find the words in the list below within the grid of letters. Words can appear horizontally, vertically, or diagonally.*

acera
avenida
calle
callejón
cuadra
edificio
esquina
fuente
manzana
puente
rascacielos
vitrina

```
L Y X Z B P J C U I G X F Q X
F S C S W J O I C I F I D E V
U A C E R A A E B N K Y P R N
E A W E I E C V E A N S A E K
N R R I M T T M E J U B W W T
T D N A D L K N I N A V D M J
E A V O S Y S J E E I I G G J
D U I A J C Y V A U H D G G E
E C T X K E A S D N P S A V L
F D R U C H L C N W I B W U L
D S I J D U N L I G P U D N A
C U N O C Z H B A E S H Q G C
K J A B K C M N J C L I Y S X
A N A Z N A M J C C Y O U N E
H O Q C I M G O W M K Y S D T
```

B *Complete the following crossword puzzle.*

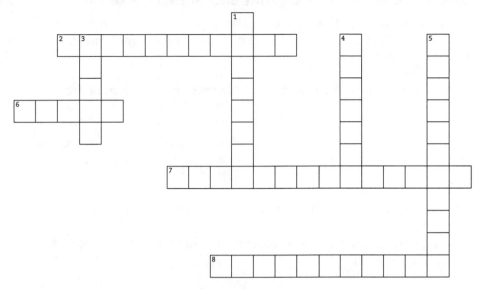

Across
2. at the intersection of
6. west
7. pedestrian crossing
8. nearby

Down
1. traffic light
3. north
4. facing
5. far from here

C *While on a bus trip, you need to give some instructions to your students. What would you say to them? Review the **Ud./Uds.** command forms, and write the correct command for each instruction given.*

1. to wait for the green light

_____

2. to get on the bus

_____

3. not to push

_____

4. to walk, not run

_____

5. not to shout

_____

GRAMMAR · Expressing What Someone Has to Do

To tell someone what he or she has to do, use the pattern "you have to" + infinitive (**Ud. tiene que** [oos-TEHD TYEH-neh keh] or **tú tienes que** [too TYEH-nehs keh] + infinitive).

You have to cross at the corner.	**Ud. tiene que cruzar en la esquina.** oos-TEHD TYEH-neh keh kroo-SAHR ehn lah ehs-KEE-nah
	Tú tienes que cruzar en la esquina. too TYEH-nehs keh kroo-SAHR ehn lah ehs-KEE-nah

For the present tense of the verb **tener**, see page 33 in this chapter.

When giving instructions to someone traveling on foot, you can use the following expressions.

You have to …	**Usted tiene que…** oos-TEHD TYEH-neh keh
	Tú tienes que… too TYEH-nehs keh
continue straight ahead	**seguir derecho** seh-GEER deh-REH-choh
cross	**cruzar** kroo-SAHR
go up to	**ir hasta** eer AHS-tah
go down to	**bajar hasta** bah-HAHR AHS-tah
turn right	**doblar a la derecha** doh-BLAHR ah lah deh-REH-chah
turn left	**doblar a la izquierda** doh-BLAHR ah lah ees-KYEHR-dah

If someone is taking public transportation, use the following expressions.

You should take …	**Ud. debe tomar...**
	oos-TEHD DEH-beh toh-MAHR
	Tú debes tomar...
	too DEH-behs toh-MAHR
the bus	**el autobús**
	ehl ah-oo-toh-BOOS
the (a) cab	**el (un) taxi**
	ehl (oon) TAHK-see
the train/subway	**el tren/metro**
	ehl trehn/MEH-troh
You should get off at _____.	**Ud. debe bajarse en _____.**
	oos-TEHD DEH-beh bah-HAHR-seh ehn

Practice 1-8

To complete the following exercise, write the correct form of the verb **tener** *in the first blank. Then, using the English cues in parentheses, choose the correct expression from the list below and write it in the second blank.*

ir hasta la esquina	llegar a tiempo a la parada
doblar a la izquierda	cruzar la calle
esperar la luz verde	tomar el metro
doblar a la derecha	

1. Juan, _____ (tú) que _____.
   (cross the street)

2. Nosotros _____ que _____.
   (wait for the green light)

3. Ellos _____ que _____.
   (get to the bus stop on time)

4. Ella _____ que _____.
   (go up to the corner)

5. Yo _____ que _____.
   (turn right)

Summary Practice

Using the correct form of the verb(s) in parentheses, write a sentence in Spanish that is equivalent to each of the following.

1. Does your child have any condition that requires special attention? (**tener/requerir**)

   _____

2. How many people live in your house? (**vivir**)

   _____

3. I am in a hurry. (**tener**)

   _____

4. How old is she? (**tener**)

   _____

5. The office is two blocks away. (**estar**)

   _____

6. Where are you (**Ud.**) from? (**ser**)

   _____

7. You (**Ud.**) have to continue straight ahead. (**tener**)

   _____

8. How does your daughter get to school? (**llegar**)

   _____

9. You (**Ud.**) have to wait for the bus at the designated stop. (**tener**)

   _____

10. I am lost. (**estar**)

    _____

11. Wait (**Ud.**) for a signal from the driver before crossing. (**esperar**)

    _____

2

The School Building

La escuela

School Personnel/Staff

El *personal de la escuela*

Many people work in a school or in occupations that bring them into daily contact with school-age children. Here are some typical positions of school personnel (**el personal de la escuela** [ehl pehr-soh-NAHL deh lah ehs-KWEH-lah]).

administrator	**el administrador / la administradora** ehl ahd-mee-nees-trah-DOHR / lah ahd-mee-nees-trah-DOH-rah
advisor	**el consejero / la consejera** ehl kohn-seh-HEH-roh / lah kohn-seh-HEH-rah
aide	**el/la asistente** ehl/lah ah-sees-TEHN-teh
assistant principal	**el/la asistente al director / a la directora** ehl/lah ah-sees-TEHN-teh ahl dee-rehk-TOHR / ah lah dee-rek-TOH-rah
board member	**el miembro de la junta directiva** ehl MYEHM-broh deh lah HOON-tah dee-rehk-TEE-bah
bus driver	**el conductor / la conductora de autobús** ehl kohn-dook-TOHR / lah kohn-dook-TOH- rah deh ah-oo-toh-BOOS
cashier	**el cajero / la cajera** ehl kah-HEH-roh / lah kah-HEH-rah
chairperson (of the _____ department)	**el jefe / la jefa (de la cátedra de _____)** ehl HEH-feh / lah HEH-fah (deh lah KAH-teh-drah deh)
coach (sports)	**el entrenador / la entrenadora** ehl ehn-treh-nah-DOHR / lah ehn-treh-nah-DOH-rah
cook	**el cocinero / la cocinera** ehl koh-see-NEH-roh / lah koh-see-NEH-rah
counselor	**el consejero / la consejera** ehl kohn-seh-HEH-roh / lah kohn-seh-HEH-rah
crossing guard	**la persona encargada de ayudar a los niños a cruzar la calle** lah pehr-SOH-nah ehn-kahr-GAH-dah deh ah-yoo-DAHR ah lohs NEE-nyohs ah kroo-SAHR lah KAH-yeh

custodian	**el guardián / la guardiana** ehl gwahr-DYAHN / lah gwahr-DYAH-nah
headmaster/headmistress	**el director / la directora** ehl dee-rehk-TOHR / lah dee-rehk-TOH-rah
instructor	**el instructor / la instructora** ehl eens-trook-TOHR / lah eens-trook-TOH-rah
interpreter	**el/la intérprete** ehl/lah een-TEHR-preh-teh
janitor	**el/la conserje** ehl/lah kohn-SEHR-heh
librarian	**el bibliotecario / la bibliotecaria** ehl bee-blyoh-teh-KAH-ryoh / lah bee-blyoh-teh-KAH-ryah
nurse	**el enfermero / la enfermera** ehl ehn-fehr-MEH-roh / lah ehn-fehr-MEH-rah
principal	**el director / la directora** ehl dee-rehk-TOHR / lah dee-rehk-TOH-rah
psychologist	**el psicólogo / la psicóloga** ehl see-KOH-loh-goh / lah see-KOH-loh-gah
receptionist	**el/la recepcionista** ehl/lah rreh-sehp-syoh-NEES-tah
secretary	**el secretario / la secretaria** ehl seh-kreh-TAH-ryoh / lah seh-kreh-TAH-ryah
security guard	**el/la guardia de seguridad** ehl/lah GWAHR-dyah deh seh-goo-ree-DAHD
superintendent	**el/la superintendente** ehl/lah soo-peh-reen-tehn-DEHN-teh
supervisor	**el supervisor / la supervisora** ehl soo-pehr-bee-SOHR / lah soo-pehr-bee-SOH-rah
teacher	**el maestro / la maestra** ehl mah-EHS-troh / lah mah-EHS-trah

teacher's aide	**el/la asistente del maestro /**
	de la maestra
	ehl/lah ah-sees-TEHN-teh dehl
	mah-EHS-troh / deh lah mah-EHS-trah
therapist	**el/la terapista**
	ehl/lah teh-rah-PEES-tah
trainer	**el entrenador / la entrenadora**
	ehl ehn-treh-nah-DOHR /
	lah ehn-treh-nah-DOH-rah
translator	**el traductor / la traductora**
	ehl trah-dook-TOHR /
	lah trah-dook-TOH-rah
volunteer	**el voluntario / la voluntaria**
	ehl boh-loon-TAH-ryoh /
	lah boh-loon-TAH-ryah

Grammar · To Find Out "Who?"

When you need to find out who is in charge or who does a particular job in the school building, you will need to ask the following questions.

Who is _____?	**¿Quién es _____?**
	kyehn ehs
Who are _____?	**¿Quiénes son _____?**
	KYEH-nehs sohn

Note that **quiénes** [KYEH-nehs] is used when you expect the answer to be more than one person.

Who is the teacher?	**¿Quién es el maestro / la maestra?**
	kyehn ehs ehl mah-EHS-troh /
	lah mah-EHS-trah
It is Mr. _____ /	**Es el señor _____ /**
Mrs. _____ / Miss _____.	**la señora _____ / la señorita _____.**
	ehs ehl seh-NYOHR / lah seh-NYOH-rah /
	lah seh-nyoh-REE-tah
Who are the members of the school board?	**¿Quiénes son los miembros de la junta directiva?**
	KYEH-nehs sohn lohs MYEHM-brohs deh
	lah HOON-tah dee-rehk-TEE-bah
Several parents are the members of the school board.	**Varios padres son los miembros de la junta directiva.**
	BAH-ryohs PAH-drehs sohn lohs
	MYEHM-brohs deh lah HOON-tah
	dee-rehk-TEE-bah

Practice 2-1

Write the Spanish words that identify the people being described. Remember to use the appropriate definite articles.

1. Who works in the library? _____

2. Who fixes problems with the boiler? _____

3. Who cleans the school building? _____

4. Who translates? _____

5. Who helps the children cross the street? _____

6. Who answers the phones? _____

7. Who maintains the security? _____

8. Who works in the cafeteria? _____

9. Who instructs the students in a sport? _____

10. Who drives the bus? _____

School Supplies

Los materiales necesarios para la escuela

Here is a list of many of the supplies needed for school (**los materiales necesarios para la escuela** [lohs mah-teh-RYAH-lehs neh-seh-SAH-ryohs PAH-rah lah ehs-KWEH-lah]).

backpack	**la mochila** lah moh-CHEE-lah
bag	**la bolsa** lah BOHL-sah
ballpoint pen	**el bolígrafo** ehl boh-LEE-grah-foh
book	**el libro** ehl LEE-broh
brush (artist's)	**el pincel** ehl peen-SEHL
calculator	**la calculadora** lah kahl-koo-lah-DOH-rah
compass	**el compás** ehl kohm-PAHS

computer	**la computadora**
	lah kohm-poo-tah-DOH-rah
dictionary	**el diccionario**
	ehl deek-syoh-NAH-ryoh
electronic organizer	**el organizador electrónico**
	ehl ohr-gah-nee-sah-DOHR
	eh-lehk-TROH-nee-koh
eraser (rubber)	**la goma de borrar**
	lah GOH-mah deh boh-RRAHR
file folder	**la carpeta**
	lah kahr-PEH-tah
highlighter	**el marcador**
	ehl mahr-kah-DOHR
lock	**el candado**
	ehl kahn-DAH-doh
notebook	**el cuaderno**
	ehl kwah-DEHR-noh
paper	**el papel**
	ehl pah-PEHL
pen	**la pluma**
	lah PLOO-mah
pencil	**el lápiz**
	ehl LAH-pees
pencil sharpener	**el sacapuntas**
	ehl sah-kah-POON-tahs
ruler	**la regla**
	lah RREH-glah
scissors	**las tijeras**
	lahs tee-HEH-rahs

GRAMMAR · Using the Verb "To Be" to Express Identification

At this point you may want to learn how to identify objects around you. There are two basic questions you can use, depending on whether you are asking about one object or about more than one object: "What is _____?" and "What are _____?" You always use the Spanish verb **ser** [sehr], meaning "to be."

What is it? (*singular*)	**¿Qué es?**
	keh ehs
What are they? (*plural*)	**¿Qué son?**
	keh sohn
It is _____.	**Es** _____.
	ehs

They are _____.	**Son** _____. sohn
What is this/that?	**¿Qué es esto/eso?** keh ehs EHS-toh/EH-soh
It is a highlighter.	**Es un marcador.** ehs oon mahr-kah-DOHR

For the conjugation of the present tense of the verb **ser** [sehr], see Chapter 1, page 42.

Practice 2-2

*Identify each of the following objects usually found in a classroom. Write a complete sentence using the verb **ser** to identify each one.*

1. _____

2. _____

3. _____

4. _____

5.  _____

6.  _____

More School-Related Vocabulary

Más vocabulario relacionado con la escuela

Here is a list of additional school-related vocabulary (**el vocabulario relacio-nado con la escuela** [ehl boh-kah-boo-LAH-ryoh rreh-lah-syoh-NAH-doh kohn lah ehs-KWEH-lah]) that will prove very useful to you.

elementary school	**la escuela primaria** lah ehs-KWEH-lah pree-MAH-ryah
grade (level)	**el grado** ehl GRAH-doh
grade (mark)	**la nota** lah NOH-tah
graduation	**la graduación** lah grah-dwah-SYOHN
high school	**la escuela secundaria** lah ehs-KWEH-lah seh-koon-DAH-ryah
homework	**la tarea** lah tah-REH-ah
lesson	**la lección** lah lehk-SYOHN
recess	**el recreo** ehl rreh-KREH-oh
report	**el informe** ehl een-FOHR-meh
report card	**el boletín** ehl boh-leh-TEEN

schedule	**el horario** ehl oh-RAH-ryoh
school year	**el año escolar** ehl AH-nyoh ehs-koh-LAHR
semester	**el semestre** ehl seh-MEHS-treh
student	**el/la estudiante** ehl/lah ehs-too-DYAHN-teh
subject	**la asignatura** lah ah-seeg-nah-TOO-rah
test	**el examen / la prueba** ehl ehk-SAH-mehn / lah PRWEH-bah

The School Building

La escuela

If you are familiar with the vocabulary related to the school building itself, you will be able to talk about where many things are located. It will also help you when you need to give directions. The following lists deal with both the building itself and its surroundings, and they will help you to communicate about situations in and around the school (**dentro y alrededor de la escuela** [DEHN-troh ee ahl-rreh-deh-DOHR deh lah ehs-KWEH-lah]).

Rooms in the School

Los cuartos de la escuela

auditorium	**el auditorio** ehl ah-oo-dee-TOH-ryoh
	el salón / la sala de actos ehl sah-LOHN / lah SAH-lah deh AHK-tohs
basement	**el sótano** ehl SOH-tah-noh
bathroom	**el cuarto de baño** ehl KWAHR-toh deh BAH-nyoh
boiler room	**la sala de calderas** lah SAH-lah deh kahl-DEH-rahs
cafeteria	**la cafetería** lah kah-feh-teh-REE-ah
classroom	**el salón de clases / el aula** ehl sah-LOHN deh KLAH-sehs / ehl AH-oo-lah

computer lab	**el laboratorio de computadoras** ehl lah-boh-rah-ᴛᴏʜ-ryoh deh kohm-poo-tah-ᴅᴏʜ-rahs
copy machine room	**el cuarto de la copiadora** ehl ᴋᴡᴀʜʀ-toh deh lah koh-pyah-ᴅᴏʜ-rah
counseling office	**la oficina del consejero / de la consejera** lah oh-fee-ꜱᴇᴇ-nah dehl kohn-seh-ʜᴇʜ-roh / deh lah kohn-seh-ʜᴇʜ-rah
gymnasium	**el gimnasio** ehl heem-ɴᴀʜ-syoh
laboratory	**el laboratorio** ehl lah-boh-rah-ᴛᴏʜ-ryoh
library	**la biblioteca** lah bee-blyoh-ᴛᴇʜ-kah
locker room	**el vestuario** ehl behs-ᴛᴡᴀʜ-ryoh
mail room	**el cuarto de correo** ehl ᴋᴡᴀʜʀ-toh deh koh-ʀʀᴇʜ-oh
nurse's office	**la oficina del enfermero / de la enfermera** lah oh-fee-ꜱᴇᴇ-nah dehl ehn-fehr-ᴍᴇʜ-roh / deh lah ehn-fehr-ᴍᴇʜ-rah
staff room	**la sala de maestros** lah ꜱᴀʜ-lah deh mah-ᴇʜꜱ-trohs

In and Around the School Building
Dentro y alrededor de la escuela

air conditioning	**el aire acondicionado** ehl ᴀʜ-ee-reh ah-kohn-dee-syoh-ɴᴀʜ-doh
carpet	**la alfombra** lah ahl-ꜰᴏʜᴍ-brah
ceiling	**el techo** ehl ᴛᴇʜ-choh
corridor	**el pasillo** ehl pah-ꜱᴇᴇ-yoh
door	**la puerta** lah ᴘᴡᴇʜʀ-tah

driveway	**la entrada (para carros)**
	lah ehn-TRAH-dah (PAH-rah KAH-rrohs)
elevator	**el ascensor**
	ehl ah-sehn-SOHR
entrance	**la entrada**
	lah ehn-TRAH-dah
escalator	**la escalera mecánica**
	lah ehs-kah-LEH-rah meh-KAH-nee-kah
exit	**la salida**
	lah sah-LEE-dah
fence	**la cerca**
	lah SEHR-kah
fire extinguisher	**el extintor**
	ehl ehs-teen-TOHR
flag	**la bandera**
	lah bahn-DEH-rah
floor (ground surface, flooring)	**el suelo**
	ehl SWEH-loh
floor (story)	**el piso**
	ehl PEE-soh
gate	**la verja**
	lah BEHR-hah
hallway	**el pasillo**
	ehl pah-SEE-yoh
heat	**la calefacción**
	lah kah-leh-fahk-SYOHN
light	**la luz**
	lah loos
lobby	**el vestíbulo**
	ehl behs-TEE-boo-loh
locker	**el cajón con llave**
	ehl kah-HOHN kohn YAH-beh
parking lot	**el estacionamiento**
	ehl ehs-tah-syoh-nah-MYEHN-toh
playground	**el patio de recreo**
	ehl PAH-tyoh deh rreh-KREH-oh
roof	**el techo**
	ehl TEH-choh
staircase	**la escalera**
	lah ehs-kah-LEH-rah

wall	**la pared**
	lah pah-REHD
water fountain	**la fuente de agua potable**
	lah FWEHN-teh deh AH-gwah
	poh-TAH-bleh
window	**la ventana**
	lah behn-TAH-nah
window shade/blind	**la persiana**
	lah pehr-SYAH-nah

In the Bathroom
En el cuarto de baño

In a school, the bathrooms (**los cuartos de baño** [lohs KWAHR-tohs deh BAH-nyoh]) that are used by the students are usually separate from those used by the adults.

boys' bathroom	**el baño para niños**
	ehl BAH-nyoh PAH-rah NEE-nyohs
girls' bathroom	**el baño para niñas**
	ehl BAH-nyoh PAH-rah NEE-nyahs
men's bathroom	**el baño para caballeros**
	ehl BAH-nyoh PAH-rah kah-bah-YEH-rohs
women's bathroom	**el baño para damas**
	ehl BAH-nyoh PAH-rah DAH-mahs

Here are some of the items you will typically find in the bathroom.

mirror	**el espejo**
	ehl ehs-PEH-hoh
paper towel	**la toalla de papel**
	lah toh-AH-yah deh pah-PEHL
sink	**el lavamanos**
	ehl lah-bah-MAH-nohs
soap	**el jabón**
	ehl hah-BOHN
toilet	**el servicio**
	ehl sehr-BEE-syoh
toilet paper	**el papel higiénico**
	ehl pah-PEHL ee-HYEH-nee-koh
urinal	**el orinal**
	ehl oh-ree-NAHL

Verbs

to ask for permission	**pedir (i) permiso**	peh-DEER pehr-MEE-soh
to dry your hands	**secarse las manos**	seh-KAHR-seh lahs MAH-nohs
to flush the toilet	**descargar**	dehs-kahr-GAHR
to wash your hands	**lavarse las manos**	lah-BAHR-seh lahs MAH-nohs

GRAMMAR · To Find Out "Where?"

If the parents or students you encounter are not familiar with the school building, you will probably be asked questions such as the following, depending on whether someone is asking about the location of one thing or about the location of more than one thing: "Where is _____?" or "Where are _____?"

Remember that to tell the location of a person, place, or thing, you use the verb **estar** [ehs-TAHR], meaning "to be."

Where is _____? (*singular*)	**¿Dónde está _____?** DOHN-deh ehs-TAH
Where are _____? (*plural*)	**¿Dónde están _____?** DOHN-deh ehs-TAHN
Where is the bathroom?	**¿Dónde está el cuarto de baño?** DOHN-deh ehs-TAH ehl KWAHR-toh deh BAH-nyoh
It is there.	**Está allí.** ehs-TAH ah-YEE
Where are the elevators?	**¿Dónde están los ascensores?** DOHN-deh ehs-TAHN lohs ah-sehn-SOH-rehs
They are over there.	**Están allá.** ehs-TAHN ah-YAH

You will also need to become familiar with several expressions that indicate location or give directions. Here is a list of several of them.

It is ... / They are ...	**Está.../Están...** ehs-TAH/ehs-TAHN
behind	**detrás de** deh-TRAHS deh
downstairs	**abajo** ah-BAH-hoh
in front of	**enfrente de** ehn-FREHN-teh deh
in the corner	**en el rincón** ehn ehl rreen-KOHN

It is … / They are …	Está…/Están… ehs-TAH/ehs-TAHN
inside	**adentro** ah-DEHN-troh
next to	**al lado de** ahl LAH-doh deh
on the corner	**en la esquina** ehn lah ehs-KEE-nah
on the first/second/third floor	**en el primer/segundo/tercer piso** ehn ehl pree-MEHR/seh-GOON-doh/ tehr-SEHR PEE-soh
outside	**afuera** ah-FWEH-rah
over there	**allá** ah-YAH
there	**allí** ah-YEE
to the right	**a la derecha** ah lah deh-REH-chah
to the left	**a la izquierda** ah lah ees-KYEHR-dah
at the end of	**al final de** ahl fee-NAHL deh
upstairs	**arriba** ah-RREE-bah

For more expressions indicating location, see Chapter 1, pages 59–60.

In the Classroom / In the Office
En la sala de clase / En la oficina

Many of the objects you find in a classroom (**la sala de clase** [lah SAH-lah deh KLAH-seh]) can also be found in any office (**la oficina** [lah oh-fee-SEE-nah]). The following list will come in handy when you are talking about either place.

bell (electric)	**el timbre** ehl TEEM-breh
bell (hand)	**la campana** lah kahm-PAH-nah
bookcase	**la estantería** lah ehs-tahn-teh-REE-ah
box	**la caja** lah KAH-hah

chair	**la silla**
	lah SEE-yah
chalk	**la tiza**
	lah TEE-sah
chalkboard	**la pizarra**
	lah pee-SAH-rrah
clock	**el reloj**
	ehl rreh-LOH
closet	**el armario**
	ehl ahr-MAH-ryoh
computer	**la computadora**
	lah kohm-poo-tah-DOH-rah
copy machine	**la copiadora**
	lah koh-pyah-DOH-rah
copy machine toner	**la tinta de copiar**
	lah TEEN-tah deh koh-PYAHR
counter	**el mostrador**
	ehl mohs-trah-DOHR
desk	**el escritorio**
	ehl ehs-kree-TOH-ryoh
desk (student)	**el pupitre**
	ehl poo-PEE-treh
drawer	**el cajón**
	ehl kah-HOHN
envelope	**el sobre**
	ehl SOH-breh
eraser (chalkboard)	**el borrador (de la pizarra)**
	ehl boh-rrah-DOHR
	(deh lah pee-SAH-rrah)
fax machine	**el telefax**
	ehl teh-leh-FAHKS
file cabinet	**el fichero**
	ehl fee-CHEH-roh
file folder	**la carpeta**
	lah kahr-PEH-tah
files	**el archivo**
	ehl ahr-CHEE-boh
ink	**la tinta**
	lah TEEN-tah
letter	**la carta**
	lah KAHR-tah
loudspeaker	**el altavoz**
	ehl ahl-tah-BOHS

overhead projector	**el retroproyector**	
	ehl rreh-troh-proh-yehk-TOHR	
paper	**el papel**	
	ehl pah-PEHL	
paper clip	**el sujetapapeles**	
	ehl soo-heh-tah-pah-PEH-lehs	
pass (permission)	**el pase / el permiso**	
	ehl PAH-seh / ehl pehr-MEE-soh	
picture	**el cuadro**	
	ehl KWAH-droh	
poster	**el cartel**	
	ehl kahr-TEHL	
printer	**la impresora**	
	lah eem-preh-SOH-rah	
rug	**la alfombra**	
	lah ahl-FOHM-brah	
sheet of paper	**la hoja de papel**	
	lah OH-hah deh pah-PEHL	
stamp	**el sello**	
	ehl SEH-yoh	
staple	**la grapa**	
	lah GRAH-pah	
stapler	**la grapadora**	
	lah grah-pah-DOH-rah	
table	**la mesa**	
	lah MEH-sah	
telephone	**el teléfono**	
	ehl teh-LEH-foh-noh	
trash can	**el cubo de la basura**	
	ehl KOO-boh deh lah bah-SOO-rah	
wastepaper basket	**la papelera**	
	lah pah-peh-LEH-rah	

Verbs

to announce	**anunciar**	ah-noon-SYAHR
to call	**llamar**	yah-MAHR
to copy	**copiar**	koh-PYAHR
to fax	**mandar por fax**	mahn-DAHR pohr fahks
to file	**archivar**	ahr-chee-BAHR
to fill out	**llenar**	yeh-NAHR
to photocopy	**fotocopiar**	foh-toh-koh-PYAHR
to staple	**sujetar con grapas**	soo-heh-TAHR kohn GRAH-pahs

Practice 2-3

A Using the English cues in parentheses, unscramble each string of letters to form a Spanish word or expression, including its definite article. Then use the numbered letters to fill in the blanks below. What is the phrase?

aaucrñeoetlbod (bathroom)

[ ][ ][ ][ ][ ][ ][ ][ ][ ][ ][ ][ ][ ][ ][ ][ ][ ][ ]
    4

dallaearsotamses (staff room)

[ ][ ][ ][ ][ ][ ][ ][ ][ ][ ][ ][ ][ ][ ][ ][ ][ ][ ][ ]
              7

ontasoel (basement)

[ ][ ][ ][ ][ ][ ][ ][ ]
    10

soellasnceadsle (classroom)

[ ][ ][ ][ ][ ][ ][ ][ ][ ][ ][ ][ ][ ][ ][ ][ ][ ]
    9

aciltboalbei (library)

[ ][ ][ ][ ][ ][ ][ ][ ][ ][ ][ ][ ][ ][ ]
      8

tadilioouer (auditorium)

[ ][ ][ ][ ][ ][ ][ ][ ][ ][ ][ ][ ][ ]
    5

dreuecltreocoora (mail room)

[ ][ ][ ][ ][ ][ ][ ][ ][ ][ ][ ][ ][ ][ ][ ][ ][ ][ ]
 12 1 17 18 14   11 15   19

onsigemlia (gymnasium)

[ ][ ][ ][ ][ ][ ][ ][ ][ ][ ][ ][ ]
      6

lvisuraoete (locker room)

[ ][ ][ ][ ][ ][ ][ ][ ][ ][ ][ ][ ][ ]
    3

feioienrnsdcjoacaleol (counselor's office)

[ ]
 13 21 2   20   16

___ ___ ___ ___ ___ ___ ___ ___ ___ ___ ___ ___ ___ ___ ___ ___ ___ ___ ___ ___ ___
 1 2 3   4 5 6 7 8 9 10 11 12 13 14 15 16 17 18 19 20 21

B *Complete the following crossword puzzle.*

Across
   5. carpet
   7. mirror
   11. exit
   12. flag
   13. ceiling
   14. light
   15. wall

Down
   1. sink
   2. window
   3. bathroom
   4. door
   6. hallway
   8. entrance
   9. staircase
   10. soap

C *Using the English cues in parentheses, write complete sentences in Spanish to tell where the following people, places, or things are located. Use the verb* **estar**.

   1. ¿Dónde está el gimnasio? (*in the basement*)

   _____

   2. ¿Dónde están las fuentes de agua potable? (*there*)

   _____

3. ¿Dónde están las toallas de papel? (*in the drawer*)

   _____

4. ¿Dónde está la oficina del director? (*in front of the auditorium*)

   _____

5. ¿Dónde está el sujetapapeles? (*next to the printer*)

   _____

6. ¿Dónde está el cubo de la basura? (*in the corner*)

   _____

7. ¿Dónde están los carteles? (*on the wall*)

   _____

8. ¿Dónde está la consejera? (*next to the nurse*)

   _____

9. ¿Dónde está el escritorio? (*in front of the students' desks*)

   _____

10. ¿Dónde están las estanterías? (*behind the copy machine*)

   _____

D Write the correct English word for the people, places, or things that are being asked about in each item in Exercise C.

1. _____
2. _____
3. _____
4. _____
5. _____
6. _____
7. _____
8. _____
9. _____
10. _____

In the Library
En la biblioteca

book	**el libro** ehl LEE-broh
fine	**la multa** lah MOOL-tah
library card	**la tarjeta de biblioteca** lah tahr-HEH-tah deh bee-blyoh-TEH-kah
magazine	**la revista** lah rreh-BEES-tah
newspaper	**el periódico** ehl peh-RYOH-dee-koh
page	**la página** lah PAH-hee-nah
return date	**la fecha de devolución** lah FEH-chah deh deh-boh-loo-SYOHN
shelf	**el estante** ehl ehs-TAHN-teh
subscription	**la suscripción** lah soos-kreep-SYOHN
volume (book)	**el tomo** ehl TOH-moh

Verbs

to borrow	**pedir (i) prestado/prestada**	peh-DEER prehs-TAH-doh/ prehs-TAH-dah
to find	**encontrar (ue)**	ehn-kohn-TRAHR
to keep silent	**guardar silencio**	gwahr-DAHR see-LEHN-syoh
to look for	**buscar**	boos-KAHR
to lose	**perder (ie)**	pehr-DEHR
to pay the fine	**pagar la multa**	pah-GAHR lah MOOL-tah
to research	**investigar**	een-behs-tee-GAHR
to return, give back	**devolver (ue)**	deh-bohl-BEHR

In the Auditorium
En el auditorio / el salón de actos / la sala de actos

aisle	**el pasillo** ehl pah-SEE-yoh
box office	**la taquilla** lah tah-KEE-yah

curtain	**el telón**
	ehl teh-LOHN
lighting	**las luces**
	lahs LOO-sehs
microphone	**el micrófono**
	ehl mee-KROH-foh-noh
row	**la fila**
	lah FEE-lah
seat	**la butaca**
	lah boo-TAH-kah
stage	**el escenario**
	ehl eh-seh-NAH-ryoh

Verbs

to applaud	**aplaudir**	ah-plah-oo-DEER
to listen	**escuchar**	ehs-koo-CHAHR
to watch	**mirar**	mee-RAHR

Practice 2-4

Write the Spanish word for what is being described. Remember to use the correct definite article.

1. where the student's grades appear

   _____

2. where we buy tickets for a play

   _____

3. where we sit in a theatre

   _____

4. what we have to pay when we have an overdue book

   _____

5. the break students get during the school day

   _____

6. what teachers give students to do at home

   _____

7. what we read to get the news every day

   _____

8. what students take to see what they have learned

   _____

9. the list of classes and times they meet

   _____

10. the number or letter students get on an exam

    _____

In the Cafeteria
En la cafetería

Meals · Las comidas

Meals (**las comidas** [lahs koh-MEE-dahs]) served to students in the school cafeteria are typically lunch (**el almuerzo** [ehl ahl-MWEHR-soh]), snacks (**la merienda** [lah meh-RYEHN-dah]), and sometimes breakfast (**el desayuno** [ehl deh-sah-YOO-noh]). Students rarely eat dinner (**la cena** [lah SEH-nah]) at school.

Foodstuffs (**los comestibles** [lohs koh-mehs-TEE-blehs]) that you may find in the cafeteria include the following.

bread	**el pan** ehl pahn
chicken	**el pollo** ehl POH-yoh
fish	**el pescado** ehl pehs-KAH-doh
hamburger	**la hamburguesa** lah ahm-boor-GEH-sah
hot dog	**el perro caliente** ehl PEH-rroh kah-LYEHN-teh
meat	**la carne** lah KAHR-neh
pepper	**la pimienta** lah pee-MYEHN-tah
rice	**el arroz** ehl ah-RROHS
salad	**la ensalada** lah ehn-sah-LAH-dah
salt	**la sal** lah sahl

sandwich	**el emparedado / el sándwich**
	ehl ehm-pah-reh-DAH-doh /
	ehl SAHND-weech
soup	**la sopa**
	lah SOH-pah
spaghetti	**los espaguetis**
	lohs ehs-pah-GEH-tees
vegetables	**los vegetales**
	los beh-heh-TAH-lehs

The following list includes some popular (and some not so popular) vegetables (**los vegetales** [lohs beh-heh-TAH-lehs]) that you may find in school cafeterias.

bean	**el frijol**
	ehl free-HOHL
broccoli	**el brécol**
	ehl BREH-kohl
carrot	**la zanahoria**
	lah sah-nah-OH-ryah
corn	**el maíz**
	ehl mah-EES
cucumber	**el pepino**
	ehl peh-PEE-noh
green pea	**el guisante**
	ehl gee-SAHN-teh
lettuce	**la lechuga**
	lah leh-CHOO-gah
potato	**la papa / la patata**
	lah PAH-pah / lah pah-TAH-tah
spinach	**la espinaca**
	lah ehs-pee-NAH-kah
tomato	**el tomate**
	ehl toh-MAH-teh

Dessert · *El postre*

You may find the following desserts (**los postres** [lohs POHS-trehs]) in a school cafeteria.

cake	**el bizcocho** ehl bees-KOH-choh
cookie	**la galletita** lah gah-yeh-TEE-tah
fruit	**la fruta** lah FROO-tah

Some fruits (**las frutas** [lahs FROO-tahs]) that might be found in the school cafeteria are the following.

apple	**la manzana** lah mahn-SAH-nah
banana	**el plátano** ehl PLAH-tah-noh
grape	**la uva** lah OO-bah
melon	**el melón** ehl meh-LOHN
orange	**la naranja** lah nah-RAHN-hah
peach	**el melocotón** ehl meh-loh-koh-TOHN
pear	**la pera** lah PEH-rah
strawberry	**la fresa** lah FREH-sah

Drinks · *Las bebidas*

Here are some drinks (**las bebidas** [lahs beh-BEE-dahs]) that you may find in the cafeteria.

juice	**el jugo** ehl HOO-goh
lemonade	**la limonada** lah lee-moh-NAH-dah

milk	**la leche**
	lah LEH-cheh
punch	**el ponche**
	ehl POHN-cheh
soft drink	**el refresco**
	ehl rreh-FREHS-koh
water	**el agua**
	ehl AH-gwah

GRAMMAR · "There Is" and "There Are"

Hay... [AH-ee] means "There is ..." and "There are ...".
¿Hay...? [AH-ee] means "Is there ...?" and "Are there ...?"

Is there soup today?	**¿Hay sopa hoy?**
	AH-ee SOH-pah OH-ee
Yes, there is chicken soup.	**Sí, hay sopa de pollo.**
	see, AH-ee SOH-pah deh POH-yoh
How many bottles of water are there on the table?	**¿Cuántas botellas de agua hay en la mesa?**
	KWAHN-tahs boh-TEH-yahs deh AH-gwah AH-ee ehn lah MEH-sah
There are two.	**Hay dos.**
	AH-ee dohs

More Information · *Más información*

In many school cafeterias you will find Spanish-speaking personnel. It is a good idea to talk to them in Spanish. You will make them feel good, and at the same time you will be practicing your Spanish. And, who knows? You may get an extra apple.

How much does it cost?	**¿Cuánto cuesta?**
	KWAHN-toh KWEHS-tah
What is for dessert today?	**¿Cuál es el postre hoy?**
	kwahl ehs ehl POHS-treh OH-ee
What is today's special?	**¿Cuál es el plato del día?**
	kwahl ehs ehl PLAH-toh dehl DEE-ah

Breakfast · El desayuno

Breakfast (**el desayuno** [ehl deh-sah-YOO-noh]) is considered to be the most important meal of the day, and yet many students do not eat a good breakfast. Included below is a separate section dedicated to breakfast.

What do you eat for breakfast?	**¿Qué comes de desayuno?** keh KOH-mehs deh deh-sah-YOO-noh
For breakfast I eat _____.	**De desayuno yo como** _____. deh deh-sah-YOO-noh yoh KOH-moh
What do you want for breakfast?	**¿Qué quieres de desayuno?** keh KYEH-rehs deh deh-sah-YOO-noh
For breakfast I want _____.	**De desayuno yo quiero** _____. deh deh-sah-YOO-noh yoh KYEH-roh
Do you bring your breakfast/ lunch from home?	**¿Traes el desayuno / el almuerzo de tu casa?** TRAH-ehs ehl deh-sah-YOO-noh / ehl ahl-MWEHR-soh deh too KAH-sah
Do you eat breakfast at home?	**¿Desayunas en casa?** deh-sah-YOO-nahs ehn KAH-sah

Typical Breakfast Foods · La comida típica del desayuno

Although a big breakfast is usually left for the weekend, even a weekday "American" breakfast is much heavier than what is usually eaten in Spanish-speaking countries. A typical breakfast in a Spanish-speaking country is likely to be coffee (**el café** [ehl kah-FEH]) and some type of bread (**el pan** [ehl pahn]).

Some typical breakfast foods (**la comida típica del desayuno** [lah koh-MEE-dah TEE-pee-kah dehl deh-sah-YOO-noh]) in the United States are the following.

bacon	**el tocino** ehl toh-SEE-noh
bread	**el pan** ehl pahn
butter	**la mantequilla** lah mahn-teh-KEE-yah
cereal	**el cereal** ehl seh-reh-AHL
cheese	**el queso** ehl KEH-soh
coffee	**el café** ehl kah-FEH

cream cheese	**el queso crema**
	ehl KEH-soh KREH-mah
egg	**el huevo**
	ehl WEH-boh
ham	**el jamón**
	ehl hah-MOHN
margarine	**la margarina**
	lah mahr-gah-REE-nah
milk	**la leche**
	lah LEH-cheh
oatmeal	**la avena**
	lah ah-BEH-nah
omelet	**la tortilla**
	lah tohr-TEE-yah
roll	**el panecillo**
	ehl pah-neh-SEE-yoh
sausage	**la salchicha**
	lah sahl-CHEE-chah
skim milk	**la leche desnatada**
	lah LEH-cheh dehs-nah-TAH-dah
tea	**el té**
	ehl teh
toast	**el pan tostado**
	ehl pahn tohs-TAH-doh
yogurt	**el yogurt**
	ehl yoh-GOOR

Verbs

to bring	**traer** (*irreg.*)	trah-EHR
to chew	**masticar**	mahs-tee-KAHR
to clean	**limpiar**	leem-PYAHR
to cost	**costar (ue)**	kohs-TAHR
to drink	**beber**	beh-BEHR
to eat	**comer**	koh-MEHR
to eat breakfast	**desayunar**	deh-sah-yoo-NAHR
to eat lunch	**almorzar (ue)**	ahl-mohr-SAHR
to eat dinner	**cenar**	seh-NAHR
to pay	**pagar**	pah-GAHR
to pick up	**recoger** (*irreg.*)	rreh-koh-HEHR
to share	**compartir**	kohm-pahr-TEER
to swallow	**tragar**	trah-GAHR

GRAMMAR · Expressing "To Like"

In Spanish, the verb **gustar** [goos-TAHR] is used to convey "to like," but its usage is slightly different from the other verbs you have encountered. You will use only two forms of the verb **gustar**: **gusta** [goos-tah] and **gustan** [goos-tahn].

When you want to express what you like *to do*, use **gusta** [goos-tah]. If you want to say that you like a certain *thing* use **gusta** [goos-tah]. However, if you want to say that you like *more than one thing*, use **gustan** [goos-tahn].

The pronouns **me, te, le, nos, les** [meh, teh, leh, nohs, lehs] are placed before the verb in order to indicate the person who is expressing his or her opinion.

I like	**me gusta/gustan**	meh goos-tah/goos-tahn
you (*familiar*) like	**te gusta/gustan**	teh goos-tah/goos-tahn
he likes	**le gusta/gustan**	leh goos-tah/goos-tahn
she likes	**le gusta/gustan**	leh goos-tah/goos-tahn
you (*formal*) like	**le gusta/gustan**	leh goos-tah/goos-tahn
we like	**nos gusta/gustan**	nohs goos-tah/goos-tahn
they like	**les gusta/gustan**	lehs goos-tah/goos-tahn
you (*plural*) like	**les gusta/gustan**	lehs goos-tah/goos-tahn

I like the music class.	**Me gusta la clase de música.** meh goos-tah lah KLAH-seh deh MOO-see-kah
She likes to study in the evening.	**Le gusta estudiar por la noche.** leh goos-tah ehs-too-DYAHR pohr lah NOH-cheh

Remember that when you like more than one thing, **gustan** [goos-tahn] is used instead of **gusta** [goos-tah].

I like hardworking students.	**Me gustan los estudiantes trabajadores.** meh goos-tahn lohs ehs-too-DYAHN-tehs trah-bah-hah-DOH-rehs

Read the examples above again. Did you notice that when a noun follows **gusta** [goos-tah] or **gustan** [goos-tahn], its definite article (**el, la, los, las** [ehl, lah, lohs, lahs]) is always included?

When talking about what you *don't* like, put **no** [noh] before **me, te, le, nos, les** [meh, teh, leh, nohs, lehs].

I don't like to study in the library.	**No me gusta estudiar en la biblioteca.** noh meh goos-tah ehs-too-DYAHR ehn lah bee-blyoh-TEH-kah

She does not like homework.   **No le gusta la tarea.**
                                 noh leh GOOS-tah lah tah-REH-ah

We don't like tests.   **No nos gustan las pruebas.**
                                 noh nohs GOOS-tahn lahs PRWEH-bahs

Practice 2-5

A *Read the following lists, then circle the word that does not belong in each group.*

1. la zanahoria | la lechuga | la carne | el pepino
2. el huevo | la salchicha | el tocino | la sopa
3. el pollo | la carne | el maíz | el perro caliente
4. la manzana | el arroz | la piña | la uva
5. comer | traer | masticar | tragar
6. la leche | el pescado | el jugo | el agua
7. la naranja | la sal | el ajo | la cebolla
8. el pollo | la avena | el cereal | la leche
9. almorzar | limpiar | cenar | desayunar
10. queso | yogurt | mantequilla | jamón

B *Write complete sentences in Spanish to answer the following questions truthfully.*

1. ¿Te gusta beber té?

_____

2. ¿Le gustan las fresas?

_____

3. ¿Les gusta comer en la cafetería?

_____

4. ¿Le gustan a Ud. los postres?

_____

5. ¿Le gusta el melocotón?

_____

C *You want to find out what all of your students, as a group, like. What would you ask them?*

_____

Summary Practice

Write the Spanish question you will need to ask in order to find out the following information.

1. who the students in the hallway are

   _____

2. if a particular student likes to share his/her lunch

   _____

3. if there is salad for (**para**) lunch

   _____

4. where the women's bathroom is

   _____

5. what the dessert is

   _____

6. if the students, as a group, don't like to bring their lunch from home

   _____

7. where the pencil sharpener is

   _____

8. what those (**esos**) papers are

   _____

9. if the principal's office is to the right of the entrance

   _____

10. if there is a light in the parking lot

   _____

3

The Primary Grades

Los grados primarios

In preschool or nursery school (**la guardería** [lah gwahr-deh-REE-ah]), kinder-garten (**el kinder / el jardín de infancia** [ehl KEEN-dehr / ehl hahr-DEEN deh een-FAHN-syah]), and the early years of elementary school (**la escuela primaria** [lah ehs-KWEH-lah pree-MAH-ryah]), children are busy learning about the world around them and they increase their vocabulary daily. Among many other things, they learn about the city or town in which they live and the people who are found there. Some important areas of learning for young children are the following.

animals	**los animales** lohs ah-nee-MAH-lehs
body	**el cuerpo** ehl KWEHR-poh
buildings	**los edificios** lohs eh-dee-FEE-syohs
city	**la ciudad** lah see-oo-DAHD
clothing	**la ropa** lah RROH-pah
colors	**los colores** lohs koh-LOH-rehs
date (on calendar)	**la fecha** lah FEH-chah
days of the week	**los días de la semana** lohs DEE-ahs deh lah seh-MAH-nah
family	**la familia** lah fah-MEE-lyah
food	**la comida** lah koh-MEE-dah
holidays	**los días feriados** lohs DEE-ahs feh-RYAH-dohs
home	**el hogar** ehl oh-GAHR
house	**la casa** lah KAH-sah
months of the year	**los meses del año** lohs MEH-sehs dehl AH-nyoh
musical instruments	**los instrumentos musicales** lohs eens-troo-MEHN-tohs moo-see-KAH-lehs
occupations	**las profesiones** lahs proh-feh-SYOH-nehs

people	**la gente / las personas**
	lah HEHN-teh / lahs pehr-SOH-nahs
seasons of the year	**las estaciones del año**
	lahs ehs-tah-SYOH-nehs dehl ah-nyoh
sports	**los deportes**
	lohs deh-POHR-tehs
time (clock)	**la hora**
	lah OH-rah
town	**el pueblo**
	ehl PWEH-bloh
transportation	**el transporte**
	ehl trahns-POHR-teh
weather	**el tiempo**
	ehl TYEHM-poh

Health and safety are also important topics in all grades. For these topics, see Chapter 6.

The School Calendar

El calendario escolar

The school calendar (**el calendario escolar** [ehl kah-lehn-DAH-ryoh ehs-koh-LAHR]), together with the schedule of classes, is an important document with which parents and students must become very familiar. Families plan their vacations around the school calendar. It is also important to be familiar with the different holidays so that when students have a day off from school, someone will be taking care of them. Important vocabulary and expressions relating to the school calendar follow.

Months
Los meses

To express dates in Spanish, you first need to know the months (**los meses** [lohs MEH-sehs]) of the year. Note that in Spanish, the months of the year are not capitalized.

January	**enero**	eh-NEH-roh
February	**febrero**	feh-BREH-roh
March	**marzo**	MAHR-soh
April	**abril**	ah-BREEL
May	**mayo**	MAH-yoh
June	**junio**	HOO-nyoh

July	**julio**	HOO-lyoh
August	**agosto**	ah-GOHS-toh
September	**septiembre**	sehp-TYEHM-breh
October	**octubre**	ohk-TOO-breh
November	**noviembre**	noh-BYEHM-breh
December	**diciembre**	dee-SYEHM-breh

Expressing Dates
Para expresar la fecha

There are a different ways you can phrase a question when you want to find out the date (**la fecha** [lah FEH-chah]).

What is today's date?	**¿Cuál es la fecha de hoy?**
	kwahl ehs lah FEH-chah deh OH-ee
	¿A cómo estamos hoy?
	ah KOH-moh ehs-TAH-mohs OH-ee

To respond with what date it is, use the following patterns.

Today is the fourth of March.	**Hoy es el cuatro de marzo.**
	OH-ee ehs ehl KWAH-troh deh MAHR-soh
	Estamos a cuatro de marzo.
	ehs-TAH-mohs ah KWAH-troh deh MAHR-soh

To find out on what date an event takes place, you may ask a question as follows.

What is the date of _____?	**¿Cuál es la fecha de _____?**
	kwahl ehs lah FEH-chah deh
What is the date of the exam?	**¿Cuál es la fecha del examen?**
	kwahl ehs lah FEH-chah dehl ehk-SAH-mehn
The exam is on June 3.	**El examen es el tres de junio.**
	ehl ehk-SAH-mehn ehs ehl trehs deh HOO-nyoh

Note that "on" + (*day of the month*) is translated as **el** [ehl] + (*day of the month*).

A complete date is expressed in the following manner.

| June 1, 2006 | **el primero de junio del dos mil seis** |
| | ehl pree-MEH-roh deh HOO-nyoh dehl dohs meel SEH-ehs |

In Spanish you will only use an ordinal number for the first of the month (**el primero del mes** [ehl pree-MEH-roh dehl mehs]). For all other dates you must use cardinal numbers.

For a complete list of numbers, see Chapter 4, pages 157–158.

Holidays
Los días feriados

Here is a list of holidays (**los días feriados** [lohs DEE-ahs feh-RYAH-dohs]), many of which are recognized by schools in the United States; several are public holidays.

Christmas	**la Navidad** lah nah-bee-DAHD
Columbus Day	**el día de la Raza** ehl DEE-ah deh lah RRAH-sah
Easter	**la Pascua de Resurrección** lah PAHS-kwah deh rreh-soo-rrehk-SYOHN
Father's Day	**el día de los Padres** ehl DEE-ah deh lohs PAH-drehs
Halloween	**la Víspera de Todos los Santos** lah BEES-peh-rah deh TOH-dohs lohs SAHN-tohs
Hanukkah	**la Fiesta de las Luces** lah FYEHS-tah deh lahs LOO-sehs
Labor Day	**el día del Trabajador** ehl DEE-ah dehl trah-bah-hah-DOHR
Mother's Day	**el día de las Madres** ehl DEE-ah deh lahs MAH-drehs
New Year's Day	**el día de Año Nuevo** ehl DEE-ah deh AH-nyoh NWEH-boh
Passover	**la Pascua (de los judíos)** lah PAHS-kwah (deh lohs hoo-DEE-ohs)
President's Day	**el día de los Presidentes** ehl DEE-ah deh lohs preh-see-DEHN-tehs
Ramadan	**Ramadán** rrah-mah-DAHN
Rosh Hashanah	**el día de Año Nuevo Judío** ehl DEE-ah deh AH-nyoh NWEH-boh hoo-DEE-oh
Thanksgiving	**el día de Acción de Gracias** ehl DEE-ah deh ahk-SYOHN deh GRAH-syahs

Valentine's Day   **el día de los Enamorados**
                                ehl DEE-ah deh lohs
                                eh-nah-moh-RAH-dohs

To express good wishes, say **feliz** [feh-LEES], meaning "happy," followed by the name of the holiday. In these cases you don't use the definite article.

Happy New Year!   **¡Feliz Año Nuevo!**
                                feh-LEES AH-nyoh NWEH-boh

Days of the Week
Los días de la semana

In Spanish, the days of the week (**los días de la semana** [lohs DEE-ahs deh lah seh-MAH-nah]) are always masculine and, like the months of the year, they are not capitalized. You will also find it helpful to know that in the Spanish-speaking world, the week begins on Monday.

Monday	**lunes**	LOO-nehs
Tuesday	**martes**	MAHR-tehs
Wednesday	**miércoles**	MYEHR-koh-lehs
Thursday	**jueves**	HWEH-behs
Friday	**viernes**	BYEHR-nehs
Saturday	**sábado**	SAH-bah-doh
Sunday	**domingo**	doh-MEEN-goh

If you want to find out the day of an event, you may ask a question using the following pattern.

What day is _____?   **¿Qué día es _____?**
                                keh DEE-ah ehs

What day is the meeting?   **¿Qué día es la reunión?**
                                keh DEE-ah ehs lah rreh-oo-NYOHN

The art class is on Monday.   **La clase de arte es el lunes.**
                                lah KLAH-seh deh AHR-teh ehs ehl
                                LOO-nehs

The art class is on Mondays.   **La clase de arte es los lunes.**
                                lah KLAH-seh deh AHR-teh ehs lohs
                                LOO-nehs

Note that "on" is translated as **el** [ehl] when used with the day of the week in its singular form, but it is translated as **los** [lohs] when the day of the week is in the plural form, as indicated by the definite article.

Telling Time
Para expresar la hora

Learning how to tell time (**expresar la hora** [ehs-preh-SAHR lah OH-rah]) in Spanish is quite simple. Remember that you will always use the verb **ser** [sehr], and that you will use only two forms of the verb. You will use **es** [ehs] between one o'clock and one thirty, and **son** [sohn] for stating all other times.

To ask or state what time it is, use the following patterns.

What time is it?	**¿Qué hora es?** keh OH-rah ehs
It's one o'clock.	**Es la una.** ehs lah oo-nah
It's two o'clock.	**Son las dos.** sohn lahs dohs

The Spanish word **y** [ee], meaning "and," is used to tell time between the hour and half past the hour, when you want to say how many minutes after the hour it is.

It is one ten.	**Es la una y diez.** ehs lah oo-nah ee dyehs
It's nine twenty.	**Son las nueve y veinte.** sohn lahs NWEH-beh ee BEH-een-teh

The Spanish word **menos** [MEH-nohs], meaning "minus," is used after the half hour to tell how many minutes it is before the next hour.

It's one thirty-five (twenty-five minutes until two).	**Son las dos menos veinte y cinco.** sohn lahs dohs MEH-nohs BEH-een-teh ee SEEN-koh

The quarter-hour and half-hour in Spanish can be expressed by using specific words instead of the number of minutes they represent.

quarter	**cuarto** KWAHR-toh
half	**media** MEH-dyah
It's a quarter to one.	**Es la una menos cuarto.** ehs lah oo-nah MEH-nohs KWAHR-toh
It's half past twelve.	**Son las doce y media.** sohn lahs DOH-seh ee MEH-dyah

If you want to differentiate between morning, afternoon, and evening, use the following expressions.

in the morning	**de la mañana** deh lah mah-NYAH-nah
in the afternoon	**de la tarde** deh lah TAHR-deh
in the evening	**de la noche** deh lah NOH-cheh
It is seven o'clock in the morning.	**Son las siete de la mañana.** sohn lahs SYEH-teh deh lah mah-NYAH-nah

To ask at what time an event takes place, you can pattern your question as follows.

(At) what time is _____?	**¿A qué hora es _____?** ah keh OH-rah ehs
(At) what time is the English class?	**¿A qué hora es la clase de inglés?** ah keh OH-rah ehs lah KLAH-seh deh een-GLEHS
(It is) at two o'clock.	**(Es) a las dos.** (ehs) ah lahs dohs
(It is) at one o'clock.	**(Es) a la una.** (ehs) ah lah OO-nah

To express noon (**el mediodía** [ehl meh-dyoh-DEE-ah]) and midnight (**la medianoche** [lah meh-dyah-NOH-cheh]), you use the following specific expressions.

at noon	**al mediodía** ahl meh-dyoh-DEE-ah
at midnight	**a la medianoche** ah lah meh-dyah-NOH-cheh

The following expressions related to telling time will prove very useful.

at about	**a eso de** ah EH-soh deh
sharp / on the dot	**en punto** ehn POON-toh

GRAMMAR · To Find Out "When?"

If you do not need to know a specific time or date when something is taking place, use **¿Cuándo?** [KWAHN-doh] to ask "When?"

When is the fair?	**¿Cuándo es el festival?** KWAHN-doh ehs ehl fehs-tee-BAHL
It is at the beginning of December.	**Es a principios de diciembre.** ehs ah preen-SEE-pyohs deh dee-SYEHM-breh

The following expressions can be used to answer the question "When?" (**¿Cuándo?** [KWAHN-doh]). When you answer, you will be giving a specific time period.

at the beginning of	**a principios de** ah preen-SEE-pyohs deh
at the end of	**a fines de** ah FEE-nehs deh
daily	**a diario / diariamente** ah DYAH-ryoh / dyah-ryah-MEHN-teh
each day	**cada día** KAH-dah DEE-ah
every day	**todos los días** TOH-dohs lohs DEE-ahs
in a minute / an hour	**en un minuto / una hora** ehn oon mee-NOO-toh / OO-nah OH-rah
in/about the middle of	**a mediados de** ah meh-DYAH-dohs deh
now	**ahora** ah-OH-rah
right now	**ahora mismo** ah-OH-rah MEES-moh
starting from (one o'clock) on	**a partir de (la una)** ah pahr-TEER deh (lah OO-nah)

The following words and phrases also answer questions asked with **¿Cuándo?** [KWAHN-doh], but they are not as specific as the expressions included in the list above.

afterward	**después** dehs-PWEHS
already	**ya** yah
at once	**en seguida** ehn seh-GEE-dah
before	**antes** AHN-tehs
from time to time	**de vez en cuando** deh behs ehn KWAHN-doh
immediately	**inmediatamente** een-meh-dyah-tah-MEHN-teh
not yet	**todavía no** toh-dah-BEE-ah noh
often	**a menudo** ah meh-NOO-doh
soon	**pronto** PROHN-toh
whenever you can	**cuando pueda** KWAHN-do PWEH-dah
whenever you have time	**cuando tenga tiempo** KWAHN-doh TEHN-gah TYEHM-poh
whenever you like	**cuando quiera** KWAHN-doh KYEH-rah

Practice 3-1

A *Express the following dates in Spanish. (If you need help with numbers, see Chapter 4, pages 157–158.)*

1. September 15, 1990 _____

2. October 25, 2001 _____

3. July 1, 2006 _____

4. January 31, 1984 _____

B Fill in the missing days of the week. Remember that in Spanish-speaking countries, the week begins on Monday.

_____ martes _____ jueves

_____ sábado _____

C Write complete sentences to express the following times in Spanish. Remember to use the verb **ser**.

1. 9:10 A.M.   _____

2. noon   _____

3. 2:35 P.M.   _____

4. 5:00 P.M.   _____

5. midnight   _____

6. 7:30 P.M.   _____

7. 11:15 A.M.   _____

D Complete the following sentences with the Spanish word(s) for the expressions in parentheses.

1. Nosotros desayunamos _____ (every day).

2. Ella visita a sus parientes _____ (at the beginning of) marzo.

3. Uds. tienen que leer _____ (right now).

4. Las vacaciones son _____ (starting from) hoy.

5. Tenemos un examen _____ (about the middle of) abril.

E Write a question in Spanish to ask for the following information.

1. the time

_____

2. today's date

_____

3. when an event is taking place

_____

4. the time of the Spanish class

_____

Talking About the Weather

Para hablar del tiempo

It is a good idea to become familiar with the different ways to talk about the weather (**el tiempo** [ehl TYEHM-poh]). Let's begin by becoming familiar with the seasons (**las estaciones** [lahs ehs-tah-SYOH-nehs]).

spring	**la primavera**	lah pree-mah-BEH-rah
summer	**el verano**	ehl beh-RAH-noh
autumn	**el otoño**	ehl oh-TOH-nyoh
winter	**el invierno**	ehl een-BYEHR-noh

If you want to ask about the weather in a specific season, you might ask the question as follows.

What is the weather like in the spring?	**¿Qué tiempo hace en la primavera?** keh TYEHM-poh AH-seh ehn lah pree-mah-BEH-rah

The verb **hacer** [ah-SEHR] is used in many idiomatic expressions dealing with the weather. To talk about what the weather is like, use **hacer** as follows.

How is the weather?	**¿Qué tiempo hace?** keh TYEHM-poh AH-seh
The weather is good.	**Hace buen tiempo.** AH-seh bwehn TYEHM-poh
The weather is bad.	**Hace mal tiempo.** AH-seh mahl TYEHM-poh
It is (very) cold.	**Hace (mucho) frío.** AH-seh (MOO-choh) FREE-oh
It is (very) hot.	**Hace (mucho) calor.** AH-seh (MOO-choh) kah-LOHR
It is cool.	**Hace fresco.** AH-seh FREHS-koh
It is sunny.	**Hace sol.** AH-seh sohl
It is windy.	**Hace viento.** AH-seh BYEHN-toh

To talk about what the weather was like in the past, use **hizo** [EE-soh] instead of **hace** [AH-seh].

What was the weather like yesterday?	**¿Qué tiempo hizo ayer?** keh TYEHM-poh EE-soh ah-YEHR
It was hot yesterday.	**Hizo calor ayer.** EE-soh kah-LOHR ah-YEHR

To find some words and expressions that are useful when talking about the past, see Chapter 6, pages 231–232.

To talk about what the weather will be like in the future, use **va a hacer** [bah ah ah-SEHR] instead of **hace** [AH-seh].

What is the weather going to be like tomorrow?	**¿Qué tiempo va a hacer mañana?** keh TYEHM-poh bah ah ah-SEHR mah-NYAH-nah
Tomorrow it is going to be windy.	**Mañana va a hacer viento.** mah-NYAH-nah bah ah ah-SEHR BYEHN-toh

To find some words and expressions that are useful when talking about the future, see Chapter 5, pages 197–198.

With the following weather expressions, you need to use the verb **estar** [ehs-TAHR], meaning "to be."

It is cloudy.	**Está nublado.** ehs-TAH noo-BLAH-doh
It is clear.	**Está despejado.** ehs-TAH dehs-peh-HAH-doh
It is sunny.	**Está soleado.** ehs-TAH soh-leh-AH-doh
It is rainy.	**Está lluvioso.** ehs-TAH yoo-BYOH-soh
It is snowing.	**Está nevando.** ehs-TAH neh-BAHN-doh
It is drizzling.	**Está lloviznando.** ehs-TAH yoh-bees-NAHN-doh
It is raining.	**Está lloviendo.** ehs-TAH yoh-BYEHN-doh

Remember to use **va a estar** [bah ah ehs-TAHR] instead of **está** [ehs-TAH] when you want to use these **estar** expressions to talk about what the weather will be like in the future.

Tomorrow it is going to be cloudy.	**Mañana va a estar nublado.** mah-NYAH-nah bah ah ehs-TAHR noo-BLAH-doh

Other weather-related events that you will want to know how to express are the following.

downpour	**el aguacero** ehl ah-gwah-SEH-roh
hail	**el granizo** ehl grah-NEE-soh
lightning	**el relámpago** ehl rreh-LAHM-pah-goh
rain	**la lluvia** lah YOO-byah
snow	**la nieve** lah NYEH-beh
thunder	**el trueno** ehl TRWEH-noh
weather forecast	**el pronóstico del tiempo** ehl proh-NOHS-tee-koh dehl TYEHM-poh

Practice 3-2

What would you say in the following situations? Express the following ideas in Spanish, either by translating a sentence or by phrasing a question to find out information.

1. You want to know what the weather was like yesterday.

   _____

2. It is cold and cloudy.

   _____

3. It is a rainy, windy day. How would you describe the weather in general?

   _____

4. You want to tell your students that tomorrow the weather is going to be good.

   _____

5. It is snowing.

   _____

Clothing

La ropa

The weather affects the clothing (**la ropa** [lah RROH-pah]) that people wear. Nowadays a lot of the clothing that children wear is the same for boys and girls.

Articles of Clothing for Boys and Girls
Las prendas de vestir para niños y niñas

The following list includes some articles of clothing (**las prendas de vestir** [lahs PREHN-dahs deh behs-TEER] that both boys (**los niños** [lohs NEE-nyohs]) and girls (**las niñas** [lahs NEE-nyahs]) may wear in many different situations.

coat	**el abrigo / el sobretodo** ehl ah-BREE-goh / ehl soh-breh-TOH-doh
jacket	**el saco / la chaqueta** ehl SAH-koh / lah chah-KEH-tah
jeans	**los blue jeans / los vaqueros** lohs bloo yeens / lohs bah-KEH-rohs
pajamas	**el piyama** ehl pee-YAH-mah
pants	**los pantalones** lohs pahn-tah-LOH-nehs
raincoat	**la gabardina / el impermeable** lah gah-bar-DEE-nah / ehl eem-pehr-meh-AH-bleh
shirt	**la camisa** lah kah-MEE-sah
shorts	**los pantalones cortos** lohs pahn-tah-LOH-nehs KOHR-tohs

socks	**los calcetines** lohs kahl-seh-TEE-nehs
suit	**el traje** ehl TRAH-heh
sweater	**el suéter** ehl SWEH-tehr
sweatshirt	**la sudadera** lah soo-dah-DEH-rah
tee shirt	**la camiseta** lah kah-mee-SEH-tah
uniform	**el uniforme** ehl oo-nee-FOHR-meh

For Girls · *Para las niñas*

blouse	**la blusa** lah BLOO-sah
bra	**el sostén** ehl sohs-TEHN
dress	**el vestido** ehl behs-TEE-doh
panties	**las bragas** lahs BRAH-gahs
pantyhose	**los pantis / las pantimedias** lohs PAHN-tees / lahs pahn-tee-MEH-dyahs
skirt	**la falda** lah FAHL-dah
tights	**los leotardos** lohs leh-oh-TAHR-dohs

For Boys · *Para los niños*

briefs	**los calzoncillos** lohs kahl-sohn-SEE-yohs
undershirt	**la camiseta** lah kah-mee-SEH-tah

Clothing Accessories
Los complementos para la ropa

accessories	**los complementos**	
	lohs kohm-pleh-MEHN-tohs	
backpack	**la mochila**	
	lah moh-CHEE-lah	
belt	**el cinturón**	
	ehl seen-too-ROHN	
cap	**la gorra**	
	lah GOH-rrah	
glove	**el guante**	
	ehl GWAHN-teh	
handkerchief	**el pañuelo**	
	ehl pah-NYWEH-loh	
hat	**el sombrero**	
	ehl sohm-BREH-roh	
pocket	**el bolsillo**	
	ehl bohl-SEE-yoh	
purse	**el monedero / el portamonedas**	
	ehl moh-neh-DEH-roh /	
	ehl pohr-tah-moh-NEH-dahs	
scarf	**la bufanda**	
	lah boo-FAHN-dah	
tie	**la corbata**	
	lah kohr-BAH-tah	
wallet	**la billetera / la cartera**	
	lah bee-yeh-TEH-rah / lah kahr-TEH-rah	

Verbs

to button up	**abrocharse**	ah-broh-CHAHR-seh
to fix	**arreglar**	ah-rreh-GLAHR
to get dressed	**vestirse (i)**	behs-TEER-seh
to put on	**ponerse** (*irreg.*)	poh-NEHR-seh
to show	**mostrar (ue)**	mohs-TRAHR
to take off	**quitarse**	kee-TAHR-seh
to tie one's shoes	**abrocharse los zapatos**	ah-broh-CHAHR-seh lohs sah-PAH-tohs
to try on	**probarse (ue)**	proh-BAHR-seh
to undress	**desvestirse (i)**	dehs-behs-TEER-seh
to wear	**llevar**	yeh-BAHR

GRAMMAR · Expressing Ownership

In Spanish, when you want to find out who owns something, you use the following patterns.

Whose _____ is it?	¿De quién es _____? deh kyehn ehs
Whose _____ are they?	¿De quién son _____? deh kyehn sohn
Whose book is it?	¿De quién es el libro? deh kyehn ehs ehl LEE-broh
Whose books are they?	¿De quién son los libros? deh kyehn sohn lohs LEE-brohs

In English, when you want to find out who owns something, you use the word "whose" regardless of whether you think the item is possessed by one person or by more than one person.

In Spanish, when you think there is more than one owner, you ask the question as follows.

Whose _____ is it?	¿De quiénes es _____? deh KYEH-nehs ehs
Whose _____ are they?	¿De quiénes son _____? deh KYEH-nehs sohn
Whose ball is it?	¿De quiénes es la pelota? deh KYEH-nehs ehs lah peh-LOH-tah
Whose balls are they?	¿De quiénes son las pelotas? deh KYEH-nehs sohn lahs peh-LOH-tahs

Note that Spanish always includes the definite article for the item possessed, though English typically does not.

To state who owns something, use the following pattern.

It is / They are _____.	Es de / Son de _____. ehs deh / sohn deh
It is / They are Ana's.	Es de / Son de Ana. ehs deh / sohn deh AH-nah
It is / They are Ana's and Paco's.	Es de / Son de Ana y Paco. ehs deh / sohn deh AH-nah ee PAH-koh
Whose is the coat?	¿De quién es el abrigo? deh kyehn ehs ehl ah-BREE-goh
It is Felipe's.	Es de Felipe. ehs deh feh-LEE-peh

GRAMMAR · **Possessive Adjectives**

Possessive adjectives are used to express ownership. In Spanish, the adjective must agree with the noun (object) that is possessed. As in English, the possessive adjectives are placed before the noun. In Chapter 1, you learned three possessive adjectives, **mi** [mee], **tu** [too], and **su** [soo].

Here is a list showing all the possessive adjectives you will need.

ONE ITEM POSSESSED	MORE THAN ONE ITEM POSSESSED
mi mochila (my backpack) mee moh-CHEE-lah	**mis mochilas** (my backpacks) mees moh-CHEE-lahs
tu mochila (your [*familiar*] backpack) too moh-CHEE-lah	**tus mochilas** (your backpacks) toos moh-CHEE-lahs
su mochila (your [*formal*] backpack) soo moh-CHEE-lah	**sus mochilas** (your backpacks) soos moh-CHEE-lahs
su mochila (his backpack) soo moh-CHEE-lah	**sus mochilas** (his backpacks) soos moh-CHEE-lahs
su mochila (her backpack) soo moh-CHEE-lah	**sus mochilas** (her backpacks) soos moh-CHEE-lahs
nuestra mochila (our backpack) NWEHS-trah moh-CHEE-lah	**nuestras mochilas** (our backpacks) NWEHS-trahs moh-CHEE-lahs
su mochila (their backpack) soo moh-CHEE-lah	**sus mochilas** (their backpacks) soos moh-CHEE-lahs

You will notice that **nuestro** [NWEHS-troh] is the only possessive adjective that has a feminine form: **nuestra** [NWEHS-trah].

our t-shirt	**nuestra camiseta** NWEHS-trah kah-mee-SEH-tah
our pants	**nuestros pantalones** NWEHS-trohs pahn-tah-LOH-nehs

GRAMMAR · **Using the Verb "To Be" to Express a Characteristic**

To find out about the characteristics of someone or something, ask a question using the following patterns.

What is _____ like?	**¿Cómo es _____?** KOH-moh ehs
What are _____ like?	**¿Cómo son _____?** KOH-moh sohn

What is the sweater like?	**¿Cómo es el suéter?** koh-moh ehs ehl sweh-tehr
What are the pants like?	**¿Cómo son los pantalones?** koh-moh sohn lohs pahn-tah-loh-nehs

When describing a person, a place, or a thing (for example, an article of clothing), use the verb **ser** [sehr] + an adjective.

The sweater is pretty.	**El suéter es bonito.** ehl sweh-tehr ehs boh-nee-toh
The pants are expensive.	**Los pantalones son caros.** lohs pahn-tah-loh-nehs sohn kah-rohs

Some adjectives that you can use to describe clothing are listed here.

dressy	**vistoso** bees-toh-soh
expensive	**caro** kah-roh
inexpensive	**barato** bah-rah-toh
long	**largo** lahr-goh
pretty	**lindo / bonito** leen-doh / boh-nee-toh
short	**corto** kohr-toh
ugly	**feo** feh-oh

GRAMMAR · Agreement of Noun and Adjective

A Spanish adjective agrees with the noun it describes in both gender and number.

The dress is long.	**El vestido es largo.** ehl behs-tee-doh ehs lahr-goh
The skirts are long.	**Las faldas son largas.** lahs fahl-dahs sohn lahr-gahs

For more information about gender and number of nouns and adjectives, see Chapter 1, page 45.

Verbs

to be in style	**estar** (*irreg.*) **de moda**	ehs-TAHR deh MOH-dah
to be out of style	**estar** (*irreg.*) **pasado de moda**	ehs-TAHR pah-SAH-doh deh MOH-dah
to fit (well)	**quedarle bien**	keh-DAHR-leh byehn
to fit (poorly)	**quedarle mal**	keh-DAHR-leh mahl
to fit loosely	**quedarle ancho**	keh-DAHR-leh AHN-choh
to fit tightly	**quedarle estrecho**	keh-DAHR-leh ehs-TREH-choh
to look good	**lucir** (*irreg.*) **bien**	loo-SEER byehn
to look bad	**lucir** (*irreg.*) **mal**	loo-SEER mahl
to match	**hacer** (*irreg.*) **juego con**	ah-SEHR HWEH-goh kohn

The indirect object pronoun **le** [leh], meaning "you," "him," or "her," can be either attached to an infinitive or placed before a conjugated verb.

The pants seem to fit you/him/her well.	**Los pantalones parecen quedarle bien.** lohs pahn-tah-LOH-nehs pah-REH-sehn keh-DAHR-leh byehn
The pants fit you/him/her well.	**Los pantalones le quedan bien.** lohs pahn-tah-LOH-nehs leh KEH-dahn byehn

Materials
Las telas

Some favorite materials (**las telas** [lahs TEH-lahs]) for clothing are the following.

cotton	**algodón** ahl-goh-DOHN
denim	**mezclilla** mehs-KLEE-yah
flannel	**franela** frah-NEH-lah
leather	**cuero** KWEH-roh
polyester	**poliéster** poh-LYEHS-tehr
wool	**lana** LAH-nah

To find out what material something (whether it is clothes or something else) is made of, ask a question as follows.

What is _____ made of?	**¿De qué es _____?** deh keh ehs
What is the blouse made of?	**¿De qué es la blusa?** deh keh ehs lah BLOO-sah

To tell about the material of which something is made, you can use the following pattern.

It is (made) of _____.	**Es de _____.** ehs deh
They are (made) of _____.	**Son de _____.** sohn deh
The blouse is made of cotton.	**La blusa es de algodón.** lah BLOO-sah ehs deh ahl-goh-DOHN
The pants are made of wool.	**Los pantalones son de lana.** lohs pahn-tah-LOH-nehs sohn deh LAH-nah

Colors
Los colores

Here is a list of colors (**los colores** [lohs koh-LOH-rehs]).

black	**negro**	NEH-groh
blue	**azul**	ah-SOOL
brown	**marrón**	mah-RROHN
gray	**gris**	grees
green	**verde**	BEHR-deh
navy blue	**azul marino**	ah-SOOL mah-REE-noh
orange	**anaranjado**	ah-nah-rahn-HAH-doh
pink	**rosado**	rroh-SAH-doh
purple	**morado**	moh-RAH-doh
red	**rojo**	RROH-hoh
violet	**morado**	moh-RAH-doh
white	**blanco**	BLAHN-koh
yellow	**amarillo**	ah-mah-REE-yoh

To talk about the color of an object in Spanish, use the following patterns.

What color is _____?	**¿De qué color es _____?** deh keh koh-LOHR ehs
What color are _____?	**¿De qué color son _____?** deh keh koh-LOHR sohn
What color is the blouse?	**¿De qué color es la blusa?** deh keh koh-LOHR ehs lah BLOO-sah
The blouse is white.	**La blusa es blanca.** lah BLOO-sah ehs BLAHN-kah
What color are the sweaters?	**¿De qué color son los suéteres?** deh keh koh-LOHR sohn lohs SWEH-teh-rehs
The sweaters are black.	**Los suéteres son negros.** lohs SWEH-teh-rehs sohn NEH-grohs

GRAMMAR · Position of Adjectives

In Spanish, adjectives are generally placed after the noun they modify. Remember that colors, as adjectives, agree with the noun they modify in gender and number.

He is wearing a white shirt and black pants.	**Lleva una camisa blanca y unos pantalones negros.** YEH-bah oo-nah kah-MEE-sah BLAHN-kah ee oo-nohs pahn-tah-LOH-nehs NEH-grohs

Practice 3-3

A *What article of clothing would these people wear in each specified situation?*

1. Hace mucho calor. Llevo _____.
2. Hace fresco. Lleva _____.
3. Está lloviendo. Llevamos _____.
4. Está nevando. Llevan _____.
5. Hace viento. Llevas _____.

B *Write complete sentences to answer the following questions, using the cues in parentheses.*

1. ¿De quién es la camiseta? (Juan)

   _____

2. ¿De quiénes son los calcetines? (Alberto *and* Pedro)

   _____

3. ¿De quién es la falda? (Graciela)

   _____

4. ¿De quién son los calzoncillos? (David)

   _____

5. ¿De quiénes son las chaquetas? (Diego *and* Tina)

   _____

C *Complete the following sentences with the Spanish words for the English cues in parentheses.*

1. _____ (my) abrigo es _____ (blue).
2. _____ (our) guantes son _____ (black).
3. _____ (his) mochila es _____ (yellow).
4. _____ (your [familiar]) pañuelos son _____ (white).
5. _____ (their) pantalones son _____ (red).

Curriculum

El plan de estudio

It is useful to learn to express the subject areas in which students in the primary grades generally receive academic instruction. A list of the typical subject areas of the primary school curriculum (**el plan de estudio** [ehl plahn deh ehs-TOO-dyoh]) follows.

art	**el arte** ehl AHR-teh
language arts	**el lenguaje** ehl lehn-GWAH-heh
mathematics	**las matemáticas** lahs mah-teh-MAH-tee-kahs

music	**la música** lah MOO-see-kah
physical education	**la educación física** lah eh-doo-kah-SYOHN FEE-see-kah
science	**la ciencia** lah SYEHN-syah
social studies	**los estudios sociales** lohs ehs-TOO-dyohs soh-SYAH-lehs

The following vocabulary will be useful as you are helping your students to become fluent in English.

How do you spell _____?	**¿Cómo se escribe / se deletrea _____?** KOH-moh seh ehs-KREE-beh / seh deh-leh-TREH-ah
alphabet	**el abecedario** ehl ah-beh-seh-DAH-ryoh
handwriting	**la caligrafía / la escritura** lah kah-lee-grah-FEE-ah / lah ehs-kree-TOO-rah
pronunciation	**la pronunciación** lah proh-noon-syah-SYOHN
reading	**la lectura** lah lehk-TOO-rah
spelling	**la ortografía** lah ohr-toh-grah-FEE-ah
spelling book	**el abecedario** ehl ah-beh-seh-DAH-ryoh

Reading time is an important learning time, as well as a relaxing activity. Children love to hear (**oír** [oh-EER]) and to tell (**contar** [kohn-TAHR]) stories (**cuentos** [KWEHN-tohs]). By the early grades they begin to read (**leer** [leh-EHR]) for themselves. Here are useful words that are related to reading.

answer	**la respuesta** lah rrehs-PWEHS-tah
beginning	**el principio** ehl preen-SEE-pyoh
chapter	**el capítulo** ehl kah-PEE-too-loh
character	**el personaje** ehl pehr-soh-NAH-heh

end	**el fin** ehl feen
page	**la página** lah PAH-hee-nah
problem	**el problema** ehl proh-BLEH-mah
question	**la pregunta** lah preh-GOON-tah
summary	**el resumen** ehl rreh-soo-mehn
theme	**el tema** ehl TEH-mah
title	**el título** ehl TEE-too-loh
word	**la palabra** lah pah-LAH-brah

Verbs

to hear / listen to stories	**oír** (*irreg.*) / **escuchar cuentos** oh-EER / ehs-koo-CHAHR KWEHN-tohs
to learn	**aprender** ah-prehn-DEHR
to print (write in block letters)	**escribir en letra de molde** ehs-kree-BEER ehn LEH-trah deh MOHL-deh
to read	**leer** (*irreg.*) leh-EHR
to spell (letter by letter)	**deletrear/escribir** deh-leh-treh-AHR/ehs-kree-BEER
to tell stories	**contar (ue) cuentos** kohn-TAHR KWEHN-tohs
to write (in longhand)	**escribir (a mano / en cursiva)** ehs-kree-BEER (ah MAH-noh / ehn koor-SEE-bah)

For a more complete list of school subjects and vocabulary related to each subject, see Chapter 4.

GRAMMAR · Verbs That Are Irregular in the yo Form

Some important verbs that are irregular only in the **yo** [yoh] form are listed here.

to be acquainted with	**conocer** koh-noh-SEHR	**yo conozco** yoh koh-NOHS-koh

to bring	**traer**	**yo traigo**
	trah-EHR	yoh TRAH-ee-goh
to do, make	**hacer**	**yo hago**
	ah-SEHR	yoh AH-goh
to fall	**caerse**	**yo me caigo**
	kah-EHR-seh	yoh meh KAH-ee-goh
to give	**dar**	**yo doy**
	dahr	yoh DOH-ee
to go out, leave	**salir**	**yo salgo**
	sah-LEER	yoh SAHL-goh
to know facts	**saber**	**yo sé**
	sah-BEHR	yoh seh
to put, place	**poner**	**yo pongo**
	poh-NEHR	yoh POHN-goh
to see	**ver**	**yo veo**
	behr	yoh VEH-oh
to translate	**traducir**	**yo traduzco**
	trah-doo-SEER	yoh trah-DOOS-koh

The verbs above are regular in all other forms of the present tense. Look carefully at the complete conjugation of the verb **traer**.

traer (*irreg.*) [trah-EHR] to bring

I bring	**yo traigo**	yoh TRAH-ee-goh
you bring	**tú traes**	too TRAH-ehs
he brings	**él trae**	ehl TRAH-eh
she brings	**ella trae**	EH-yah TRAH-eh
you bring	**Ud. trae**	oos-TEHD TRAH-eh
we bring	**nosotros traemos**	noh-SOH-trohs trah-EH-mohs
we bring	**nosotras traemos**	noh-SOH-trahs trah-EH-mohs
they bring	**ellos traen**	EH-yohs TRAH-ehn
they bring	**ellas traen**	EH-yahs TRAH-ehn
you (*plural*) bring	**Uds. traen**	oos-TEH-dehs TRAH-ehn

What do you bring to school?	**¿Qué traes a la escuela?**
	keh TRAH-ehs ah lah ehs-KWEH-lah
I bring a notebook and a pencil.	**Traigo un cuaderno y un lápiz.**
	TRAH-ee-goh oon kwah-DEHR-noh ee
	oon LAH-pees

For a list of additional objects that you might find in the classroom, see Chapter 2, pages 69–70 and 78–80.

Art Projects

Los proyectos de arte

Art projects (**los proyectos de arte** [lohs proh-YEHK-tohs deh AHR-teh]) are an everyday activity in early childhood education. When doing art projects, a student may wear an apron (**un delantal** [oon deh-lahn-TAHL]).

Some materials that are typically used in art projects are the following.

brush (artist's)	**el pincel** ehl peen-SEHL
coloring book	**el libro de colorear** ehl LEE-broh deh koh-loh-reh-AHR
crayons	**los lápices para pintar** lohs LAH-pee-sehs PAH-rah peen-TAHR
glue	**la cola** lah KOH-lah
modeling clay	**la plasticina** lah plahs-tee-SEE-nah
paper (colored)	**el papel (de colores)** ehl pah-PEHL (deh koh-LOH-rehs)
scissors (plastic)	**las tijeras (de plástico)** lahs tee-HEH-rahs (deh PLAHS-tee-koh)

Verbs

to color	**colorear**	koh-loh-reh-AHR
to cut	**cortar**	kohr-TAHR
to draw	**dibujar**	dee-boo-HAHR
to fold	**doblar**	doh-BLAHR
to paint	**pintar**	peen-TAHR
to paste	**pegar**	peh-GAHR
to tie	**amarrar**	ah-mah-RRAHR

Cleaning Up the Classroom

Para limpiar el aula

At the end of each day, and usually at the end of any art project, the children will have to gather what they have used and clean up. Some items that will be needed for cleaning up the classroom (**limpiar el aula** [leem-PYAHR ehl AH-oo-lah]) are listed here.

broom	**la escoba**
	lah ehs-KOH-bah
bucket	**el balde / el cubo**
	ehl BAHL-deh / ehl KOO-boh
dust rag	**el trapo**
	ehl TRAH-poh
dustpan	**el recogedor de basura**
	ehl rreh-koh-heh-DOHR deh bah-soo-rah
mop	**el trapeador**
	ehl trah-peh-ah-DOHR
paper towel	**la toalla de papel**
	lah toh-AH-yah deh pah-PEHL
sponge	**la esponja**
	lah ehs-POHN-hah
towel	**la toalla**
	lah toh-AH-yah
trash can	**el basurero**
	ehl bah-soo-REH-roh
water	**el agua**
	ehl AH-gwah

Here are some familiar commands you will find useful when asking a child to clean up.

Dust.	**Sacude.**
	sah-KOO-deh
Pick up.	**Recoge.**
	rreh-KOH-heh
Sweep.	**Barre.**
	BAH-rreh

To review the formation of commands, see the Introduction, pages 16–18, 20, and 21.

Verbs

to clean	**limpiar**	leem-PYAHR
to dust	**sacudir**	sah-koo-DEER
to mop	**trapear**	trah-peh-AHR
to pick up	**recoger** (*irreg.*)	rreh-koh-HEHR
to put	**poner** (*irreg.*)	poh-NEHR
to put away	**guardar**	gwahr-DAHR
to sweep	**barrer**	bah-RREHR
to throw away	**tirar**	tee-RAHR
to throw away	**botar**	boh-TAHR
to wash	**lavar**	lah-BAHR

Practice 3-4

Answer the following questions truthfully, using complete sentences.

1. ¿Sabes deletrear en español?

   _____

2. ¿Traes un sacapuntas a la escuela?

   _____

3. ¿A qué hora sales de la escuela?

   _____

4. ¿Conoces a todos los estudiantes de la escuela?

   _____

5. ¿Das mucha tarea a los estudiantes?

   _____

6. ¿Haces mucho trabajo en la escuela?

   _____

Toys and Playthings

Los juguetes y otras cosas para jugar

In early childhood programs, a good part of the day is spent in playtime and rest. There are often many toys and playthings (**los juguetes y otras cosas para jugar** [lohs hoo-GEH-tehs ee OH-trahs KOH-sahs PAH-rah hoo-GAHR]) in the classroom. The children may also have many of these playthings at home.

ball	**la pelota** lah peh-LOH-tah
balloon	**el globo** ehl GLOH-boh
blocks (wooden)	**los bloques (de madera)** lohs BLOH-kehs (deh mah-DEH-rah)
cart (small)	**el carretón** ehl kah-rreh-TOHN
costume	**el disfraz** ehl dees-FRAHS

doll	**la muñeca** lah moo-NYEH-kah
jump rope	**la cuerda de saltar** lah KWEHR-dah deh sahl-TAHR
puppet	**el títere** ehl TEE-teh-reh
puzzle (jigsaw)	**el rompecabezas** ehl rrohm-peh-kah-BEH-sahs
stuffed animal	**el animal de peluche** ehl ah-nee-MAHL deh peh-LOO-cheh
toy train	**el tren de juguete** ehl trehn deh hoo-GEH-teh
toy truck	**el camión de juguete** ehl kah-MYOHN deh hoo-GEH-teh

Spanish speakers often use the ending **-ito**, which indicates that something is little or small in size, when referring to toys.

boat	**el barquito** ehl bahr-KEE-toh
car	**el carrito** ehl kah-RREE-toh
train	**el trencito** ehl trehn-SEE-toh
truck	**el camioncito** ehl kah-myohn-SEE-toh

It is also common to use the ending **-ito** when referring to stuffed animals, but in this case it is used to indicate endearment. For example, a toy bear is **el osito** [ehl oh-SEE-toh], a toy cat is **el gatito** [ehl gah-TEE-toh], and a toy dog is **el perrito** [ehl peh-RREE-toh]. The ending **-ito** can also be used with people's names (especially children) to indicate endearment, for example, **Pedrito** instead of **Pedro** or **Juanita** instead of **Juana**.

Here is a list of other toys or playthings that children may have at home.

bicycle	**la bicicleta** lah bee-see-KLEH-tah
kite	**la cometa** lah koh-MEH-tah
skates	**los patines** lohs pah-TEE-nehs

sled	**el trineo**	
	ehl tree-NEH-oh	
toy soldier	**el soldado de juguete**	
	ehl sohl-DAH-doh deh hoo-GEH-teh	
tricycle	**el triciclo**	
	ehl tree-SEE-kloh	

Spanish-speaking children, like their English-speaking counterparts, often use English brand names to identify their favorite playthings (las Barbies, el Nintendo, los Legos, etc.).

Verbs

to bounce (the ball)	**hacer** (*irreg.*) **rebotar (la pelota)**	ah-SEHR rreh-boh-TAHR (lah peh-LOH-tah)
to play	**jugar (ue)**	hoo-GAHR
to ride	**montar**	mohn-TAHR
to throw	**tirar**	tee-RAHR
to throw	**lanzar**	lahn-SAHR

Pets in the Classroom

Los animales domésticos en el aula

There are often pets (**los animales domésticos** [lohs ah-nee-MAH-lehs doh-MEHS-tee-kohs]) in an early childhood classroom. Some common ones are listed here.

fish	**el pez / los peces**
	ehl PEHS / lohs PEH-sehs
frog	**la rana**
	lah RRAH-nah
hamster	**el hámster**
	ehl HAHMS-tehr
snake	**la culebra**
	lah koo-LEH-brah
turtle	**la tortuga**
	lah tohr-TOO-gah

On the Playground

En el patio de recreo

Naps (**la siesta** [lah SYEHS-tah]), snacks (**la merienda** [lah meh-RYEHN-dah]), and recess (**el recreo** [ehl rreh-KREH-oh]) are very important in early childhood education.

Here are some things you may find on an early childhood playground (**el patio de recreo** [ehl PAH-tyoh deh rreh-KREH-oh]).

bench	**el banco** ehl BAHN-koh
merry-go-round	**el tiovivo** ehl tee-oh-BEE-boh
sandbox	**el cajón de arena** ehl kah-HOHN deh ah-REH-nah
seesaw	**el subibaja** ehl soo-bee-BAH-hah
slide	**el tobogán** ehl toh-boh-GAHN
swing	**el columpio** ehl koh-LOOM-pyoh
water fountain	**la fuente de agua potable** lah FWEHN-teh deh AH-gwah poh-TAH-bleh

During playtime, young children also like to do these activities.

to play "dress up"	**jugar a disfrazarse** hoo-GAHR ah dees-frah-SAHR-seh
to play hide and seek	**jugar al escondite** hoo-GAHR ahl ehs-kohn-DEE-teh
to play "house"	**jugar a la casita** hoo-GAHR ah lah kah-SEE-tah
to put puzzles together	**armar rompecabezas** ahr-MAHR rrohm-peh-kah-BEH-sahs

As children get older, they often enjoy table games (**los juegos de mesa** [lohs HWEH-gohs deh MEH-sah]), some of which are listed here.

cards	**las cartas** lahs KAHR-tahs

checkers	**las damas** lahs DAH-mahs
chess	**el ajedrez** ehl ah-heh-DREHS

Here is a list of some of the things that you may say to the children.

It's time (to) …	**Es hora de…** ehs OH-rah deh
to get up	**levantarse** leh-bahn-TAHR-seh
to go to the park	**ir al parque** eer ahl PAHR-keh
to nap	**dormir la siesta** dohr-MEER lah SYEHS-tah
to play (a game)	**jugar a (un juego)** hoo-GAHR ah (oon HWEH-goh)
to relax	**relajarse** rreh-lah-HAHR-seh
to rest	**descansar** dehs-kahn-SAHR

Some commands that you may want to give a child are the following.

Behave.	**Pórtate bien.** POHR-tah-teh byehn
Get up.	**Levántate.** leh-BAHN-tah-teh
Go to sleep.	**Duérmete.** DWEHR-meh-teh
Lie down.	**Acuéstate.** ah-KWEHS-tah-teh
Don't be afraid.	**No tengas miedo.** noh TEHN-gahs MYEH-doh
Don't cry.	**No llores.** noh YOH-rehs

When children are at play, things do not always go as they should. You will sometimes need to tell a child not to behave in a certain way.

Don't behave badly.	**No te portes mal.** noh teh POHR-tehs mahl
Don't bite.	**No muerdas.** noh MWEHR-dahs

Don't fight.	**No pelees.**
	noh peh-LEH-ehs
Don't hit.	**No pegues.**
	noh PEH-gehs
Don't jump.	**No saltes.**
	noh SAHL-tehs
Don't push.	**No empujes.**
	noh ehm-POO-hehs
Don't run.	**No corras.**
	noh KOH-rrahs

Verbs

to argue	**discutir**	dees-koo-TEER
to break	**romper**	rrohm-PEHR
to curse	**decir** (*irreg.*) **malas palabras**	deh-SEER MAH-lahs pah-LAH-brahs
to grab	**agarrar**	ah-gah-RRAHR
to hit	**pegar**	peh-GAHR
to hit	**golpear**	gohl-peh-AHR
to hit (against)	**dar** (*irreg.*) **(contra)**	dahr (KOHN-trah)
to hit (against)	**chocar (contra)**	choh-KAHR (KOHN-trah)
to jump	**saltar**	sahl-TAHR
to kick	**patear**	pah-teh-AHR
to pull	**tirar de**	tee-RAHR deh
to pull	**jalar**	hah-LAHR
to push	**empujar**	ehm-poo-HAHR
to run	**correr**	koh-RREHR
to shake	**sacudir**	sah-koo-DEER
to spit	**escupir**	ehs-koo-PEER
to yell	**gritar**	gree-TAHR

For an explanation of how to form commands, see the Introduction, pages 16–18, 20, and 21.

GRAMMAR · Reflexive Verbs I

When Spanish speakers talk about many of their daily activities, you will find that they often need to use reflexive verbs. These verbs are called "reflexive" because they indicate that the subject is acting upon himself/herself. You will recognize reflexive verbs by the **se** [seh] that is attached to the infinitive form.

to behave oneself	**portarse bien**	pohr-TAHR-seh byehn
to brush one's hair	**cepillarse el pelo**	seh-pee-YAHR-seh ehl PEH-loh
to brush one's teeth	**cepillarse los dientes**	seh-pee-YAHR-seh lohs DYEHN-tehs

to get up	**levantarse**	leh-bahn-TAHR-seh
to go to sleep	**dormirse (ue)**	dohr-MEER-seh
to lie down, go to bed	**acostarse (ue)**	ah-kohs-TAHR-seh
to misbehave	**portarse mal**	pohr-TAHR-seh mahl
to sit down	**sentarse (ie)**	sehn-TAHR-seh
to wake up	**despertarse (ie)**	dehs-pehr-TAHR-seh
to wash up	**lavarse**	lah-BAHR-seh

When used without the **se**, many reflexive verbs change meaning. For example, **dormir** [dohr-MEER] means "to sleep," **levantar** [leh-bahn-TAHR] means "to raise," and **portar** [pohr-TAHR] means "to carry."

Many sections of this book have lists of verbs that are related to the theme of a particular section. Remember that the reflexive verbs will have **se** [seh] attached to the infinitive ending. When you use these verbs, don't forget to use the reflexive pronouns, shown here.

myself	**me**	meh	ourselves	**nos**	nohs
yourself (*familiar*)	**te**	teh			
himself	**se**	seh	themselves (*masc.*)	**se**	seh
herself	**se**	seh	themselves (*fem.*)	**se**	seh
yourself (*formal*)	**se**	seh	yourselves	**se**	seh

levantarse [leh-bahn-TAHR-seh] to get up (raise oneself)

I get up	**(yo) me levanto**	meh leh-BAHN-toh
you get up	**(tú) te levantas**	teh leh-BAHN-tahs
he gets up	**(él) se levanta**	seh leh-BAHN-tah
she gets up	**(ella) se levanta**	seh leh-BAHN-tah
you get up	**(Ud.) se levanta**	seh leh-BAHN-tah
we get up	**(nosotros) nos levantamos**	nohs leh-bahn-TAH-mohs
we get up	**(nosotras) nos levantamos**	nohs leh-bahn-TAH-mohs
they get up	**(ellos) se levantan**	seh leh-BAHN-tahn
they get up	**(ellas) se levantan**	seh leh-BAHN-tahn
you (*plural*) get up	**(Uds.) se levantan**	seh leh-BAHN-tahn

Yesterday you (*plural*) behaved.　**Ayer se portaron bien.**
ah-YEHR seh pohr-TAH-rohn byehn

Are you going to wake up early?　**¿Te vas a despertar temprano?**
teh bahs ah dehs-pehr-TAHR tehm-PRAH-noh

Don't get up.　**No te levantes.**
noh teh leh-BAHN-tehs

Note that reflexive pronouns are usually placed immediately before a conjugated verb. The only exception to this placement is with an affirmative command. The reflexive pronoun is attached to the end of an affirmative command.

Do not lie down.	**No te acuestes.**
	noh teh ah-KWEHS-tehs
Lie down.	**Acuéstate.**
	ah-KWEHS-tah-teh

GRAMMAR · Direct Object Pronouns

In Spanish, as in English, direct object pronouns can replace nouns representing the person or thing that is the direct object of the verb. Here is a list of the direct object pronouns.

me	**me**	meh	us	**nos**	nohs
you (*familiar*)	**te**	teh			
him	**lo**	loh	them (*masc.*)	**los**	lohs
her	**la**	lah	them (*fem.*)	**las**	lahs
you (*formal, masc.*)	**lo**	loh	you (*formal, masc.*)	**los**	lohs
you (*formal, fem.*)	**la**	lah	you (*formal, fem.*)	**las**	lahs
it (*masc.*)	**lo**	loh	them (*masc.*)	**los**	lohs
it (*fem.*)	**la**	lah	them (*fem.*)	**las**	lahs

With the exception of affirmative commands, direct object pronouns are placed directly before a conjugated verb.

Did you buy the book?	**¿Compraste el libro?**
	kohm-PRAHS-teh ehl LEE-broh
Yes, I bought it.	**Sí, lo compré.**
	see, loh kohm-PREH

With an affirmative command, the direct object pronoun follows and is attached to the command.

| Return it! | **¡Devuélvelo!** |
| | deh-BWEHL-beh-loh |

Note that when a direct object pronoun is attached to an affirmative command, a written accent is used in order to keep the stress on the same syllable of the verb that carries the stress in the non-command form. Verbs that only have one syllable do not need this accent.

In a negative sentence, the direct object pronoun is preceded by **no**.

I did not buy it.	**No lo compré.**
	noh loh kohm-PREH
Do not buy it!	**¡No lo compres!**
	noh loh KOHM-prehs

Grammar · Personal *a*

When the direct object of the verb is a person, the word **a** [ah] is placed before the word that represents the person. This **a** is called *the personal a* and it is not translated into English.

I know Pedro.   **Conozco a Pedro.**
                        koh-NOHS-koh ah PEH-droh

When the direct object pronoun is used for a person, it replaces both the personal **a** and the direct object noun.

Do you know Elena?   **¿Conoces a Elena?**
                        koh-NOH-sehs ah eh-LEH-nah

No, I do not know her.   **No, no la conozco.**
                        noh, noh lah koh-NOHS-koh

Practice 3-5

A *Using the English phrase in parentheses as a clue, fill in the blanks from the strings of letters below.*

1. eemurdet
   (*go to sleep*)

2. rolsel
   (*don't cry*)   n o

3. attenaelv
   (*get up*)

4. sleepe
   (*don't fight*)   n o

5. srarco
   (*don't run*)   n o

6. ratelopmets
   (*don't behave badly*) n o

7. eatcestau
   (*lie down*)

8. obeitranept
   (*behave*)

B *Write the reflexive pronoun that completes each phrase.*

1. Yo _____ porto bien.

2. Ellos _____ levantan a las diez.

3. Nosotros _____ acostamos a las once.

4. Tú _____ cepillas el pelo.

5. Ella _____ despierta a las siete.

C *Answer each of the following questions by replacing the underlined words with the correct pronoun.*

1. ¿Conoces a Juan? Sí, _____ conozco.

2. ¿Lees las novelas? No, no _____ leo.

3. ¿Me vas a despertar a las diez? Sí, _____ voy a despertar a las ocho.

4. ¿Visitas a tu tía? Sí, _____ visito.

5. ¿Empujas a tus amigos? No, no _____ empujo.

D *Write the personal* **a** *on the line provided if it is needed to complete the sentence. If it is not needed, just write an X.*

1. Conocen _____ los estudiantes.

2. Traigo _____ los lápices.

3. Nosotros dormimos _____ la siesta.

4. El director visita _____ los profesores.

5. Juan se cepilla _____ los dientes.

6. Tú ves _____ tus compañeros de clase.

Summary Practice

What would you say in the following situations? Write your responses in Spanish, using complete sentences.

1. You want to know if a student knows the principal.

   _____

2. You need to find out when the meeting is.

   _____

3. You ask someone what the weather is going to be like tomorrow.

   _____

4. You tell a friend that it is raining.

   _____

5. You tell your students that your scarf is black and red.

   _____

6. You want to find out to whom the coat belongs.

   _____

7. You tell a student that the dress is in style.

   _____

8. You ask a student what the color of a shirt is.

   _____

9. You tell a student to write it [*masculine*] on the chalkboard.

   _____

10. Tell a student not to put them [*feminine*] in his/her backpack.

    _____

11. Tell your students to put away the toys.

    _____

12. Tell your students to behave.

    _____

4

The Curriculum

El plan de estudio

School Subjects

Las asignaturas

The following is an extensive, though not exhaustive, list of school subjects (**las asignaturas** [lahs ah-seeg-nah-TOO-rahs] that a typical student encounters in the school curriculum (**el plan de estudio** [ehl plahn deh ehs-TOO-dyoh]), together with some useful related vocabulary.

algebra	**el álgebra**
	ehl AHL-heh-brah
arithmetic	**la aritmética**
	lah ah-reet-MEH-tee-kah
art	**el arte**
	ehl AHR-teh
astronomy	**la astronomía**
	lah ahs-troh-noh-MEE-ah
biology	**la biología**
	lah byoh-loh-HEE-ah
calculus	**el cálculo**
	ehl KAHL-koo-loh
chemistry	**la química**
	lah KEE-mee-kah
Chinese	**el chino**
	ehl CHEE-noh
computer science	**la informática**
	lah een-fohr-MAH-tee-kah
dance	**el baile**
	ehl BAH-ee-leh
drama	**el drama**
	ehl DRAH-mah
economics	**la economía**
	lah eh-koh-noh-MEE-ah
English	**el inglés**
	ehl een-GLEHS
French	**el francés**
	ehl frahn-SEHS

geography	**la geografía**
	lah heh-oh-grah-FEE-ah
geometry	**la geometría**
	lah heh-oh-meh-TREE-ah
German	**el alemán**
	ehl ah-leh-MAHN
history	**la historia**
	lah ees-TOH-ryah
Italian	**el italiano**
	ehl ee-tah-LYAH-noh
Korean	**el coreano**
	ehl koh-reh-AH-noh
Latin	**el latín**
	ehl lah-TEEN
literature	**la literatura**
	lah lee-teh-rah-TOO-rah
mathematics	**las matemáticas**
	lahs mah-teh-MAH-tee-kahs
music	**la música**
	lah MOO-see-kah
physical education	**la educación física**
	lah eh-doo-kah-SYOHN FEE-see-kah
physics	**la física**
	lah FEE-see-kah
science	**la ciencia**
	lah SYEHN-syah
social studies	**los estudios sociales**
	lohs ehs-TOO-dyohs soh-SYAH-lehs
Spanish	**el español**
	ehl ehs-pah-NYOHL
theater	**el teatro**
	ehl teh-AH-troh
trigonometry	**la trigonometría**
	lah tree-goh-noh-meh-TREE-ah

GRAMMAR · The Verb "To Know"

In Spanish, there are two verbs that mean "to know," but these two verbs are not interchangeable.

Saber [sah-BEHR] is used to express the idea of knowing a *fact,* such as where a place is, a lesson, a rule, etc.

I know there are no classes today.	**Yo sé que no hay clases hoy.** yoh seh keh noh AH-ee KLAH-sehs OH-ee

To express the idea of knowing *how* to do something, use **saber** [sah-BEHR] followed by an infinitive.

We know how to play the guitar.	**Nosotros sabemos tocar la guitarra.** noh-SOH-trohs sah-BEH-mohs toh-KAHR lah gee-TAH-rrah

To express knowing a place or a person in the sense of being *acquainted with* or *familiar with,* you will always use **conocer** [koh-noh-SEHR].

She knows the school very well.	**Ella conoce la escuela muy bien.** EH-yah koh-NOH-seh lah ehs-KWEH-lah MOO-ee byehn
I know the biology teacher.	**Yo conozco al maestro de biología / a la maestra de biología.** yoh koh-NOHS-koh ahl mah-EHS-troh deh byoh-loh-HEE-ah / ah lah mah-EHS-trah deh byoh-loh-HEE-ah

Remember that when **conocer** [koh-noh-SEHR] is followed by a person, as in the example above, you must add the personal **a** [ah] after the verb. If **a** [ah] is followed by **el** [ehl], remember to use the contraction **al** [ahl].

Following is the present tense of the two Spanish verbs that mean "to know."

saber (*irreg.*) [sah-BEHR] to know (information, facts, how to do something)

I know	**yo sé**	yoh seh
you know	**tú sabes**	too SAH-behs
he knows	**él sabe**	ehl SAH-beh
she knows	**ella sabe**	EH-yah SAH-beh
you know	**Ud. sabe**	oos-TEHD SAH-beh
we know	**nosotros sabemos**	noh-SOH-trohs sah-BEH-mohs
we know	**nosotras sabemos**	noh-SOH-trahs sah-BEH-mohs
they know	**ellos saben**	EH-yohs SAH-behn
they know	**ellas saben**	EH-yahs SAH-behn
you (*plural*) know	**Uds. saben**	oos-TEH-dehs SAH-behn

conocer (*irreg.*) [koh-noh-SEHR] to know, be acquainted/familiar with

I know	**yo conozco**	yoh koh-NOHS-koh
you know	**tú conoces**	too koh-NOH-sehs
he knows	**él conoce**	ehl koh-NOH-seh
she knows	**ella conoce**	EH-yah koh-NOH-seh
you know	**Ud. conoce**	oos-TEHD koh-NOH-seh
we know	**nosotros conocemos**	noh-SOH-trohs koh-noh-SEH-mohs
we know	**nosotras conocemos**	noh-SOH-trahs koh-noh-SEH-mohs
they know	**ellos conocen**	EH-yohs koh-NOH-sehn
they know	**ellas conocen**	EH-yahs koh-NOH-sehn
you (*plural*) know	**Uds. conocen**	oos-TEH-dehs koh-NOH-sehn

Practice 4-1

Complete the following sentences with the correct form of **saber** *or* **conocer**.

1. Yo no _____ a tus padres.

2. Nosotros _____ la respuesta a la pregunta.

3. Ellos _____ jugar al tenis.

4. ¿_____ tú a mi familia?

5. El director no _____ quién es el presidente del club.

6. Yo _____ hablar español muy bien.

7. Uds. _____ los restaurantes buenos en Lima.

8. Ella _____ a todos los profesores de la escuela.

In Language Class

En la clase de lenguas

Following is vocabulary that is particularly relevant to language class (**la clase de lenguas** [lah KLAH-seh deh LEHN-gwahs]).

accent	**el acento**
	ehl ah-SEHN-toh
adjective	**el adjetivo**
	ehl ahd-heh-TEE-boh
adverb	**el adverbio**
	ehl ahd-BEHR-byoh
colon	**los dos puntos**
	lohs dohs POON-tohs

comma	**la coma** lah KOH-mah
command	**el mandato** ehl mahn-DAH-toh
composition	**la composición** lah kohm-poh-see-SYOHN
conjugation	**la conjugación** lah kohn-hoo-gah-SYOHN
conjunction	**la conjunción** lah kohn-hoon-SYOHN
consonant	**la consonante** lah kohn-soh-NAHN-teh
essay	**el ensayo** ehl ehn-SAH-yoh
gerund	**el gerundio** ehl heh-ROON-dyoh
grammar	**la gramática** lah grah-MAH-tee-kah
infinitive	**el infinitivo** ehl een-fee-nee-TEE-boh
interjection	**la interjección** lah een-tehr-hehk-SYOHN
language	**el lenguaje** ehl lehn-GWAH-heh
letter (alphabet)	**la letra** lah LEH-trah
letter (capital)	**la letra mayúscula** lah LEH-trah mah-YOOS-koo-lah
letter (lowercase)	**la letra minúscula** lah LEH-trah mee-NOOS-koo-lah
meaning	**el significado** ehl seeg-nee-fee-KAH-doh
noun	**el sustantivo** ehl soos-tahn-TEE-boh
paragraph	**el párrafo** ehl PAH-rrah-foh
participle	**el participio** ehl pahr-tee-SEE-pyoh
passive voice	**la voz pasiva** lah bohs pah-SEE-bah
period	**el punto** ehl POON-toh

preposition	**la preposición**
	lah preh-poh-see-SYOHN
pronoun	**el pronombre**
	ehl proh-NOHM-breh
semicolon	**el punto y coma**
	ehl POON-toh ee KOH-mah
sentence	**la oración / la frase completa**
	lah oh-rah-SYOHN /
	lah FRAH-seh kohm-PLEH-tah
subject	**el sujeto**
	ehl soo-HEH-toh
syllable	**la sílaba**
	lah SEE-lah-bah
tense	**el tiempo**
	ehl TYEHM-poh
verb	**el verbo**
	ehl BEHR-boh
vocabulary	**el vocabulario**
	ehl boh-kah-boo-LAH-ryoh
vowel	**la vocal**
	lah boh-KAHL
word	**la palabra**
	lah pah-LAH-brah
writing	**la escritura**
	lah ehs-kree-TOO-rah

In Literature Class

En la clase de literatura

Following is vocabulary that is particularly relevant to literature class (**la clase de literatura** [lah KLAH-seh deh lee-teh-rah-TOO-rah]).

anonymous	**anónimo**
	ah-NOH-nee-moh
anthology	**la antología**
	lah ahn-toh-loh-HEE-ah
author	**el autor / la autora**
	ehl ah-oo-TOHR / lah ah-oo-TOH-rah
best seller	**el libro de gran éxito / el bestseller**
	ehl LEE-broh deh grahn EHK-see-toh /
	ehl behst-SEH-lehr

biography	**la biografía**
	lah byoh-grah-FEE-ah
chapter	**el capítulo**
	ehl kah-PEE-too-loh
character	**el personaje**
	ehl pehr-soh-NAH-heh
comedy	**la comedia**
	lah koh-MEH-dyah
edition	**la edición**
	lah eh-dee-SYOHN
hero	**el héroe**
	ehl EH-roh-eh
heroine	**la heroína**
	lah eh-roh-EE-nah
in print	**en venta**
	ehn BEHN-tah
index	**el índice**
	ehl EEN-dee-seh
literary prize	**el premio literario**
	ehl PREH-myoh lee-teh-RAH-ryoh
literature	**la literatura**
	lah lee-teh-rah-TOO-rah
masterpiece	**la obra maestra**
	lah OH-brah mah-EHS-trah
narrator	**el narrador / la narradora**
	ehl nah-rrah-DOHR /
	lah nah-rrah-DOH-rah
novel	**la novela**
	lah noh-BEH-lah
out of print	**agotado**
	ah-goh-TAH-doh
paperback	**el libro de bolsillo**
	ehl LEE-broh deh bohl-SEE-yoh
period (literary)	**el período**
	ehl peh-REE-oh-doh
play	**la obra de teatro**
	lah OH-brah deh teh-AH-troh
plot	**el argumento**
	ehl ahr-goo-MEHN-toh
poetry	**la poesía**
	lah poh-eh-SEE-ah

prose	**la prosa** lah PROH-sah
reader	**el lector / la lectora** ehl lehk-TOHR / lah lehk-TOH-rah
reading	**la lectura** lah lehk-TOO-rah
script	**el guión** ehl gee-OHN
short story	**el cuento** ehl KWEHN-toh
style	**el estilo** ehl ehs-TEE-loh
theme	**el tema** ehl TEH-mah
title	**el título** ehl TEE-too-loh
tragedy	**la tragedia** lah trah-HEH-dyah
volume	**el volumen** ehl boh-LOO-mehn
work (of art)	**la obra (de arte)** lah OH-brah (deh AHR-teh)

Poetry
La poesía

metaphor	**la metáfora** lah meh-TAH-foh-rah
ode	**la oda** lah OH-dah
poem	**el poema** ehl poh-EH-mah
poet	**el poeta / la poetiza** ehl poh-EH-tah / lah poh-eh-TEE-sah
rhyme	**la rima** lah RREE-mah
sonnet	**el soneto** ehl soh-NEH-toh
stanza	**la estrofa** lah ehs-TROH-fah
verse	**el verso** ehl BEHR-soh

In Social Studies Class

En la clase de estudios sociales

Following are general topics that are particularly relevant to social studies class (**la clase de estudios sociales** [lah KLAH-seh deh ehs-TOO-dyohs soh-SYAH-lehs]).

ages	**las edades** lahs eh-DAH-dehs
compass points	**los puntos cardinales** lohs POON-tohs kahr-dee-NAH-lehs
eras	**las eras** lahs EH-rahs
geography	**la geografía** lah heh-oh-grah-FEE-ah
government	**el gobierno** ehl goh-BYEHR-noh
history	**la historia** lah ees-TOH-ryah
monarchy	**la monarquía** lah moh-nahr-KEE-ah
religion	**la religión** lah rreh-lee-HYOHN
war and conflict	**la guerra y el conflicto** lah GEH-rrah ee ehl kohn-FLEEK-toh

Eras/Ages

Las eras / Las edades

Age of Enlightenment	**el Siglo de las Luces** ehl SEE-gloh deh lahs LOO-sehs
Bronze Age	**la Edad de Bronce** lah eh-DAHD deh BROHN-seh
Feudalism	**el feudalismo** ehl feh-oo-dah-LEES-moh
Golden Age	**el Siglo de Oro** ehl SEE-gloh deh OH-roh
Middle Ages	**la Edad Media** lah eh-DAHD MEH-dyah
Renaissance	**el Renacimiento** ehl rreh-nah-see-MYEHN-toh
Stone Age	**la Edad de Piedra** lah eh-DAHD deh PYEH-drah

Government
El gobierno

congress	**el congreso** ehl kohn-GREH-soh
council	**el concilio** ehl kohn-SEE-lyoh
coup d'etat	**el golpe de estado** ehl GOHL-peh deh ehs-TAH-doh
court	**la corte** lah KOHR-teh
house of representatives	**la cámara de representantes** lah KAH-mah-rah deh rreh-preh-sehn-TAHN-tehs
leader	**el jefe / la jefa** ehl HEH-feh / lah HEH-fah **el/la líder** ehl/lah LEE-dehr
nation	**la nación** lah nah-SYOHN
parliament	**el parlamento** ehl pahr-lah-MEHN-toh
policy	**la política** lah poh-LEE-tee-kah
possession	**la posesión** lah poh-seh-SYOHN
power	**la potencia** lah poh-TEHN-syah
president	**el presidente** ehl preh-see-DEHN-teh
prime minister	**el primer ministro / la primera ministra** ehl pree-MEHR mee-NEES-troh / lah pree-MEH-rah mee-NEES-trah
republic	**la república** lah rreh-POO-blee-kah
ruler	**el/la gobernante** ehl/lah goh-behr-NAHN-teh
senate	**el senado** ehl seh-NAH-doh
state	**el estado** ehl ehs-TAH-doh

statesman	**el hombre de estado / la mujer de estado**
	ehl OHM-breh deh ehs-TAH-doh /
	lah moo-HEHR deh ehs-TAH-doh

Monarchy
La monarquía

castle	**el castillo**
	ehl kahs-TEE-yoh
coronation	**la coronación**
	lah koh-roh-nah-SYOHN
court	**la corte**
	lah KOHR-teh
crown	**la corona**
	lah koh-ROH-nah
heir	**el heredero**
	ehl eh-reh-DEH-roh
king	**el rey**
	ehl RREH-ee
queen	**la reina**
	lah RREH-ee-nah
reign	**el reinado**
	ehl rreh-ee-NAH-doh
throne	**el trono**
	ehl TROH-noh

Religion
La religión

atheism	**el ateísmo**
	ehl ah-teh-EES-moh
Bible	**la Biblia**
	lah BEE-blyah
Catholicism	**el catolicismo**
	ehl kah-toh-lee-SEES-moh
Christianity	**el cristianismo**
	ehl krees-tyah-NEES-moh
church	**la iglesia**
	lah ee-GLEH-syah
faith	**la fe**
	lah feh
God	**Dios**
	dyohs

Hinduism	**el hinduismo** ehl een-doo-EES-moh
Imam	**el imán** ehl ee-MAHN
Islam	**el Islam** ehl ees-LAHM
Judaism	**el judaísmo** ehl hoo-dah-EES-moh
minister	**el/la ministro** ehl/lah mee-NEES-troh
New/Old Testament	**el Nuevo / el Antiguo Testamento** ehl NWEH-boh / ehl ahn-TEE-gwoh tehs-tah-MEHN-toh
paganism	**el paganismo** ehl pah-gah-NEES-moh
pope	**el papa** ehl PAH-pah
priest	**el sacerdote / el cura** ehl sah-sehr-DOH-teh / ehl KOO-rah
Protestantism	**el protestantismo** ehl proh-tehs-tahn-TEES-moh
rabbi	**el rabino** ehl rrah-BEE-noh

War and Conflict
La guerra y el conflicto

ally	**el aliado** ehl ah-LYAH-doh
army	**el ejército** ehl eh-HEHR-see-toh
battle	**la batalla** lah bah-TAH-yah
century	**el siglo** ehl SEE-gloh
civil war	**la guerra civil** lah GEH-rrah see-BEEL
conqueror	**el conquistador / la conquistadora** ehl kohn-kees-tah-DOHR / lah kohn-kees-tah-DOH-rah
defeat	**la derrota** lah deh-RROH-tah

dynasty	**la dinastía** lah dee-nahs-ᴛᴇᴇ-ah
empire	**el imperio** ehl eem-ᴘᴇʜ-ryoh
enemy	**el enemigo / la enemiga** ehl eh-neh-ᴍᴇᴇ-goh / lah eh-neh-ᴍᴇᴇ-gah
execution	**la ejecución** lah eh-heh-ᴋᴏᴏ-sʏᴏʜɴ
invasion	**la invasión** lah een-bah-sʏᴏʜɴ
navy	**la armada** lah ahr-ᴍᴀʜ-dah
patriot	**el/la patriota** ehl/lah pah-ᴛʀʏᴏʜ-tah
peace	**la paz** lah pahs
rebel	**el/la rebelde** ehl/lah rreh-ʙᴇʜʟ-deh
revolution	**la revolución** lah rreh-boh-loo-sʏᴏʜɴ
settler	**el colonizador / la colonizadora** ehl koh-loh-nee-sah-ᴅᴏʜʀ / lah koh-loh-nee-sah-ᴅᴏʜ-rah
siege	**el sitio** ehl sᴇᴇ-tyoh
slave	**el esclavo / la esclava** ehl ehs-ᴋʟᴀʜ-boh / lah ehs-ᴋʟᴀʜ-bah
slavery	**la esclavitud** lah ehs-klah-bee-ᴛᴏᴏᴅ
succession	**la sucesión** lah soo-seh-sʏᴏʜɴ
surrender	**la rendición** lah rrehn-dee-sʏᴏʜɴ
traitor	**el traidor / la traidora** ehl trah-ee-ᴅᴏʜʀ / lah trah-ee-ᴅᴏʜ-rah
treason	**la traición** lah trah-ee-sʏᴏʜɴ
treaty	**el tratado** ehl trah-ᴛᴀʜ-doh
unity	**la unidad** lah oo-nee-ᴅᴀʜᴅ
victory	**la victoria** lah beek-ᴛᴏʜ-ryah

Verbs

to conquer	**conquistar**	kohn-kees-TAHR
to defeat	**derrotar**	deh-rroh-TAHR
to execute	**ejecutar**	eh-heh-koo-TAHR
to found	**fundar**	foon-DAHR
to invade	**invadir**	een-bah-DEER
to rebel	**rebelarse**	rreh-beh-LAHR-seh
to restore	**restaurar**	rrehs-tah-oo-RAHR
to rule	**gobernar (ie)**	goh-behr-NAHR
to surrender	**rendirse (i)**	rrehn-DEER-seh

Geography
La geografía

atmosphere — **la atmósfera**
lah aht-MOHS-feh-rah

bay — **la bahía**
lah bah-EE-ah

beach — **la playa**
lah PLAH-yah

cave — **la caverna / la cueva**
lah kah-BEHR-nah / lah KWEH-bah

coastline — **el litoral**
ehl lee-toh-RAHL

continent — **el continente**
ehl kohn-tee-NEHN-teh

desert — **el desierto**
ehl deh-SYEHR-toh

earth — **la tierra**
lah TYEH-rrah

earthquake — **el terremoto**
ehl teh-rreh-MOH-toh

forest — **la selva**
lah SEHL-bah

gulf — **el golfo**
ehl GOHL-foh

hill — **la colina**
lah koh-LEE-nah

island — **la isla**
lah EES-lah

jungle — **la jungla**
lah HOON-glah

lake	**el lago**	ehl LAH-goh
land	**la tierra**	lah TYEH-rrah
map	**el mapa**	ehl MAH-pah
mountain	**la montaña**	lah mohn-TAH-nyah
mountain range	**la cordillera**	lah kohr-dee-YEH-rah
ocean	**el océano**	ehl oh-SEH-ah-noh
peninsula	**la península**	lah peh-NEEN-soo-lah
plain	**la llanura**	lah yah-NOO-rah
region	**la región**	lah rreh-HYOHN
river	**el río**	ehl RREE-oh
sea	**el mar**	ehl mahr
stream	**el arroyo**	ehl ah-RROH-yoh
valley	**el valle**	ehl BAH-yeh
vegetation	**la vegetación**	lah beh-heh-tah-SYOHN
volcano	**el volcán**	ehl bohl-KAHN
woods	**el bosque**	ehl BOHS-keh

Compass Points
Los puntos cardinales

north	**el norte**	ehl NOHR-teh
south	**el sur**	ehl soor
east	**el este**	ehl EHS-teh
west	**el oeste**	ehl oh-EHS-teh

In Mathematics Class

En la clase de matemáticas

Among other areas of study, mathematics class (**la clase de matemáticas** [lah KLAH-seh deh mah-teh-MAH-tee-kahs]) may include the following.

algebra	**el álgebra** ehl AHL-heh-brah
arithmetic	**la aritmética** lah ah-reet-MEH-tee-kah
calculus	**el cálculo** ehl KAHL-koo-loh
geometry	**la geometría** lah heh-oh-meh-TREE-ah
trigonometry	**la trigonometría** lah tree-goh-noh-meh-TREE-ah

Here is some additional vocabulary that is particularly useful when talking about mathematics.

arithmetical operations	**las operaciones aritméticas** lahs oh-peh-rah-SYOH-nehs ah-reet-MEH-tee-kahs
arithmetical signs	**los signos aritméticos** lohs SEEG-nohs ah-reet-MEH-tee-kohs
decimal	**el número decimal** ehl NOO-meh-roh deh-see-MAHL
denominator	**el denominador** ehl deh-noh-mee-nah-DOHR
difference	**la diferencia** lah dee-feh-REHN-syah
dividend	**el dividendo** ehl dee-bee-DEHN-doh
divisor	**el divisor** ehl dee-bee-SOHR
equation	**la ecuación** lah eh-kwah-SYOHN
factor	**el factor** ehl fahk-TOHR

fraction	**el quebrado / la fracción** ehl keh-BRAH-doh / lah frahk-SYOHN
geometric figures	**las figuras geométricas** lahs fee-GOO-rahs heh-oh-MEH-tree-kahs
integer	**el número entero** ehl NOO-meh-roh ehn-TEH-roh
logarithm	**el logaritmo** ehl loh-gah-REET-moh
multiple	**el múltiplo** ehl MOOL-tee-ploh
number	**el número** ehl NOO-meh-roh
numerator	**el numerador** ehl noo-mee-rah-DOHR
operation	**la operación** lah oh-peh-rah-SYOHN
parenthesis	**el paréntesis** ehl pah-REHN-teh-sees
problem	**el problema** ehl proh-BLEH-mah
product	**el producto** ehl proh-DOOK-toh
proportion	**la proporción** lah proh-pohr-SYOHN
quantity	**la cantidad** lah kahn-tee-DAHD
quotient	**el cociente** ehl koh-SYEHN-teh
remainder	**el resto** ehl RREHS-toh
result	**el resultado** ehl rreh-sool-TAH-doh
ruler	**la regla** lah RREH-glah
solution	**la solución** lah soh-loo-SYOHN
sum	**la suma** lah SOO-mah
table	**la tabla** lah TAH-blah
total	**el total** ehl toh-TAHL

Arithmetical Signs
Los signos aritméticos

addition sign **el signo de la suma**
ehl SEEG-noh deh lah SOO-mah

division sign **el signo de la división**
ehl SEEG-noh deh lah dee-bee-SYOHN

equal sign **el signo de igualdad**
ehl SEEG-noh deh ee-gwahl-DAHD

multiplication sign **el signo de la multiplicación**
ehl SEEG-noh deh lah
mool-tee-plee-kah-SYOHN

subtraction sign **el signo de la resta**
ehl SEEG-noh deh lah RREHS-tah

Arithmetical Operations
Las operaciones aritméticas

addition **la suma**
lah SOO-mah

divided by **dividido por**
dee-bee-DEE-doh pohr

division **la división**
lah dee-bee-SYOHN

minus **menos**
MEH-nohs

multiplication **la multiplicación**
lah mool-tee-plee-kah-SYOHN

multiplied by **multiplicado por**
mool-tee-plee-KAH-doh pohr

plus **más**
mahs

subtraction **la resta**
lah RREHS-tah

Geometry
La geometría

Some terms used in geometry class are the following.

acute angle **el ángulo agudo**
ehl AHN-goo-loh ah-GOO-doh

altitude	**la altura**
	lah ahl-TOO-rah
angle	**el ángulo**
	ehl AHN-goo-loh
arc	**el arco**
	ehl AHR-koh
area	**el área**
	ehl AH-reh-ah
axiom	**el axioma**
	ehl ahk-SYOH-mah
base	**la base**
	lah BAH-seh
center	**el centro**
	ehl SEHN-troh
chord	**la cuerda**
	lah KWEHR-dah
circumference	**la circunferencia**
	lah seer-koon-feh-REHN-syah
curve	**la curva**
	lah KOOR-bah
diagonal	**diagonal**
	dyah-goh-NAHL
diameter	**el diámetro**
	ehl DYAH-meh-troh
dimension	**la dimensión**
	lah dee-mehn-SYOHN
ellipse	**el elipse**
	ehl eh-LEEP-seh
equilateral	**equilátero**
	eh-kee-LAH-teh-roh
geometric figures	**las figuras geométricas**
	lahs fee-GOO-rahs heh-oh-MEH-tree-kahs
height	**la altura**
	lah ahl-TOO-rah
horizontal	**horizontal**
	oh-ree-sohn-TAHL
hyperbola	**la hipérbola**
	lah ee-PEHR-boh-lah
hypotenuse	**la hipotenusa**
	lah ee-poh-teh-NOO-sah
intersection	**la intersección**
	lah een-tehr-sehk-SYOHN

length	**la longitud** lah lohn-hee-TOOD
line	**la línea** lah LEE-neh-ah
line segment	**el segmento de la línea** ehl sehg-MEHN-toh deh lah LEE-neh-ah
obtuse angle	**el ángulo obtuso** ehl AHN-goo-loh ohb-TOO-soh
parabola	**la parábola** lah pah-RAH-boh-lah
parallel	**paralelo** pah-rah-LEH-loh
perpendicular	**perpendicular** pehr-pehn-dee-koo-LAHR
plane	**el plano** ehl PLAH-noh
point	**el punto** ehl POON-toh
radius	**el radio** ehl RRAH-dyoh
right angle	**el ángulo recto** ehl AHN-goo-loh RREHK-toh
secant	**la secante** lah seh-KAHN-teh
side	**el lado** ehl LAH-doh
symmetry	**la simetría** lah see-meh-TREE-ah
tangent	**la tangente** lah tahn-HEHN-teh
vertical	**vertical** behr-tee-KAHL

Geometric Figures · *Las figuras geométricas*

circle	**el círculo** ehl SEER-koo-loh
parallelogram	**el paralelogramo** ehl pah-rah-leh-loh-GRAH-moh
pentagon	**el pentágono** ehl pehn-TAH-goh-noh
polygon	**el polígono** ehl poh-LEE-goh-noh

quadrilateral	**el cuadrilátero**	
	ehl kwah-dree-LAH-teh-roh	
rectangle	**el rectángulo**	
	ehl rrehk-TAHN-goo-loh	
rhombus	**el rombo**	
	ehl RROHM-boh	
semicircle	**el semicírculo**	
	ehl seh-mee-SEER-koo-loh	
square	**el cuadrado**	
	ehl kwah-DRAH-doh	
trapezoid	**el trapezoide**	
	ehl trah-peh-SOH-ee-deh	
triangle	**el triángulo**	
	ehl TRYAHN-goo-loh	

Verbs

to add	**sumar**	SOO-MAHR
to be correct	**estar** (*irreg.*) **correcto**	ehs-TAHR koh-RREHK-toh
to be incorrect	**estar** (*irreg.*) **incorrecto**	ehs-TAHR een-koh-RREHK-toh
to be incorrect	**equivocarse**	eh-kee-boh-KAHR-seh
to bring down (a number)	**bajar (un número)**	bah-HAHR (oon NOO-meh-roh)
to calculate	**calcular**	kahl-koo-LAHR
to carry (a number)	**llevarse (un número)**	yeh-BAHR-seh (oon NOO-meh-roh)
to check	**comprobar (ue)**	kohm-proh-BAHR
to count	**contar (ue)**	kohn-TAHR
to divide	**dividir**	dee-bee-DEER
to multiply	**multiplicar**	mool-tee-plee-KAHR
to prove	**probar (ue)**	proh-BAHR
to solve	**resolver (ue)**	rreh-sohl-BEHR
to subtract	**restar**	rrehs-TAHR

Numbers
Los números

To describe numbers (**los números** [lohs NOO-meh-rohs], use these terms.

cardinal	**cardinal**	
	kahr-dee-NAHL	
composite	**compuesto**	
	kohm-PWEHS-toh	

even	**par**
	pahr
integral	**entero**
	ehn-TEH-roh
irrational	**irracional**
	ee-rrah-syoh-NAHL
odd	**impar**
	eem-PAHR
ordinal	**ordinal**
	ohr-dee-NAHL
prime	**primo**
	PREE-moh
rational	**racional**
	rrah-syoh-NAHL

Cardinal Numbers · *Los números cardinales*

0	**cero**	SEH-roh	16	**dieciséis**	dyeh-see-SEH-ees
1	**uno**	OO-noh	17	**diecisiete**	dyeh-see-SYEH-teh
2	**dos**	dohs	18	**dieciocho**	dyeh-see-OH-choh
3	**tres**	trehs	19	**diecinueve**	dyeh-see-NWEH-beh
4	**cuatro**	KWAH-troh	20	**veinte**	BEH-een-teh
5	**cinco**	SEEN-koh	21	**veinte y uno**	BEH-een-teh ee OO-noh
6	**seis**	SEH-ees	22	**veinte y dos**	BEH-een-teh ee dohs
7	**siete**	SYEH-teh	23	**veinte y tres**	BEH-een-teh ee trehs
8	**ocho**	OH-choh	24	**veinte y cuatro**	BEH-een-teh ee KWAH-troh
9	**nueve**	NWEH-beh	25	**veinte y cinco**	BEH-een-teh ee SEEN-koh
10	**diez**	dyehs	26	**veinte y seis**	BEH-een-teh ee SEH-ees
11	**once**	OHN-seh	27	**veinte y siete**	BEH-een-teh ee SYEH-teh
12	**doce**	DOH-seh	28	**veinte y ocho**	BEH-een-teh ee OH-choh
13	**trece**	TREH-seh	29	**veinte y nueve**	BEH-een-teh ee NWEH-beh
14	**catorce**	kah-TOHR-seh	30	**treinta**	TREH-een-tah
15	**quince**	KEEN-seh			

40	**cuarenta**	kwah-REHN-tah
50	**cincuenta**	seen-KWEHN-tah
60	**sesenta**	seh-SEHN-tah
70	**setenta**	seh-TEHN-tah
80	**ochenta**	oh-CHEHN-tah
90	**noventa**	noh-BEHN-tah
100	**ciento/cien**	SYEHN-toh/syehn

101	**ciento uno**	SYEHN-toh oo-noh
102	**ciento dos**	SYEHN-toh dohs
200	**doscientos/doscientas**	doh-SYEHN-tohs/doh-SYEHN-tahs
300	**trescientos/trescientas**	treh-SYEHN-tohs/treh-SYEHN-tahs
400	**cuatrocientos/cuatrocientas**	kwah-troh-SYEHN-tohs/ kwah-troh-SYEHN-tahs
500	**quinientos/quinientas**	kee-NYEHN-tohs/kee-NYEHN-tahs
600	**seiscientos/seiscientas**	seh-ee-SYEHN-tohs/seh-ee-SYEHN-tahs
700	**setecientos/setecientas**	seh-teh-SYEHN-tohs/seh-teh-SYEHN-tahs
800	**ochocientos/ochocientas**	oh-choh-SYEHN-tohs/oh-choh-SYEHN-tahs
900	**novecientos/novecientas**	noh-beh-SYEHN-tohs/noh-beh-SYEHN-tahs

1,000	**mil**	meel
2,000	**dos mil**	dohs meel
100,000	**cien mil**	syehn meel
200,000	**doscientos mil / doscientas mil**	doh-SYEHN-tohs meel / doh-SYEHN-tahs meel
1,000,000	**un millón**	oon mee-YOHN
2,000,000	**dos millones**	dohs mee-YOH-nehs
1,000,000,000	**mil millones**	meel mee-YOH-nehs

To express a quantity in terms of millions or billions, you use a **de** [deh] + noun construction as follows: a million books is **un millón de libros** [oon mee-YOHN deh LEE-brohs]; two million balls is **dos millones de pelotas** [dohs mee-YOH-nehs deh peh-LOH-tahs]; a billion dollars is **mil millones de dólares** [meel mee-YOH-nehs deh DOH-lah-rehs].

Fractions · *Las fracciones*

½	**un medio**	oon MEH-dyoh
1½	**uno y medio**	oo-noh ee MEH-dyoh
⅓	**un tercio**	oon TEHR-syoh
⅔	**dos tercios**	dohs TEHR-syohs
¼	**un cuarto**	oon KWAHR-toh
¾	**tres cuartos**	trehs KWAHR-tohs
⅕	**un quinto**	oon KEEN-toh
⅘	**cuatro quintos**	KWAH-troh KEEN-tohs
⅙	**un sexto**	oon SEHS-toh
⅚	**cinco sextos**	SEEN-koh SEHS-tohs
⅐	**un séptimo**	oon SEHP-tee-moh

⁶⁄₇	**seis séptimos**	SEH-ees SEHP-tee-mohs
⅛	**un octavo**	oon ohk-TAH-boh
⅞	**siete octavos**	SYEH-teh ohk-TAH-bohs
⅑	**un noveno**	oon noh-BEH-noh
⁸⁄₉	**ocho novenos**	OH-choh noh-BEH-nohs
⅒	**un décimo**	oon DEH-see-moh
⁹⁄₁₀	**nueve décimos**	NWEH-beh DEH-see-mohs

Ordinal Numbers · *Los números ordinales*

first	**primero/primera**	pree-MEH-roh/pree-MEH-rah
second	**segundo/segunda**	seh-GOON-doh/seh-GOON-dah
third	**tercero/tercera**	tehr-SEH-roh/tehr-SEH-rah
fourth	**cuarto/cuarta**	KWAHR-toh/KWAHR-tah
fifth	**quinto/quinta**	KEEN-toh/KEEN-tah
sixth	**sexto/sexta**	SEHS-toh/SEHS-tah
seventh	**séptimo/séptima**	SEHP-tee-moh/SEHP-tee-mah
eighth	**octavo/octava**	ohk-TAH-boh/ohk-TAH-bah
ninth	**noveno/novena**	noh-BEH-noh/noh-BEH-nah
tenth	**décimo/décima**	DEH-see-moh/DEH-see-mah

However, to express "first" or "third" before a masculine singular noun, you use **primer** [pree-MEHR] and **tercer** [tehr-SEHR].

In Computer Science Class

En la clase de informática

Many terms associated with computers are English words. In computer science class (**la clase de informática** [lah KLAH-seh deh een-fohr-MAH-tee-kah], students learn that although "download" is translated as **bajar** [bah-HAHR], many people use the English word "download" [DAH-oon-loh-ood].

@	**la arroba**
	lah ah-RROH-bah
address book	**la libreta de direcciones**
	lah lee-BREH-tah deh
	dee-rehk-SYOH-nehs
antivirus	**el antivirus**
	ehl ahn-tee-BEE-roos

attached file	**el archivo adjunto** ehl ahr-CHEE-boh ahd-HOON-toh
backup disk	**el disco de respaldo** ehl DEES-koh deh rrehs-PAHL-doh
backup file	**el archivo de reserva** ehl ahr-CHEE-boh deh rreh-SEHR-bah
button	**el botón** ehl boh-TOHN
computer	**la computadora** lah kohm-poo-tah-DOH-rah
database	**la base de datos** lah BAH-seh deh DAH-tohs
disk	**el disco** ehl DEES-koh
disk drive	**la unidad de discos** lah oo-nee-DAHD deh DEES-kohs
e-mail	**el correo electrónico** ehl koh-RREH-oh eh-lehk-TROH-nee-koh
e-mail address	**la dirección de correo electrónico** lah dee-rehk-SYOHN deh koh-RREH-oh eh-lehk-TROH-nee-koh
exit	**la salida** lah sah-LEE-dah
file	**el archivo / el fichero** ehl ahr-CHEE-boh / ehl fee-CHEH-roh
file transfer	**la transferencia de ficheros** lah trahns-feh-REHN-syah deh fee-CHEH-rohs
floppy disk	**el disco flexible** ehl DEES-koh flehk-SEE-bleh
folder	**la carpeta** lah kahr-PEH-tah
handle (nickname)	**el apodo** ehl ah-POH-doh
hard disk	**el disco duro** ehl DEES-koh DOO-roh
home page	**la página principal / la página inicial** lah PAH-hee-nah preen-see-PAHL / lah PAH-hee-nah ee-nee-SYAHL
inkjet printer	**la impresora de chorro de tinta** lah eem-preh-SOH-rah deh CHOH-rroh deh TEEN-tah

Internet	**la red / el internet** lah rrehd / ehl een-tehr-NEHT
key	**la tecla** lah TEH-klah
keyboard	**el teclado** ehl teh-KLAH-doh
keyword	**la palabra clave** lah pah-LAH-brah KLAH-beh
laser printer	**la impresora por láser** lah eem-preh-SOH-rah pohr LAH-sehr
link	**el enlace / el vínculo** ehl ehn-LAH-seh / ehl BEEN-koo-loh
memory	**la memoria** lah meh-MOH-ryah
menu	**el menú** ehl meh-NOO
modem	**el módem** ehl MOH-dehm
monitor	**la consola** lah kohn-SOH-lah
mouse	**el ratón** ehl rrah-TOHN
mouse button	**el botón del ratón** ehl boh-TOHN dehl rrah-TOHN
mouse pad	**la alfombrilla de ratón** lah ahl-fohm-BREE-yah deh rrah-TOHN
password	**la contraseña** lah kohn-trah-SEH-nyah
printer	**la impresora** lah eem-preh-SOH-rah
screen	**la pantalla** lah pahn-TAH-yah
search engine	**el motor de búsqueda** ehl moh-TOHR deh BOOS-keh-dah
shift lock	**el sujetador de mayúsculas** ehl soo-heh-tah-DOHR deh mah-YOOS-koo-lahs
space bar	**el espaciador** ehl ehs-pah-syah-DOHR
spam	**el mensaje no deseado** ehl mehn-SAH-heh noh deh-seh-AH-doh

toolbar	**la barra de herramientas**	
	lah BAH-rrah deh eh-rrah-MYEHN-tahs	
user name	**el nombre de usuario**	
	ehl NOHM-breh deh oo-SWAH-ryoh	
virus	**el virus**	
	ehl BEE-roos	
Web page	**la página web**	
	lah PAH-hee-nah wehb	
Web site	**el sitio web**	
	ehl SEE-tyoh wehb	
window	**la ventana**	
	lah behn-TAH-nah	

Verbs

to attach	**adjuntar**	ahd-hoon-TAHR
to attach	**unir**	OO-NEER
to back up	**hacer** (*irreg.*) **un backup**	ah-SEHR oon BAHK-ahp
to backspace	**retroceder**	rreh-troh-seh-DEHR
to chat	**conversar**	kohn-behr-SAHR
to chat	**charlar**	chahr-LAHR
to check	**verificar**	beh-ree-fee-KAHR
to check	**examinar**	ehk-sah-mee-NAHR
to clear	**borrar**	boh-RRAHR
to clear	**despejar**	dehs-peh-HAHR
to click	**pulsar**	pool-SAHR
to compute	**computar**	kohm-poo-TAHR
to delete	**borrar**	boh-RRAHR
to download	**hacer** (*irreg.*) **un download**	ah-SEHR oon DAH-oon-loh-ood
to download	**bajar archivos**	bah-HAHR ahr-CHEE-bohs
to drag	**arrastrar**	ah-rrahs-TRAHR
to file	**archivar**	ahr-chee-BAHR
to file	**guardar**	gwahr-DAHR
to go back	**regresar**	rreh-greh-SAHR
to load	**cargar**	kahr-GAHR
to log on	**comenzar** (ie) **una sesión**	koh-mehn-SAHR OO-nah seh-SYOHN
to log out	**terminar la sesión**	tehr-mee-NAHR lah seh-SYOHN
to paste	**pegar**	peh-GAHR
to print	**imprimir**	eem-pree-MEER
to quit	**salir** (*irreg.*)	sah-LEER
to save a file	**hacer** (*irreg.*) **un archivo de reserva**	ah-SEHR oon ahr-CHEE-boh deh rreh-SEHR-bah
to surf	**navegar**	nah-beh-GAHR

to upload	**subir**	SOO-BEER
to upload	**cargar**	kahr-GAHR
to upload	**copiar**	koh-PYAHR

In Chemistry Class

En la clase de química

acid
el ácido
ehl AH-see-doh

atom
el átomo
ehl AH-toh-moh

atomic
atómico
ah-TOH-mee-koh

chemical
químico
KEE-mee-koh

chemical reaction
la reacción química
lah rreh-ahk-SYOHN KEE-mee-kah

dioxide
el dióxido
ehl dee-OHK-see-doh

element
el elemento
ehl eh-leh-MEHN-toh

flask
el frasco de laboratorio
ehl FRAHS-koh deh lah-boh-rah-TOH-ryoh

gas
el gas
ehl gahs

gaseous
gaseoso
gah-seh-OH-soh

inorganic
inorgánico
ee-nohr-GAH-nee-koh

matter
la materia
lah mah-TEH-ryah

molecule
la molécula
la moh-LEH-koo-lah

nitrate
el nitrato
ehl nee-TRAH-toh

organic
orgánico
ohr-GAH-nee-koh

oxide
el óxido
ehl OHK-see-doh

particle
la partícula
lah pahr-TEE-koo-lah

salt	**la sal**	lah sahl
solid	**sólido**	SOH-lee-doh
substance	**la sustancia**	lah soos-TAHN-syah
test tube	**la probeta**	lah proh-BEH-tah

Chemical Elements
Los elementos químicos

aluminum	**el aluminio**	ehl ah-loo-MEE-nyoh
barium	**el bario**	ehl BAH-ryoh
calcium	**el calcio**	ehl KAHL-syoh
carbon	**el carbono**	ehl kahr-BOH-noh
chlorine	**el cloro**	ehl KLOH-roh
chromium	**el cromo**	ehl KROH-moh
copper	**el cobre**	ehl KOH-breh
gold	**el oro**	ehl OH-roh
helium	**el helio**	ehl EH-lyoh
hydrogen	**el hidrógeno**	ehl ee-DROH-heh-noh
iodine	**el yodo**	ehl YOH-doh
iron	**el hierro**	ehl YEH-rroh
lead	**el plomo**	ehl PLOH-moh
magnesium	**el magnesio**	ehl mahg-NEH-syoh
mercury	**el mercurio**	ehl mehr-KOO-ryoh

oxygen	**el oxígeno** ehl ohk-SEE-heh-noh
potassium	**el potasio** ehl poh-TAH-syoh
radium	**el radio** ehl RRAH-dyoh
silicon	**el silicio** ehl see-LEE-syoh
silver	**la plata** lah PLAH-tah
sodium	**el sodio** ehl SOH-dyoh
sulfur	**el azufre** ehl ah-SOO-freh
tin	**el estaño** ehl ehs-TAH-nyoh
zinc	**el zinc** ehl seenk

Verbs

to balance (an equation)	**balancear (una ecuación)** bah-lahn-seh-AHR (OO-nah eh-kwah-SYOHN)
to do an experiment	**hacer (*irreg.*) un experimento** ah-SEHR oon ehs-peh-ree-MEHN-toh
to mix	**mezclar** mehs-KLAHR

In Art Class

En la clase de arte

abstract	**abstracto** ahbs-TRAHK-toh
art	**el arte** ehl AHR-teh
artist	**el/la artista** ehl/lah ahr-TEES-tah
artwork	**la obra de arte** lah OH-brah deh AHR-teh
background	**el fondo** ehl FOHN-doh

brush	**el pincel**
	ehl peen-SEHL
bust	**el busto**
	ehl BOOS-toh
canvas	**el lienzo**
	ehl LYEHN-soh
chisel	**el cincel**
	ehl seen-SEHL
clay	**la arcilla**
	lah ahr-SEE-yah
color	**el color**
	ehl koh-LOHR
design	**el diseño**
	ehl dee-SEH-nyoh
drawing	**el dibujo**
	ehl dee-BOO-hoh
easel	**el caballete**
	ehl kah-bah-YEH-teh
exhibit	**la exposición**
	lah ehs-poh-see-SYOHN
gallery	**la galería**
	lah gah-leh-REE-ah
illustration	**la ilustración**
	lah ee-loos-trah-SYOHN
landscape	**el paisaje**
	ehl pah-ee-SAH-heh
light	**la luz**
	lah loos
marble	**el mármol**
	ehl MAHR-mohl
model	**el/la modelo**
	ehl/lah moh-DEH-loh
oil paint	**el óleo**
	ehl OH-leh-oh
oil painting	**el cuadro al óleo**
	ehl KWAH-droh ahl OH-leh-oh
paint	**la pintura**
	lah peen-TOO-rah
painter	**el pintor / la pintora**
	ehl peen-TOHR / lah peen-TOH-rah

painting (activity)	la pintura
	lah peen-TOO-rah
painting (picture)	la pintura / el cuadro
	lah peen-TOO-rah / ehl KWAH-droh
palette	la paleta
	lah pah-LEH-tah
portrait	el retrato
	ehl rreh-TRAH-toh
pottery	la cerámica
	lah seh-RAH-mee-kah
sculptor	el escultor / la escultora
	ehl ehs-kool-TOHR / lah ehs-kool-TOH-rah
sculpture	la escultura
	lah ehs-kool-TOO-rah
shadow	la sombra
	lah SOHM-brah
statue	la estatua
	lah ehs-TAH-twah
still life	el bodegón / la naturaleza muerta
	ehl boh-deh-GOHN / lah nah-too-rah-LEH-sah MWEHR-tah
stone	la piedra
	lah PYEH-drah
style	el estilo
	ehl ehs-TEE-loh
watercolor paint	la acuarela
	lah ah-kwah-REH-lah

Verbs

to admire	admirar	ahd-mee-RAHR
to carve	tallar	tah-YAHR
to cast	fundir	foon-DEER
to comment on	comentar sobre	koh-mehn-TAHR SOH-breh
to criticize	criticar	kree-tee-KAHR
to model	modelar	moh-deh-LAHR
to paint	pintar	peen-TAHR
to see	ver (*irreg.*)	behr
to watch	mirar	mee-RAHR

In Music Class

En la clase de música

Following is vocabulary that is particularly relevant to music class (**la clase de música** [lah ᴋʟᴀʜ-seh deh ᴍᴏᴏ-see-kah]).

auditorium	**el auditorio** ehl ah-oo-dee-ᴛᴏʜ-ryoh **el salón / la sala de actos** ehl sah-ʟᴏʜɴ / lah sᴀʜ-lah deh ᴀʜᴋ-tohs
band	**el conjunto** ehl kohn-ʜᴏᴏɴ-toh
baton	**la batuta** lah bah-ᴛᴏᴏ-tah
choir	**el coro** ehl ᴋᴏʜ-roh
composer	**el compositor / la compositora** ehl kohm-poh-see-ᴛᴏʜʀ / lah kohm-poh-see-ᴛᴏʜ-rah
concert	**el concierto** ehl kohn-sʏᴇʜʀ-toh
conductor	**el director / la directora de orquesta** ehl dee-rehk-ᴛᴏʜʀ / lah dee-rehk-ᴛᴏʜ-rah deh ohr-ᴋᴇʜs-tah
harmony	**la armonía** lah ahr-moh-ɴᴇᴇ-ah
key	**la tecla** lah ᴛᴇʜ-klah
keyboard	**el teclado** ehl teh-ᴋʟᴀʜ-doh
melody	**la melodía** lah meh-loh-ᴅᴇᴇ-ah
music	**la música** lah ᴍᴏᴏ-see-kah
musical instruments	**los instrumentos musicales** lohs eens-troo-ᴍᴇʜɴ-tohs moo-see-ᴋᴀʜ-lehs
musical staff	**el pentagrama** ehl pehn-tah-ɢʀᴀʜ-mah
musical styles	**los estilos de música** lohs ehs-ᴛᴇᴇ-lohs deh ᴍᴏᴏ-see-kah

musician	**el músico / la música** ehl MOO-see-koh / lah MOO-see-kah
note	**la nota** lah NOH-tah
orchestra	**la orquesta** lah ohr-KEHS-tah
refrain	**el estribillo** ehl ehs-tree-BEE-yoh
rhythm	**el ritmo** ehl RREET-moh
scale	**la escala** lah ehs-KAH-lah
score	**la partitura** lah pahr-tee-TOO-rah
singer	**el/la cantante** ehl/lah kahn-TAHN-teh
song	**la canción** lah kahn-SYOHN
sound	**el sonido** ehl soh-NEE-doh
theory	**la teoría** lah teh-oh-REE-ah
tune	**la melodía** lah meh-loh-DEE-ah
voice	**la voz** lah bohs

Musical Styles
Los estilos de música

blues	**los blues** lohs bloos
chamber music	**la música de cámara** lah MOO-see-kah deh KAH-mah-rah
classical music	**la música clásica** lah MOO-see-kah KLAH-see-kah
country music	**la música country** lah MOO-see-kah KOHN-tree
folk music	**la música folk** lah MOO-see-kah FOH-ook
jazz	**la música de jazz** lah MOO-see-kah deh yahs

opera	**la ópera** la OH-peh-rah
popular music	**la música popular** lah MOO-see-kah poh-poo-LAHR
rock	**la música rock** lah MOO-see-kah rrohk

Musical Instruments
Los instrumentos musicales

accordion	**el acordeón** ehl ah-kohr-deh-OHN
bassoon	**el bajón** ehl bah-HOHN
castanets	**las castañuelas** lahs kahs-tah-NYWEH-lahs
cello	**el violoncelo** ehl byoh-lohn-SEH-loh
clarinet	**el clarinete** ehl klah-ree-NEH-teh
drum	**el tambor** ehl tahm-BOHR
drums (set)	**la batería** lah bah-teh-REE-ah
electric guitar	**la guitarra eléctrica** lah gee-TAH-rrah eh-LEHK-tree-kah
flute	**la flauta** lah FLAH-oo-tah
guitar	**la guitarra** lah gee-TAH-rrah
horn	**la trompa** lah TROHM-pah
oboe	**el oboe** ehl oh-BOH-eh
organ	**el órgano** ehl OHR-gah-noh
piano	**el piano** ehl PYAH-noh
saxophone	**el saxofón** ehl sahk-soh-FOHN
trombone	**el trombón** ehl trohm-BOHN

trumpet	la trompeta
	lah trohm-PEH-tah
tuba	la tuba
	lah TOO-bah
viola	la viola
	lah BYOH-lah
violin	el violín
	ehl byoh-LEEN

Verbs

to applaud	aplaudir	ah-plah-oo-DEER
to hear	oír (*irreg.*)	oh-EER
to listen	escuchar	ehs-koo-CHAHR
to play (a musical instrument)	tocar	toh-KAHR
to sing	cantar	kahn-TAHR
to sound	sonar (ue)	soh-NAHR
to tune (a musical instrument)	afinar	ah-fee-NAHR

In Dance Class

En la clase de baile

Following is vocabulary that is particularly relevant to dance class (**la clase de baile** [lah KLAH-seh deh BAH-ee-leh]).

ballet	el ballet
	ehl bah-LEH
choreographer	el coreógrafo / la coreógrafa
	ehl koh-reh-OH-grah-foh /
	lah koh-reh-OH-grah-fah
choreography	la coreografía
	lah koh-reh-oh-grah-FEE-ah
dancer	el bailarín / la bailarina
	ehl bah-ee-lah-REEN /
	lah bah-ee-lah-REE-nah
ethnic	étnico
	EHT-nee-koh
jump	el salto
	ehl SAHL-toh
modern	moderno
	moh-DEHR-noh
movement	el movimiento
	ehl moh-bee-MYEHN-toh

partner	**el compañero / la compañera** ehl kohm-pah-NYEH-roh / lah kohm-pah-NYEH-rah
slippers	**las zapatillas** lahs sah-pah-TEE-yahs
step	**el paso** ehl PAH-soh
tap	**el tap** ehl tahp

Verbs

to choreograph	**coreografiar**	koh-reh-oh-grah-fee-AHR
to dance	**bailar**	bah-ee-LAHR
to move	**moverse (ue)**	moh-BEHR-seh

In Drama Class

En la clase de drama

Following is vocabulary that is particularly relevant to drama class (**la clase de drama** [lah KLAH-seh deh DRAH-mah]).

act	**el acto** ehl AHK-toh
actor	**el actor** ehl ahk-TOHR
actress	**la actriz** lah ahk-TREES
applause	**el aplauso** ehl ah-PLAH-oo-soh
audience	**el público** ehl POO-blee-koh
character	**el personaje** ehl pehr-soh-NAH-heh
comedy	**la comedia** lah koh-MEH-dyah
costumes	**el vestuario** ehl behs-TWAH-ryoh
dialogue	**el diálogo** ehl DYAH-loh-goh
director	**el director / la directora** ehl dee-rehk-TOHR / lah dee-rehk-TOH-rah

end	**el fin** ehl FEEN
ending	**el final** ehl fee-NAHL
performance	**la función** lah foon-SYOHN
play	**la obra de teatro** lah OH-brah deh teh-AH-troh
playwright	**el dramaturgo / la dramaturga** ehl drah-mah-TOOR-goh / lah drah-mah-TOOR-gah
plot	**la trama** lah TRAH-mah
row	**la fila** lah FEE-lah
scene	**la escena** lah eh-SEH-nah
screen	**la pantalla** lah pahn-TAH-yah
script	**el guión** ehl gee-OHN
seat	**el asiento** ehl ah-SYEHN-toh
show	**la función** lah foon-SYOHN
stage	**el escenario** ehl eh-seh-NAH-ryoh
theme	**el tema** ehl TEH-mah
title	**el título** ehl TEE-too-loh
tragedy	**la tragedia** lah trah-HEH-dyah

Verbs

to build scenery	**construir** (*irreg.*) **un escenario** kohns-troo-EER oon eh-seh-NAH-ryoh
to play (perform) a role	**hacer** (*irreg.*) **/ representar un papel** ah-SEHR / rreh-preh-sehn-TAHR oon pah-PEHL
to put on a play	**representar una obra** rreh-preh-sehn-TAHR OO-nah OH-brah

In Physical Education Class

En la clase de educación física

Following is vocabulary that is particularly relevant to physical education class (**la clase de educación física** [lah KLAH-seh deh eh-doo-kah-SYOHN FEE-see-kah]).

gym	**el gimnasio** ehl heem-NAH-syoh
sports	**los deportes** lohs deh-POHR-tehs
stadium	**el estadio** ehn ehl ehs-TAH-dyoh

Sports

Los deportes

athletics	**el atletismo** ehl ah-tleh-TEES-moh
baseball	**el béisbol** ehl BEH-ees-bohl
basketball	**el básquetbol** ehl BAHS-keht-bohl
fencing	**la esgrima** lah ehs-GREE-mah
football	**el fútbol americano** ehl FOOT-bohl ah-meh-ree-KAH-noh
ice hockey	**el hockey sobre (el) hielo** ehl HOH-kee SOH-breh (ehl) YEH-loh
race (contest)	**la carrera** lah kah-RREH-rah
soccer	**el fútbol** ehl FOOT-bohl
sport	**el deporte** ehl deh-POHR-teh
swimming	**la natación** lah nah-tah-SYOHN
tennis	**el tenis** ehl TEH-nees
volleyball	**el volibol** ehl boh-lee-BOHL

weightlifting	**el levantamiento de pesas** ehl leh-bahn-tah-MYEHN-toh deh PEH-sahs
wrestling	**la lucha libre** lah LOO-chah LEE-breh

At the Stadium / At the Gym
En el estadio / En el gimnasio

athlete	**el/la atleta** ehl/lah ah-TLEH-tah
ball	**la pelota / el balón** lah peh-LOH-tah / ehl bah-LOHN
baseball	**la pelota de béisbol** lah peh-LOH-tah deh BEH-ees-bohl
basketball	**el balón de básquetbol** ehl bah-LOHN deh BAHS-keht-bohl
soccer ball	**el balón de fútbol** ehl bah-LOHN deh FOOT-bohl
tennis ball	**la pelota de tenis** lah peh-LOH-tah deh TEH-nees
basket	**la canasta** lah kah-NAHS-tah
bat	**el bate** ehl BAH-teh
champion	**el campeón / la campeona** ehl kahm-peh-OHN / lah kahm-peh-OH-nah
coach	**el entrenador / la entrenadora** ehl ehn-treh-nah-DOHR / lah ehn-treh-nah-DOH-rah
court	**la cancha** lah KAHN-chah
exercise	**el ejercicio** ehl eh-hehr-SEE-syoh
field	**el campo deportivo** ehl KAHM-poh deh-pohr-TEE-boh
game	**el partido / el encuentro** ehl pahr-TEE-doh / ehl ehn-KWEHN-troh
helmet	**el casco** ehl KAHS-koh

match	**el partido / el encuentro**	
	ehl pahr-TEE-doh / ehl ehn-KWEHN-troh	
net	**la red**	
	lah rrehd	
player	**el jugador / la jugadora**	
	ehl hoo-gah-DOHR / lah hoo-gah-DOH-rah	
racket	**la raqueta**	
	lah rrah-KEH-tah	
referee	**el árbitro**	
	ehl AHR-bee-troh	
runner	**el corredor / la corredora**	
	ehl koh-rreh-DOHR /	
	lah koh-rreh-DOH-rah	
team	**el equipo**	
	ehl eh-KEE-poh	
tournament	**el torneo**	
	ehl tohr-NEH-oh	
track	**la pista**	
	lah PEES-tah	
trainer	**el entrenador / la entrenadora**	
	ehl ehn-treh-nah-DOHR /	
	lah ehn-treh-nah-DOH-rah	

Verbs

to bat	**batear**	bah-teh-AHR
to bowl	**bolear**	boh-leh-AHR
to catch	**coger** (*irreg.*)	koh-HEHR
to catch	**agarrar**	ah-gah-RRAHR
to dive	**clavar**	klah-BAHR
to do aerobics	**hacer** (*irreg.*) **ejercicios aeróbicos**	ah-SEHR eh-hehr-SEE-syohs ah-eh-ROH-bee-kohs
to exercise	**hacer** (*irreg.*) **ejercicios**	ah-SEHR eh-hehr-SEE-syohs
to get in shape	**ponerse** (*irreg.*) **en forma**	poh-NEHR-seh ehn FOHR-mah
to jog	**trotar**	troh-TAHR
to jump	**saltar**	sahl-TAHR
to keep score	**apuntar los tantos**	ah-poon-TAHR lohs TAHN-tohs
to lift weights	**levantar pesas**	leh-bahn-TAHR PEH-sahs
to lose	**perder (ie)**	pehr-DEHR
to play a game/ match	**jugar (ue) un partido**	hoo-GAHR oon pahr-TEE-doh
to practice	**practicar**	prahk-tee-KAHR
to run	**correr**	koh-RREHR
to score a goal	**marcar un tanto**	mahr-KAHR oon TAHN-toh

to skate	**patinar**	pah-tee-NAHR
to sweat	**sudar**	SOO-DAHR
to swim	**nadar**	nah-DAHR
to throw	**lanzar**	lahn-SAHR
to train	**entrenarse**	ehn-treh-NAHR-seh
to win	**ganar**	gah-NAHR

Extracurricular Activities

Las actividades extracurriculares

The number of extracurricular activities (**las actividades extracurriculares** [lahs ahk-tee-bee-DAH-dehs ehs-trah-koo-rree-koo-LAH-rehs]) varies from school to school, but this is a list of the most common activities that take place during or after school.

the … club	**el club de…**
	ehl kloob deh
chess	**ajedrez**
	ah-heh-DREHS
computer	**informática**
	een-fohr-MAH-tee-kah
dance	**baile**
	BAH-ee-leh
debate	**debate**
	deh-BAH-teh
drama	**drama**
	DRAH-mah
ecology	**ecología**
	eh-koh-loh-HEE-ah
film	**cine**
	SEE-neh
foreign languages	**lenguas extranjeras**
	LEHN-gwahs ehs-trahn-HEH-rahs
history	**historia**
	ees-TOH-ryah
mathematics	**matemáticas**
	mah-teh-MAH-tee-kahs
poetry	**poesía**
	poh-eh-SEE-ah
science	**ciencias**
	SYEHN-syahs

Encouraging students to take part in extracurricular activities allows them to make new friends and learn new information.

Do you want to participate in the _____ club?	**¿Quieres participar en el club de _____?** KYEH-rehs pahr-tee-see-PAHR ehn ehl kloob deh
The club's meetings take place at (*time*).	**Las reuniones del club tienen lugar a la(s) (*time*).** lahs rreh-oo-NYOH-nehs dehl kloob TYEH-nehn loo-GAHR ah lah(s)
When does the club meet?	**¿Cuándo se reúne el club?** KWAHN-doh seh rreh-oo-neh ehl kloob
The meeting is at three thirty.	**La reunión es a las tres y media.** lah rreh-oo-NYOHN ehs ah lahs trehs ee MEH-dyah
Who is the advisor to the club?	**¿Quién es el consejero / la consejera del club?** kyehn ehs ehl kohn-seh-HEH-roh / lah kohn-seh-HEH-rah dehl kloob
The requirements for the club are _____.	**Los requisitos para el club son _____.** lohs rreh-kee-SEE-tohs PAH-rah ehl kloob sohn
There are no requirements to belong to the club.	**No hay requisitos para pertenecer al club.** noh AH-ee rreh-kee-SEE-tohs PAH-rah pehr-teh-neh-SEHR ahl kloob

Many students like to get involved in their community and can join organizations through the school.

In our school we have an organization to help ...	**En nuestra escuela tenemos una organización para ayudar a...** ehn NWEHS-trah ehs-KWEH-lah teh-NEH-mohs oo-nah ohr-gah-nee-sah-SYOHN PAH-rah ah-yoo-DAHR ah
avoid drinking and driving	**evitar beber y conducir** eh-bee-TAHR beh-BEHR ee kohn-doo-SEER
build houses	**construir casas** kohns-TRWEER KAH-sahs

the elderly	**los ancianos** lohs ahn-SYAH-nohs
the homeless	**los destituidos** lohs dehs-tee-TWEE-dohs
people with AIDS	**las personas con SIDA** lahs pehr-SOH-nahs kohn SEE-dah
to raise money	**recaudar fondos** rreh-kah-oo-DAHR FOHN-dohs
students with academic problems	**los estudiantes con problemas académicos** lohs ehs-too-DYAHN-tehs kohn proh-BLEH-mahs ah-kah-DEH-mee-kohs

Clubs and other organizations often have fundraisers, which may include events such as the following.

auction	**la subasta** lah soo-BAHS-tah
banquet	**el banquete** ehl bahn-KEH-teh
carnival	**el carnaval** ehl kahr-nah-BAHL
contest	**el concurso** ehl kohn-KOOR-soh
dance	**el baile** ehl BAH-ee-leh
fair	**la feria** lah FEH-ryah
party	**la fiesta** lah FYEHS-tah
performance	**la función** lah foon-SYOHN
raffle	**la rifa / el sorteo** lah RREE-fah / ehl sohr-TEH-oh
show	**la función / el espectáculo** lah foon-SYOHN / ehl ehs-pehk-TAH-koo-loh
trip	**el viaje** ehl BYAH-heh

On a Trip

De excursión

Regardless of the grade you teach, there is often an opportunity to take trips outside of school. There is a lot of planning that takes place before any trip (**la excursión** [lah ehs-koor-SYOHN]). Here are some phrases that will prove useful.

You have to take the permission letter home.	**Tienes que llevar la carta de permiso a casa.** TYEH-nehs keh yeh-BAHR lah KAHR-tah deh pehr-MEE-soh ah KAH-sah
One of your parents has to sign the letter.	**Uno de tus padres tiene que firmar la carta.** OO-noh deh toos PAH-drehs TYEH-neh keh feer-MAHR lah KAHR-tah
Your guardian has to sign the letter.	**Tu tutor tiene que firmar la carta.** too too-TOHR TYEH-neh keh feer-MAHR lah KAHR-tah
You have to bring your lunch.	**Tienes que traer el almuerzo.** TYEH-nehs keh trah-EHR ehl ahl-MWEHR-soh
You have to be here on time.	**Tienes que estar aquí a tiempo.** TYEH-nehs keh ehs-TAHR ah-KEE ah TYEHM-poh
We are going to leave at (*time*).	**Vamos a salir a la(s) (*time*).** BAH-mohs ah sah-LEER a lah(s)
We are going to return at (*time*).	**Vamos a regresar a la(s) (*time*).** BAH-mohs ah rreh-greh-SAHR ah lah(s)

Permission Form

El formulario de permiso

Most schools require a permission form (**el formulario de permiso** [ehl fohr-moo-LAH-ryoh deh pehr-MEE-soh]) before a student is allowed to go on a school trip. The form letter and permission form on page 181 can be sent home with students. Other phrases you may need to include, depending on the situation, are included on the following pages.

Note that in many Spanish-speaking countries you will find the date written as DD/MM/YY, rather than as MM/DD/YY, which you are more used to. When in doubt, write the date with the name of the month spelled out, as shown here.

June 7, 2005　　　　　　　　　**Junio 7, 2005**

(*Date*)

Dear Mr./Mrs. _____ ,
Estimado Sr. / Estimada Sra.,

On _____ (*date*) our class is going to participate in a visit to
_____ (*place*).
El _____ (date) nuestra clase va a participar en una visita a
_____ (place).

We are going to leave school at _____ (*time*) and we are going to
return at _____ (*time*).
*Vamos a salir de la escuela a la(s) _____ (time) y vamos a regresar
a la(s) _____ (time).*

All of the students have to bring their lunch, since we are not going to be able
to eat lunch in the school cafeteria.
*Todos los estudiantes tienen que traer el almuerzo ya que no vamos a poder
almorzar en la cafetería de la escuela.*

Please sign the form below and return it with your child before
_____ (*date*) .
Por favor, firme el formulario abajo y devuélvalo con su hijo/hija antes del
_____ (date).

Sincerely,
Sinceramente,

_____

_____ (*student's name*) has my permission to attend the field
trip to _____ (*place*) on _____ (*date*).
_____ (student's name) *tiene mi permiso para asistir a la*
excursión a _____ (place) el _____ (date).

_____
Parent/Guardian signature
Firma del padre / de la madre / del tutor

Other sentences you may need to include or say are the following.

Each student must pay for the entrance fee.	**Cada estudiante tiene que pagar la entrada.** KAH-dah ehs-too-DYAHN-teh TYEH-neh keh pah-GAHR lah ehn-TRAH-dah
The cost is _____.	**El costo es de _____.** ehl KOHS-toh ehs deh
Please enclose a check or cash.	**Por favor, incluya un cheque o dinero en efectivo.** pohr fah-BOHR, een-KLOO-yah oon CHEH-keh oh dee-NEH-roh ehn eh-fehk-TEE-boh
If you send a check, make it payable to _____.	**Si envía un cheque, hágalo a nombre de _____.** see ehn-BEE-ah oon CHEH-keh, AH-gah-loh ah NOHM-breh deh
If you can't afford it, please send me a note.	**Si Ud. no puede hacer este gasto, por favor envíeme una nota.** see OOS-TEHD noh PWEH-deh ah-SEHR EHS-teh GAHS-toh, pohr fah-BOHR ehn-BEE-eh-meh oo-nah NOH-tah
We can use the school's funds to cover the cost.	**Podemos usar los fondos de la escuela para cubrir el costo.** poh-DEH-mohs oo-SAHR lohs FOHN-dohs deh lah ehs-KWEH-lah PAH-rah koo-BREER ehl KOHS-toh
We need volunteers.	**Necesitamos voluntarios.** neh-seh-see-TAH-mohs boh-loon-TAH-ryohs
Please let me know if you are willing to accompany us on the trip.	**Por favor, avíseme si Ud. está dispuesto a acompañarnos en el viaje.** por fah-BOHR, ah-BEE-seh-meh see OOS-TEHD ehs-TAH dees-PWEHS-toh ah ah-kohm-pah-NYAHR-nohs ehn ehl BYAH-heh
All students have to bring _____.	**Todos los estudiantes tienen que traer _____.** TOH-dohs lohs ehs-too-DYAHN-tehs TYEH-nehn keh trah-EHR

Please remind your child that he/she must respect all the school's rules of behavior during the trip.	**Por favor, recuérdele a su hijo/hija que tiene que respetar todas las reglas de comportamiento de la escuela durante el viaje.**
	pohr fah-BOHR, rreh-KWEHR-deh-leh ah soo EE-hoh/EE-hah keh TYEH-neh keh rrehs-peh-TAHR TOH-dahs lahs RREH-glahs deh kohm-pohr-tah-MYEHN-toh deh lah ehs-KWEH-lah doo-RAHN-teh ehl BYAH-heh
If you have any questions, you can call me at (*phone number*) between (*time*) and (*time*).	**Si Ud. tiene alguna pregunta, me puede llamar a (***phone number***) entre la(s) (***time***) y la(s) (***time***).**
	see OOS-TEHD TYEH-neh ahl-GOO-nah preh-GOON-tah, meh PWEH-deh yah-MAHR ahl NOO-meh-roh (*number*) EHN-treh lah(s) (*time*) ee lah(s) (*time*)

These are some places you may visit on a school trip.

amusement park	**el parque de atracciones**
	ehl PAHR-keh deh ah-trahk-SYOH-nehs
aquarium	**el acuario**
	ehl ah-KWAH-ryoh
beach	**la playa**
	lah PLAH-yah
botanical garden	**el jardín botánico**
	ehl hahr-DEEN boh-TAH-nee-koh
city hall	**el ayuntamiento**
	ehl ah-yoon-tah-MYEHN-toh
courthouse	**la corte**
	lah KOHR-teh
factory	**la fábrica**
	lah FAH-bree-kah
farm	**la granja**
	lah GRAHN-hah
firehouse	**la casa de bomberos**
	lah KAH-sah deh bohm-BEH-rohs
library	**la biblioteca**
	lah bee-blyoh-TEH-kah

movie theater	**el cine** ehl SEE-neh
museum	**el museo** ehl moo-SEH-oh
park	**el parque** ehl PAHR-keh
police station	**el cuartel de policía** ehl kwahr-TEHL deh poh-lee-SEE-ah
restaurant	**el restaurante** ehl rrehs-tah-oo-RAHN-teh
theater	**el teatro** ehl teh-AH-troh
zoo	**el parque zoológico** ehl PAHR-keh soh-LOH-hee-koh

Here are some things you may want to say to some of the students who may not be familiar with English. The commands included here address a group (more than one person). You may want to refer to the Introduction, pages 16–18, 20, and 21, to review the singular commands.

We have arrived.	**Hemos llegado.** EH-mohs yeh-GAH-doh
Does anyone have to go to the bathroom?	**¿Alguien tiene que ir al baño?** AHL-gyehn TYEH-neh keh eer ahl BAH-nyoh
Get off the bus.	**Bájense del autobús.** BAH-hehn-seh dehl ah-oo-toh-BOOS
Line up.	**Pónganse en fila.** POHN-gahn-seh ehn FEE-lah
Take your partner by the hand.	**Tomen a su compañero de la mano.** TOH-mehn ah soo kohm-pah-NYEH-roh deh lah MAH-noh
Do not separate from the group.	**No se separen del grupo.** noh seh seh-PAH-rehn dehl GROO-poh
Hurry up.	**Apúrense. / Dense prisa.** ah-POO-rehn-seh / DEHN-seh PREE-sah
Get on the bus.	**Súbanse al autobús.** SOO-bahn-seh ahl ah-oo-toh-BOOS

Practice 4-2

A *List four activities that you could suggest to your students as a way to raise funds for a club.*

1. _____

2. _____

3. _____

4. _____

B *Write in Spanish where you would take your students if they wanted to do the following things.*

1. visit an art exhibit

   _____

2. see animals in their habitat

   _____

3. have fun and go on different rides

   _____

4. visit the office of the mayor

   _____

5. learn about fire prevention

   _____

6. learn about books and do research

   _____

C *You and your students are taking a trip. Write three sentences in Spanish in which you tell the students or their parents what they must do before the trip.*

1. _____

2. _____

3. _____

D *While on a trip, students need to know the rules. Write what you would tell them if you wanted them to do the following things. Use the Spanish command form.*

1. walk in pairs

   _____

2. get on the bus

   _____

3. walk in a line

   _____

Success in School: Enlisting Parental Support

El éxito en la escuela:
para ganarse el apoyo de los padres

Most teachers communicate regularly with parents in order to enlist their support (**ganarse el apoyo de los padres** [gah-NAHR-seh ehl ah-POH-yoh deh lohs PAH-drehs]). Most parents will gladly help if they know what they can do to help their child reach his/her full potential and enjoy success in school (**el éxito en la escuela** [ehl EHK-see-toh ehn lah ehs-KWEH-lah]). One important area in which parents can help is school attendance (**la asistencia a la escuela** [lah ah-sees-TEHN-syah ah lah ehs-KWEH-lah]).

School/Class Attendance

La asistencia a la escuela / a las clases

Children can't learn if they are not in class. It is of primary importance to communicate the need to attend school and arrive on time. Let's begin with some things you can tell the parents.

School attendance is mandatory.	**La asistencia a la escuela es obligatoria.** lah ah-sees-TEHN-syah ah lah ehs-KWEH-lah ehs oh-blee-gah-TOH-ryah
Your child must arrive on time.	**Su hijo/hija tiene que llegar a tiempo.** soo EE-hoh/EE-hah TYEH-neh keh yeh-GAHR ah TYEHM-poh
If your child is absent, call the school at (*phone number*).	**Si su hijo/hija está ausente, llame a la escuela al número** (*phone number*). see soo EE-hoh/EE-hah ehs-TAH ah-oo-SEHN-teh, YAH-meh ah lah ehs-KWEH-lah ahl NOO-meh-roh
Upon returning, your child must bring a note signed by you.	**Al regresar, su hijo/hija tiene que traer una nota firmada por Ud.** ahl rreh-greh-SAHR, soo EE-hoh/EE-hah TYEH-neh keh trah-EHR OO-nah NOH-tah feer-MAH-dah pohr oos-TEHD
If possible, your child should call a classmate in order to find out the assignment.	**Si es posible, su hijo/hija debe llamar a un compañero de clase para saber la tarea.** see ehs poh-SEE-bleh, soo EE-hoh/EE-hah DEH-beh yah-MAHR ah oon kohm-pah-NYEH-roh deh KLAH-seh PAH-rah sah-BEHR lah tah-REH-ah
If the absence is prolonged, you should call the teacher.	**Si la ausencia es larga, Ud. debe llamar al maestro / a la maestra.** see lah ah-oo-SEHN-syah ehs LAHR-gah, oos-TEHD DEH-beh yah-MAHR ahl mah-EHS-troh / ah lah mah-EHS-trah

If the absence is more than (*number*) days, your child needs a note from the doctor.	**Si la ausencia es de más de** (*number*) **días, su hijo/hija necesita una nota del médico / de la médica.**

see lah ah-oo-SEHN-syah ehs deh mahs deh… DEE-ahs, soo EE-hoh/EE-hah neh-seh-SEE-tah oo-nah NOH-tah dehl MEH-dee-koh / deh lah MEH-dee-kah

Classroom Rules

Las reglas de la clase

Another area in which parents can help is in adherence to classroom rules (**las reglas de la clase** [lahs RREH-glahs deh lah KLAH-seh]). You can begin the process by making them aware of the rules set by the administration and the teachers in your school so that they can understand what they can do to help. Here are some things that you might say to the parents.

I need your help in making sure that your child follows the rules of our school.	**Necesito su ayuda para asegurar que su hijo/hija siga las reglas de nuestra escuela.**

neh-seh-SEE-toh soo ah-YOO-dah PAH-rah ah-seh-goo-RAHR keh soo EE-hoh/EE-hah SEE-gah lahs RREH-glahs deh NWEHS-trah ehs-KWEH-lah

There are general behavior rules that can apply to most situations.

It is important …	**Es importante…**
	ehs eem-pohr-TAHN-teh
to ask permission	**pedir permiso**
	peh-DEER pehr-MEE-soh
to be respectful	**ser respetuoso/respetuosa**
	sehr rrehs-peh-TWOH-soh/ rrehs-peh-TWOH-sah
to behave	**portarse bien**
	pohr-TAHR-seh byehn
to pay attention	**prestar atención**
	prehs-TAHR ah-tehn-SYOHN

GRAMMAR · Impersonal Expressions + Infinitive

Using an impersonal expression such as "it is important" (**es importante** [ehs eem-pohr-TAHN-teh]) followed by an infinitive, as shown in the examples above, is one way to express how students are expected to behave. Using an impersonal expression allows you to make a general statement about expected behavior without addressing anyone in particular.

Here are some other impersonal expressions you can use this way.

It is necessary …	**Es necesario…** ehs neh-seh-SAH-ryoh
It is better …	**Es mejor…** ehs meh-HOHR
It is advisable …	**Es aconsejable…** ehs ah-kohn-seh-HAH-bleh
It is good …	**Es bueno…** ehs BWEH-noh
It is bad …	**Es malo…** ehs MAH-loh

What Must Be Done

Lo que hay que hacer

Using the expression **hay que** [AH-ee keh], meaning "one must," + an infinitive is another way to express the rules of classroom behavior without addressing a particular person. It allows you to say what must be done (**lo que hay que hacer** [loh keh AH-ee keh ah-SEHR]).

To speak, one must raise one's hand.	**Para hablar hay que levantar la mano.** PAH-rah ah-BLAHR AH-ee keh leh-bahn-TAHR lah MAH-noh
To leave the class, one must ask permission.	**Para salir de la clase hay que pedir permiso.** PAH-rah sah-LEER deh lah KLAH-seh AH-ee keh peh-DEER pehr-MEE-soh
To get good grades, one must …	**Para sacar buenas notas hay que…** PAH-rah sah-KAHR BWEH-nahs NOH-tahs AH-ee keh
study regularly	**estudiar regularmente** ehs-too-DYAHR rreh-goo-lahr-MEHN-teh

| do the homework every day | **hacer la tarea todos los días** |
| | ah-SEHR lah tah-REH-ah TOH-dohs lohs DEE-ahs |

| take notes in class | **hacer apuntes en la clase** |
| | ah-SEHR ah-POON-tehs ehn KLAH-seh |

| bring the necessary supplies to class every day | **traer los materiales necesarios a clase todos los días** |
| | trah-EHR lohs mah-teh-RYAH-lehs neh-seh-SAH-ryohs ah KLAH-seh TOH-dohs lohs DEE-ahs |

| pay attention in class | **prestar atención en clase** |
| | prehs-TAHR ah-tehn-SYOHN ehn KLAH-seh |

| ask questions when one does not understand | **hacer preguntas cuando uno no entiende** |
| | ah-SEHR preh-GOON-tahs KWAHN-doh oo-noh noh ehn-TYEHN-deh |

Practice 5-1

Use one of the impersonal expressions below to state what must be done or what students need to do in each case. Write complete sentences in Spanish.

es mejor   es bueno
es aconsejable   es necesario
hay que

1. bring a note from your father

   _____

2. call a classmate

   _____

3. pay attention

   _____

4. do the homework every day

   _____

5. study regularly

   _____

Rules of Behavior

Las reglas de comportamiento

In addition to classroom rules, all schools have general rules of behavior (**las reglas de comportamiento** [lahs RREH-glahs deh kohm-pohr-tah-MYEHN-toh]) that must be followed to ensure the safety and well-being of everyone in the school. Many of these rules apply to any school or any classroom, and they often specify what students cannot do (**lo que los estudiantes no pueden hacer** [loh que lohs ehs-too-DYAHN-tehs noh PWEH-dehn ah-SEHR]).

What Students Cannot Do

Lo que los estudiantes no pueden hacer

In our school, students cannot ...	En nuestra escuela los estudiantes no pueden...
	ehn NWEHS-trah ehs-KWEH-lah lohs ehs-too-DYAHN-tehs noh PWEH-dehn
arrive late	**llegar tarde**
	yeh-GAHR TAHR-deh
be disrespectful to others	**faltarle el respeto a otros**
	fahl-TAHR-leh ehl rrehs-PEH-toh ah OH-trohs
bring cell phones	**traer teléfonos celulares**
	trah-EHR teh-LEH-foh-nohs seh-loo-LAH-rehs
cut class	**ausentarse de clase**
	ah-oo-sehn-TAHR-seh deh KLAH-seh
destroy school property	**destruir la propiedad de la escuela**
	dehs-troo-EER lah proh-pyeh-DAHD deh lah ehs-KWEH-lah
disobey school rules	**desobedecer las reglas de la escuela**
	dehs-oh-beh-deh-SEHR lahs RREH-glahs deh lah ehs-KWEH-lah
eat outside the cafeteria	**comer fuera de la cafetería**
	koh-MEHR FWEH-rah deh lah kah-feh-teh-REE-ah

fight with others	**pelear con otros**
	peh-leh-AHR kohn OH-trohs
leave without permission	**salir sin permiso**
	sah-LEER seen pehr-MEE-soh
play in the hallways	**jugar en los pasillos**
	hoo-GAHR ehn lohs pah-SEE-yohs
smoke	**fumar**
	foo-MAHR
speak in a loud voice	**hablar en voz alta**
	ah-BLAHR ehn bohs AHL-tah
use bad language	**usar malas palabras**
	oo-SAHR MAH-lahs pah-LAH-brahs

If you want to express what behavior is forbidden in a way that is not intended for any particular student, use the expression **se prohíbe** [seh proh-EE-beh] + an infinitive.

It is forbidden ...	**Se prohíbe...**
	seh proh-EE-beh
to fight	**pelear**
	peh-leh-AHR
to kick	**dar patadas**
	dahr pah-TAH-dahs
to laugh at another person	**reírse de otra persona**
	rreh-EER-seh deh OH-trah pehr-SOH-nah
to make fun of another person	**burlarse de otra persona**
	boor-LAHR-seh deh OH-trah pehr-SOH-nah
to push	**empujar**
	ehm-poo-HAHR
to spit	**escupir**
	ehs-koo-PEER
to yell	**gritar**
	gree-TAHR

Gʀᴀᴍᴍᴀʀ · Expressing What Someone Can(not) Do

You may have noticed that by using **(no)** + the present tense of the verb **poder** [poh-ᴅᴇʜʀ] + an infinitive, you can express many of the activities that students are and are not allowed to do in school.

poder (ue) [poh-ᴅᴇʜʀ] to be able, can (present tense)

I can	yo puedo	yoh ᴘᴡᴇʜ-doh
you can	tú puedes	too ᴘᴡᴇʜ-dehs
he can	él puede	ehl ᴘᴡᴇʜ-deh
she can	ella puede	ᴇʜ-yah ᴘᴡᴇʜ-deh
you can	Ud. puede	ᴏᴏs-ᴛᴇʜᴅ ᴘᴡᴇʜ-deh
we can	nosotros podemos	noh-sᴏʜ-trohs poh-ᴅᴇʜ-mohs
we can	nosotras podemos	noh-sᴏʜ-trahs poh-ᴅᴇʜ-mohs
they can	ellos pueden	ᴇʜ-yohs ᴘᴡᴇʜ-dehn
they can	ellas pueden	ᴇʜ-yahs ᴘᴡᴇʜ-dehn
you (*plural*) can	Uds. pueden	ᴏᴏs-ᴛᴇʜ-dehs ᴘᴡᴇʜ-dehn

For example, if you are addressing only one student, you use **(no) puedes** [(noh) ᴘᴡᴇʜ-dehs].

You may (not) bring ... to school.	**(No) puedes traer... a la escuela.** noh ᴘᴡᴇʜ-dehs trah-ᴇʜʀ... ah lah ehs-ᴋᴡᴇʜ-lah
a beeper	**un bíper** oon ʙᴇᴇ-pehr
a game	**un juego** oon ʜᴡᴇʜ-goh
a gun	**un revólver** oon rreh-ʙᴏʜʟ-behr
a knife	**un cuchillo** oon koo-ᴄʜᴇᴇ-yoh

Practice 5-2

Write the correct form of the verb **poder** *to complete the following sentences.*

1. ¿_____ nosotros fumar en el patio?

2. Tú no _____ salir del aula ahora.

3. Ellos _____ estudiar en la biblioteca.

4. Él no _____ traer la mochila al gimnasio.

5. Yo no _____ traer mis CDs a la escuela.

6. Uds. _____ salir después de las clases.

GRAMMAR · To Find Out "Why?"

It is important to know the reasons that a student takes certain actions. Here are some questions you will need to use when trying to find out why (**por qué** [pohr keh]) students do or don't do certain things in school.

Why did you arrive late?	**¿Por qué llegaste tarde?** pohr keh yeh-GAHS-teh TAHR-deh
Why were you absent?	**¿Por qué estuviste ausente?** pohr keh ehs-too-BEES-teh ah-oo-SEHN-teh
Why didn't you go to (English) class?	**¿Por qué no fuiste a la clase de (inglés)?** pohr keh noh FWEES-teh ah lah KLAH-seh deh (een-GLEHS)
Why didn't you do your homework?	**¿Por qué no hiciste la tarea?** pohr keh noh ee-SEES-teh lah tah-REH-ah
Why didn't you study for the test?	**¿Por qué no estudiaste para el examen?** pohr keh noh ehs-too-DYAHS-teh PAH-rah ehl ehk-SAH-mehn
Why didn't you come to _____?	**¿Por qué no viniste a _____?** pohr keh noh bee-NEES-teh ah

All of the verbs used in the questions above are in the preterite tense. For information about the formation of the preterite and a list of words and expressions that are useful when talking about the past, see Chapter 6, pages 230–232.

Remember that in order to find out the cause or reason for certain behavior, you can ask a question using **¿Por qué?** [pohr keh], meaning "Why?" The answer to the question may include the word **porque** [POHR-keh], meaning "because."

I arrived late because the bus was late.	**Llegué tarde porque el autobús llegó tarde.** yeh-GEH TAHR-deh POHR-keh ehl ah-oo-toh-BOOS yeh-GOH TAHR-deh

Practice 5-3

Answer the following questions according to the model.

MODELO   ¿Puedo fumar en la escuela?

        No, no puedes fumar. Se prohíbe fumar en la escuela.

1. ¿Pueden ellos pelear en el patio?

    _____

2. ¿Puedes tú llegar tarde?

    _____

3. ¿Puedo yo comer fuera de la cafetería?

    _____

4. ¿Puede ella salir sin permiso?

    _____

5. ¿Podemos nosotros jugar en los pasillos?

    _____

Consequences

Las consecuencias

There are different types of consequences, depending on the severity of the infraction. There may be academic consequences (**las consecuencias académicas** [lahs kohn-seh-KWEHN-syahs ah-kah-DEH-mee-kahs]) or consequences resulting from behavior problems (**los problemas de comportamiento** [lohs proh-BLEH-mahs deh kohm-pohr-tah-MYEHN-toh]). Note that some of the same consequences may apply in both situations.

Academic Consequences
Las consecuencias académicas

You have to …	Tienes que... TYEH-nehs keh
stay in school after classes	**quedarte en la escuela después de las clases** keh-DAHR-teh ehn lah ehs-KWEH-lah dehs-PWEHS deh lahs KLAH-sehs

go to the detention room	**ir al aula de castigo** eer ahl AH-oo-lah deh kahs-TEE-goh
work with a private teacher	**trabajar con un maestro / una maestra particular** trah-bah-HAHR kohn oon mah-EHS-troh / oo-nah mah-EHS-trah pahr-tee-koo-LAHR
take the exam again	**hacer el examen otra vez** ah-SEHR ehl ehk-SAH-mehn OH-trah behs
attend review classes	**asistir a las clases de repaso** ah-sees-TEER ah lahs KLAH-sehs deh RREH-pah-soh

As you can see, by using the expression **tener** [teh-NEHR] + **que** [keh] + an infinitive, you can express what a student *has to do*.

GRAMMAR · The Simple Future

Spanish speakers use the present tense of the verb **ir** [eer] followed by the word **a** [ah] + an infinitive to express or ask about future actions.

Are you going to study a lot tonight?	**¿Vas a estudiar mucho esta noche?** bahs ah ehs-too-DYAHR MOO-choh EHS-tah NOH-cheh
Yes, I am going to study a lot.	**Sí, voy a estudiar mucho.** see, BOH-ee ah ehs-too-DYAHR MOO-choh

You may find the following words and expressions useful when talking about the future.

later	**más tarde** mahs TAHR-deh
today	**hoy** OH-ee
tonight	**esta noche** EHS-tah NOH-cheh
tomorrow	**mañana** mah-NYAH-nah
tomorrow morning	**mañana por la mañana** mah-NYAH-nah pohr lah mah-NYAH-nah
tomorrow afternoon	**mañana por la tarde** mah-NYAH-nah pohr lah TAHR-deh

tomorrow night	**mañana por la noche**
the day after tomorrow	mah-NYAH-nah pohr lah NOH-cheh
	pasado mañana
	pah-SAH-doh mah-NYAH-nah
next week	**la semana próxima**
	lah seh-MAH-nah PROHK-see-mah
next month	**el mes próximo**
	ehl mehs PROHK-see-moh
next year	**el año próximo**
	ehl AH-nyoh PROHK-see-moh

Grammar · "If" Clauses

Spanish speakers use the following pattern when they state under what conditions certain actions, events, or situations will take place: "if" + verb in present tense, verb in (simple) future tense (**si** [see] + verb in present tense, verb in (simple) future tense).

	ENGLISH	SPANISH
CONDITION	If you do not study,	**Si no estudias,**
RESULT	you are not going to succeed.	**no vas a tener éxito.**
		see noh ehs-TOO-dyahs,
		noh bahs ah teh-NEHR
		EHK-see-toh
CONDITION	If you are late,	**Si llegas tarde,**
RESULT	you will not learn.	**no vas a aprender.**
		see YEH-gahs TAHR-deh,
		noh bahs ah ah-prehn-DEHR
CONDITION	If you use bad language,	**Si usas malas palabras,**
RESULT	I am going to call your parents.	**voy a llamar a tus padres.**
		see OO-sahs MAH-lahs
		pah-LAH-brahs, BOH-ee ah
		yah-MAHR ah toos PAH-drehs

Practice 5-4

A *Answer the following questions in order to tell what the person has to do. Use the correct form of* **tener que** + *an infinitive in your answers.*

1. ¿Por qué no puedo ir a la cafetería? (*have to study now*)

    _____

2. ¿Por qué no podemos hacer el examen hoy? (*have to attend review classes*)

    _____

3. ¿Por qué no puedes llegar a tiempo? (*have to work with a private teacher*)

   _____

4. ¿Por qué no pueden ellos ir a la clase de baile? (*have to stay in school after classes*)

   _____

B *Using the strings of words below, write sentences expressing what the different people are going to do. The words are given in no particular order.*

1. nosotros / más tarde / estudiar / en la biblioteca / ir a

   _____

2. ellos / mañana por la tarde / asistir a las clases de repaso / ir a

   _____

3. tú / ir a / la semana próxima / hacer el examen

   _____

4. yo / mañana por la mañana / ir a / hacer la tarea

   _____

5. Ud. / ir a / pasado mañana / llamar al director

   _____

C *Complete the following sentences with the correct form of the verb in parentheses.*

1. Si tú _____ (pelear) con tus amigos, tú _____ (ir) a quedarte en la escuela después de las clases.

2. Si nosotros no _____ (asistir) a clases, nosotros

   _____ (ir) a salir mal.

3. Si él _____ (usar) malas palabras, él _____ (ir) a tener muchos problemas.

4. Si Uds. _____ (salir) sin permiso, el consejero

   _____ (ir) a llamar a sus padres.

5. Si yo _____ (hablar) en voz alta, mis compañeros no

   _____ (ir) a oír a la profesora.

Other Consequences of Improper Conduct
Otras consecuencias de conducta impropia

Here are other consequences of improper conduct (**otras consecuencias de conducta impropia** [OH-trahs kohn-seh-KWEHN-syahs deh kohn-DOOK-tah eem-PROH-pyah]) that you might need to inform students about.

You can also express the consequence of certain behavior by stating what the person has to do.

If you fight with others, you have to …	**Si peleas con otros, tienes que…** see peh-LEH-ahs kohn OH-trohs, TYEH-nehs keh
apologize	**disculparte / pedir perdón** dees-kool-PAHR-teh / peh-DEER pehr-DOHN
go to the principal's office	**ir a la oficina del director / de la directora** eer ah lah oh-fee-SEE-nah dehl dee-rehk-TOHR / deh lah dee-rehk-TOH-rah

To describe some of the penalties for breaking the school rules, you should also become familiar with the following phrases.

You have to return to school with one of your parents.	**Tienes que regresar a la escuela con uno de tus padres.** TYEH-nehs keh rreh-greh-SAHR ah lah ehs-KWEH-lah kohn OO-noh deh toos PAH-drehs
You cannot participate in extracurricular activities.	**No puedes participar en las actividades extracurriculares.** noh PWEH-dehs pahr-tee-see-PAHR ehn lahs ahk-tee-bee-DAH-dehs ehs-trah-koo-rree-koo-LAH-rehs
You are suspended for (*number*) days.	**Quedas suspendido por (*number*) días.** KEH-dahs soos-pehn-DEE-doh pohr… DEE-ahs

Praising a Student's Behavior and His/Her Work

*Para alabar el buen comportamiento y el trabajo
de un alumno / una alumna*

Letting the student's parents know when their child has done well is key to reinforcing the good behavior we expect from all students. Here are some phrases you may want to use to praise a student's behavior and work (**para alabar el buen comportamiento y el trabajo de un alumno / una alumna** [PAH-rah ah-lah-BAHR ehl bwehn kohm-pohr-tah-MYEHN-toh ee ehl trah-BAH-hoh deh oon ah-LOOM-noh / oo-nah ah-LOOM-nah]).

You should be proud of (name).	**Ud. debe estar orgulloso/orgullosa de (name).** OOS-TEHD DEH-beh ehs-TAHR ohr-goo-YOH-soh/ohr-goo-YOH-sah deh
He/She ...	**Él/Ella...** ehl/EH-yah
has improved his/her behavior	**ha mejorado su comportamiento** ah meh-hoh-RAH-doh soo kohm-pohr-tah-MYEHN-toh
has improved his/her relationship with the other students	**ha mejorado su relación con otros estudiantes** ah meh-hoh-RAH-doh soo rreh-lah-SYOHN kohn OH-trohs ehs-too-DYAHN-tehs
behaves well in class	**se comporta bien en clase** seh kohm-POHR-tah byehn ehn KLAH-seh
has a positive attitude	**tiene una actitud positiva** TYEH-neh oo-nah ahk-tee-TOOD poh-see-TEE-bah
completes his/her work on time	**completa su trabajo a tiempo** kohm-PLEH-tah soo trah-BAH-hoh ah TYEHM-poh
helps others	**ayuda a otros** ah-YOO-dah ah OH-trohs
works independently	**trabaja independientemente** trah-BAH-hah een-deh-pehn-dyehn-teh-MEHN-teh
cooperates in class	**coopera en la clase** koh-oh-PEH-rah ehn lah KLAH-seh

He/She …	Él/Ella…
	ehl/EH-yah
got a good grade on the last homework / the last test	**sacó una buena nota en la última tarea / el último examen**
	sah-KOH oo-nah BWEH-nah NOH-tah ehn lah OOL-tee-mah tah-REH-ah / ehl OOL-tee-moh ehk-SAH-mehn
passed all his/her classes	**aprobó en todas sus clases**
	ah-proh-BOH ehn TOH-dahs soos KLAH-sehs

An easy way to praise the student and his/her work directly is by using ¡qué [keh] + an adjective!

How marvelous!	**¡Qué maravilloso!**
	keh mah-rah-bee-YOH-soh
How organized!	**¡Qué organizado/organizada!**
	keh ohr-gah-nee-SAH-doh/ ohr-gah-nee-SAH-dah
How wonderful!	**¡Qué estupendo!**
	keh ehs-too-PEHN-doh

You may also include the noun that you are praising. In this case, the word **tan** [tahn] or **más** [mahs] usually precedes the adjective.

What good homework!	**¡Qué tarea tan/más buena!**
	keh tah-REH-ah tahn/mahs BWEH-nah
What a marvelous composition!	**¡Qué composición tan/más maravillosa!**
	keh kohm-poh-see-SYOHN tahn/mahs mah-rah-bee-YOH-sah

Describing States and Conditions

Para describir el estado de ánimo y condiciones

When talking to parents, you will often need to describe how a student seems to be feeling at school. One way to express this idea is by using the verb **parecer** [pah-reh-SEHR] + an adjective, with the meaning of "to seem" + an adjective.

In class your child seems …	**En clase su hijo/hija parece…**
	ehn KLAH-seh soo EE-hoh/EE-hah pah-REH-seh
anxious	**ansioso**
	ahn-SYOH-soh

bored	**aburrido**
	ah-boo-RREE-doh
calm	**tranquilo**
	trahn-KEE-loh
exhausted	**agotado**
	ah-goh-TAH-doh
happy	**contento**
	kohn-TEHN-toh
nervous	**nervioso**
	nehr-BYOH-soh
relaxed	**relajado**
	rreh-lah-HAH-doh
tired	**cansado**
	kahn-SAH-doh
worried	**preocupado**
	preh-oh-koo-PAH-doh

If the child to whom you are referring is a girl, all the Spanish adjectives listed above will end in **-a** instead of **-o**.

GRAMMAR · Using the Verb "To Be" + Adjective to Express Conditions or States

The most common way to describe a condition or state in Spanish is to use the verb **estar** [ehs-TAHR] + an adjective. In addition to the adjectives listed above, other adjectives that are commonly used with **estar** are listed here.

I am ...	**Estoy...**
	ehs-TOH-ee
angry	**enojado**
	eh-noh-HAH-doh
ashamed	**avergonzado**
	ah-behr-gohn-SAH-doh
busy	**ocupado**
	oh-koo-PAH-doh
grateful	**agradecido**
	ah-grah-deh-SEE-doh
healthy	**saludable**
	sah-loo-DAH-bleh
sad	**triste**
	TREES-teh
sick	**enfermo**
	ehn-FEHR-moh

I am ...	**Estoy...**
	ehs-TOH-ee
surprised	**sorprendido**
	sohr-prehn-DEE-doh

Remember that the adjective ending may need to be changed to agree with the gender and number of the noun it describes.

| We are furious. | **Estamos furiosos.** |
| | ehs-TAH-mohs foo-RYOH-sohs |

For additional vocabulary about feelings and personal problems, see Chapter 7, pages 252–253 and 257–259.

To review the present tense of the verb **estar**, see Chapter 1, page 59.

Practice 5-5

Complete the following sentences with the Spanish translation for one of the adjectives below. Remember to change the ending if necessary. One of the adjectives will not be used.

surprised	furious
ashamed	tired
busy	healthy
anxious	bored

1. Juan trabaja mucho. Él está _____.

2. Ellos tienen muchos exámenes hoy. Ellos están _____.

3. Nosotros salimos muy bien en el examen. Estamos _____.

4. Yo no estudié para el examen. Estoy _____.

5. La clase no es muy interesante. Uds. están _____.

6. Ella no puede ir al teatro porque tiene mucho trabajo. Está

   _____.

7. Estudio mucho pero no salgo bien. Estoy _____.

Giving Advice to Students

Para aconsejar a los estudiantes

As a teacher, you will sometimes give advice to students (**aconsejar a los estu-diantes** [ah-kohn-seh-HAHR ah lohs ehs-too-DYAHN-tehs]). Remember that you can use **(no) debes** [(noh) DEH-behs] + an infinitive, meaning "you should (not)" + the infinitive. Here are some expressions you may need.

You should / ought to ...

> **Debes...**
> DEH-behs

do the homework carefully

> **hacer la tarea con cuidado**
> ah-SEHR lah tah-REH-ah kohn
> kwee-DAH-doh

ask questions

> **hacer preguntas**
> ah-SEHR preh-GOON-tahs

arrive at class early / on time

> **llegar a la clase temprano / a tiempo**
> yeh-GAHR ah lah KLAH-seh
> tehm-PRAH-noh / ah TYEM-poh

pay attention in class

> **prestar atención en clase**
> prehs-TAHR ah-tehn-SYOHN ehn
> KLAH-seh

participate in class

> **participar en la clase**
> pahr-tee-see-PAHR ehn lah KLAH-seh

You should not / ought not ...

> **No debes...**
> noh DEH-behs

copy another student's homework

> **copiar la tarea de otro estudiante**
> koh-PYAHR lah tah-REH-ah deh OH-troh
> ehs-too-DYAHN-teh

talk with your friends during class

> **hablar con tus amigos durante la clase**
> ah-BLAHR kohn toos ah-MEE-gohs
> doo-RAHN-teh lah KLAH-seh

leave the class without permission

> **salir de la clase sin permiso**
> sah-LEER deh lah KLAH-seh seen
> pehr-MEE-soh

get to class late

> **llegar tarde a la clase**
> yeh-GAHR TAHR-deh ah lah KLAH-seh

look at another student's work during an exam

> **mirar el trabajo de otro estudiante**
> **durante un examen**
> mee-RAHR ehl trah-BAH-hoh deh
> OH-troh ehs-too-DYAHN-teh
> doo-RAHN-teh oon ehk-SAH-mehn

Homework

La tarea

Homework (**la tarea** [lah tah-REH-ah]) provides a link between school and home. Parents who come from Spanish-speaking countries are not always familiar with the type and length of homework assignments given in classrooms across the United States. It will prove helpful to share with them the reasons that homework is given and guidelines for what it should involve at home.

Homework is given in order …	**La tarea se da para...** lah tah-REH-ah seh dah PAH-rah
to know whether the students understood the lesson	**saber si los alumnos entendieron la lección** sah-BEHR see lohs ah-LOOM-nohs ehn-tehn-DYEH-rohn lah lehk-SYOHN
to help the students understand and review what I presented in class	**ayudar a los alumnos a entender y repasar lo que yo expliqué en clase** ah-yoo-DAHR ah lohs ah-LOOM-nohs ah ehn-tehn-DEHR ee rreh-pah-SAHR loh keh yoh ehs-plee-KEH ehn KLAH-seh
to help the students find more information on a topic	**ayudar a los alumnos a encontrar más información sobre un tema** ah-yoo-DAHR ah lohs ah-LOOM-nohs ah ehn-kohn-TRAHR mahs een-fohr-mah-SYOHN SOH-breh oon TEH-mah
Your child should spend about (number) minutes a night on homework.	**Su hijo/hija debe pasar unos (number) minutos en la tarea cada noche.** soo EE-hoh/EE-hah DEH-beh pah-SAHR oo-nohs... mee-NOO-tohs ehn lah tah-REH-ah KAH-dah NOH-cheh
Your child should spend about (number) hours a night on homework.	**Su hijo/hija debe pasar unas (number) horas en la tarea cada noche.** soo EE-hoh/EE-hah DEH-beh pah-SAHR oo-nahs... OH-rahs ehn lah tah-REH-ah KAH-dah NOH-cheh

Many of the suggestions in this chapter, such as the information about homework, could be sent home to the parents.

In order to succeed in school, children need to develop good study habits (**buenos hábitos de estudio** [BWEH-nohs AH-bee-tohs deh ehs-TOO-dyoh]) and attitudes that will help them to become lifelong learners. Teachers and parents are partners (**compañeros** [kohm-pah-NYEH-rohs]) in helping students to achieve this goal. Although you can use the direct command to tell the parents what to do, it is often better to tell them indirectly by using the subjunctive, which is explained below.

GRAMMAR · The Present Subjunctive in Indirect Commands

Spanish speakers use the subjunctive to express a desire to influence the actions of others, that is, to give an indirect command.

It is necessary for your child to study / do homework daily.	**Es necesario que su hijo/hija estudie / haga la tarea diariamente.** ehs neh-seh-SAH-ryoh keh soo EE-hoh/EE-hah ehs-TOO-dyeh / AH-gah lah tah-REH-ah dyah-ryah-MEHN-teh

The Present Subjunctive: Regular Verbs

All verbs that end in **-o** in the **yo** [yoh] form of the present tense are formed regularly in the present subjunctive. The present subjunctive is formed by removing the **-o** from the **yo** form of the present tense and adding a set of endings as follows.

* For **-ar** verbs

  Add **-e, -es, -e, -emos, -en.**

* For **-er** and **-ir** verbs

  Add **-a, -as, -a, -amos, -an.**

Conjugations of some sample verbs that are regular in the present subjunctive follow.

estudiar [ehs-too-DYAHR] to study

yo	estudie	yoh ehs-TOO-dyeh
tú	estudies	too ehs-TOO-dyehs
él	estudie	ehl ehs-TOO-dyeh
ella	estudie	EH-yah ehs-TOO-dyeh
Ud.	estudie	OOS-TEHD ehs-TOO-dyeh
nosotros	estudiemos	noh-SOH-trohs ehs-too-DYEH-mohs
nosotras	estudiemos	noh-SOH-trahs ehs-too-DYEH-mohs
ellos	estudien	EH-yohs ehs-TOO-dyehn
ellas	estudien	EH-yahs ehs-TOO-dyehn
Uds.	estudien	OOS-TEH-dehs ehs-TOO-dyehn

leer [leh-EHR] to read

yo	lea	yoh LEH-ah
tú	leas	too LEH-ahs
él	lea	ehl LEH-ah
ella	lea	EH-yah LEH-ah
Ud.	lea	OOS-TEHD LEH-ah
nosotros	leamos	noh-SOH-trohs leh-AH-mohs
nosotras	leamos	noh-SOH-trahs leh-AH-mohs
ellos	lean	EH-yohs LEH-ahn
ellas	lean	EH-yahs LEH-ahn
Uds.	lean	OOS-TEH-dehs LEH-ahn

escribir [ehs-kree-BEER] to read

yo	escriba	yoh ehs-KREE-bah
tú	escribas	too ehs-KREE-bahs
él	escriba	ehl ehs-KREE-bah
ella	escriba	EH-yah ehs-KREE-bah
Ud.	escriba	OOS-TEHD ehs-KREE-bah
nosotros	escribamos	noh-SOH-trohs ehs-kree-BAH-mohs
nosotras	escribamos	noh-SOH-trahs ehs-kree-BAH-mohs
ellos	escriban	EH-yohs ehs-KREE-bahn
ellas	escriban	EH-yahs ehs-KREE-bahn
Uds.	escriban	OOS-TEH-dehs ehs-KREE-bahn

venir [beh-NEER] to come

yo	venga	yoh BEHN-gah
tú	vengas	too BEHN-gahs
él	venga	ehl BEHN-gah
ella	venga	EH-yah BEHN-gah
Ud.	venga	OOS-TEHD BEHN-gah
nosotros	vengamos	noh-SOH-trohs behn-GAH-mohs
nosotras	vengamos	noh-SOH-trahs behn-GAH-mohs
ellos	vengan	EH-yohs BEHN-gahn
ellas	vengan	EH-yahs BEHN-gahn
Uds.	vengan	OOS-TEH-dehs BEHN-gahn

The teacher hopes that …	**El maestro / La maestra espera que…** ehl mah-EHS-troh / lah mah-EHS-trah ehs-PEH-rah keh
we will study	**estudiemos** ehs-too-DYEH-mohs

I am reading the book	**yo lea el libro**
	yoh LEH-ah ehl LEE-broh
they will write the composition	**ellos escriban la composición**
	EH-yohs ehs-KREE-bahn lah kohm-poh-see-SYOHN
you are coming early	**tú vengas temprano**
	too BEHN-gahs tehm-PRAH-noh

Note that the present subjunctive can express an action that is happening either at the same time as or after the action of the main verb.

The Present Subjunctive: Irregular Verbs

If the **yo** [yoh] form of the present tense does not end in **-o**, the present subjunctive form is irregular. The following verbs are irregular in the present subjunctive.

dar [dahr] to give

yo	dé	yoh deh
tú	des	too dehs
él	dé	ehl deh
ella	dé	EH-yah deh
Ud.	dé	oos-TEHD deh
nosotros	demos	noh-SOH-trohs DEH-mohs
nosotras	demos	noh-SOH-trahs DEH-mohs
ellos	den	EH-yohs dehn
ellas	den	EH-yahs dehn
Uds.	den	oos-TEH-dehs dehn

estar [ehs-TAHR] to be

yo	esté	yoh ehs-TEH
tú	estés	too ehs-TEHS
él	esté	ehl ehs-TEH
ella	esté	EH-yah ehs-TEH
Ud.	esté	oos-TEHD ehs-TEH
nosotros	estemos	noh-SOH-trohs ehs-TEH-mohs
nosotras	estemos	noh-SOH-trahs ehs-TEH-mohs
ellos	estén	EH-yohs ehs-TEHN
ellas	estén	EH-yahs ehs-TEHN
Uds.	estén	oos-TEH-dehs ehs-TEHN

ir [eer] to go

yo	vaya	yoh BAH-yah
tú	vayas	too BAH-yahs
él	vaya	ehl BAH-yah
ella	vaya	EH-yah BAH-yah
Ud.	vaya	OOS-TEHD BAH-yah
nosotros	vayamos	noh-SOH-trohs bah-YAH-mohs
nosotras	vayamos	noh-SOH-trahs bah-YAH-mohs
ellos	vayan	EH-yohs BAH-yahn
ellas	vayan	EH-yahs BAH-yahn
Uds.	vayan	OOS-TEH-dehs BAH-yahn

ser [sehr] to be

yo	sea	yoh SEH-ah
tú	seas	too SEH-ahs
él	sea	ehl SEH-ah
ella	sea	EH-yah SEH-ah
Ud.	sea	OOS-TEHD SEH-ah
nosotros	seamos	noh-SOH-trohs seh-AH-mohs
nosotras	seamos	noh-SOH-trahs seh-AH-mohs
ellos	sean	EH-yohs SEH-ahn
ellas	sean	EH-yahs SEH-ahn
Uds.	sean	OOS-TEH-dehs SEH-ahn

saber [sah-BEHR] to know

yo	sepa	yoh SEH-pah
tú	sepas	too SEH-pahs
él	sepa	ehl SEH-pah
ella	sepa	EH-yah SEH-pah
Ud.	sepa	OOS-TEHD SEH-pah
nosotros	sepamos	noh-SOH-trohs seh-PAH-mohs
nosotras	sepamos	noh-SOH-trahs seh-PAH-mohs
ellos	sepan	EH-yohs SEH-pahn
ellas	sepan	EH-yahs SEH-pahn
Uds.	sepan	OOS-TEH-dehs SEH-pahn

Impersonal Expressions

Here are some impersonal expressions that can be used to give indirect commands when followed by a subject + a verb in the present subjunctive.

It is advisable that … **Es aconsejable que…**
ehs ah-kohn-seh-HAH-bleh keh

It is better that … **Es mejor que…**
ehs meh-HOHR keh

It is important that …	**Es importante que…**
	ehs eem-pohr-TAHN-teh keh
It is necessary that …	**Es necesario que…**
	ehs neh-seh-SAH-ryoh keh
It is preferable that …	**Es preferible que…**
	ehs preh-feh-REE-bleh keh
It is important that you come to school every day.	**Es importante que vengas a la escuela todos los días.**
	ehs eem-pohr-TAHN-teh keh BEHN-gahs ah lah ehs-KWEH-lah TOH-dohs lohs DEE-ahs

When you're making a general statement about expected behavior without referring to anyone in particular, impersonal expressions are followed by the infinitive because they are statements rather than indirect commands.

It is important to come to school every day.	**Es importante venir a la escuela todos los días.**
	ehs eem-pohr-TAHN-teh beh-NEER ah lah ehs-KWEH-lah TOH-dohs lohs DEE-ahs

In addition to using impersonal expressions, you can give indirect commands by using the expression **Ojalá que** [oh-hah-LAH keh], meaning "I hope that," or by using conjugated forms of verbs that express a desire to influence the actions of another person. Some of those verbs are listed here.

to advise	**aconsejar**	ah-kohn-seh-HAHR
to forbid	**prohibir**	proh-ee-BEER
to hope	**esperar**	ehs-peh-RAHR
to recommend	**recomendar (ie)**	rreh-koh-mehn-DAHR
to want	**querer (ie)**	keh-REHR
to want	**desear**	deh-seh-AHR

I hope that you can help me.	**Espero que / Ojalá que Ud. me pueda ayudar.**
	ehs-PEH-roh keh / oh-hah-LAH keh OOS-TEHD meh PWEH-dah ah-yoo-DAHR
I recommend that your child do practice exercises.	**Recomiendo que su hijo/hija haga ejercicios de práctica.**
	rreh-koh-MYEHN-doh keh soo EE-hoh/ EE-hah AH-gah eh-hehr-SEE-syohs deh PRAHK-tee-kah

Other suggestions that you may want to make to parents follow.

It is important that your child …	**Es importante que su hijo/hija…**
	ehs eem-pohr-TAHN-teh keh soo EE-hoh/EE-hah
turn in the homework	**entregue la tarea**
	ehn-TREH-geh lah tah-REH-ah
review the lessons	**repase las lecciones**
	rreh-PAH-seh lahs lehk-SYOH-nehs
read a book	**lea un libro**
	LEH-ah oon LEE-broh
get at least (*number*) hours of sleep each night	**duerma por lo menos** (*number*) **horas cada noche**
	DWEHR-mah pohr loh MEH-nohs… OH-rahs KAH-dah NOH-cheh

Long-term assignments, such as research papers and oral reports, often have deadlines that are weeks away, so it is important for parents to be aware of what their children need to do in order to handle such an assignment.

It is important that you help your child organize his/her assignments by recording them on calendars or planners, along with due dates, etc.	**Es importante que ayude a su hijo/hija a organizar sus tareas poniéndolas en un calendario o planificador junto con las fechas en que se deben entregar, etc.**
	ehs eem-pohr-TAHN-teh keh ah-YOO-deh ah soo EE-hoh/EE-hah ah ohr-gah-nee-SAHR soos tah-REH-ahs poh-NYEHN-doh-lahs ehn oon kah-lehn-DAH-ryoh oh plah-nee-fee-kah-DOHR HOON-toh kohn lahs FEH-chahs ehn keh seh DEH-behn ehn-treh-GAHR
This assignment is for (*day of the week*).	**Esta tarea es para** (*day of the week*).
	EHS-tah tah-REH-ah ehs PAH-rah
If he/she does not hand in the assignment by that date …	**Si él/ella no entrega la tarea para esa fecha…**
	see ehl/EH-yah noh ehn-TREH-gah lah tah-REH-ah PAH-rah EH-sah FEH-chah
I am not going to accept it	**no la voy a aceptar**
	noh lah BOH-ee ah ah-sehp-TAHR
he/she will get a lower grade	**él/ella va a recibir una nota más baja**
	ehl/EH-yah bah a rreh-see-BEER OO-nah NOH-tah mahs BAH-hah

Practice 5-6

A *Circle the correct form of the verb from the two that are given to complete the following sentences. Once you are finished, you should say the sentence aloud so that you can practice the use of the subjunctive.*

1. Es necesario que ellos (vienen | vengan) antes de las clases.

2. Yo quiero que tú (leas | lees) esa novela.

3. El señor Thomas prohíbe que los estudiantes (comen | coman) en clase.

4. Es mejor que tú (entregues | entregas) la tarea hoy.

5. Ellos esperan que el examen no (es | sea) esta semana.

6. Yo recomiendo que Uds. (saben | sepan) el vocabulario.

7. La bibliotecaria desea que él no (habla | hable) en voz alta.

8. Es preferible que nosotros (repasemos | repasamos) la gramática.

B *Complete the following sentences with the Spanish translation for the phrase in parentheses.*

1. Es necesario que tú _____ (study early).

2. Yo espero que Uds. _____ (come on time).

3. Es mejor que tú _____ (study in the library).

4. Es aconsejable que los estudiantes

   _____ (don't go to the park today).

5. Es importante que yo _____
   (know when you are absent).

6. El director prohíbe que Uds. _____
   (eat in the hallways).

7. Yo recomiendo que ella _____
   (participate more in class).

8. El consejero desea que yo _____
   (speak with you).

9. Yo no quiero que ellos _____
   (copy another student's homework).

10. Tus padres esperan que tú _____
    (do well on the exam).

The Home Environment

El ambiente en casa

Parents can also help to establish good study habits by providing a suitable home environment (**el ambiente en casa** [ehl ahm-BYEHN-teh ehn KAH-sah]) for doing homework and for studying. Here are some guidelines you may want to give them.

Establish a regular time for studying and doing homework.	**Establezca una hora regular para estudiar y hacer la tarea.**
	ehs-tah-BLEHS-kah oo-nah OH-rah RREH-goo-lahr PAH-rah ehs-too-DYAHR ee ah-SEHR lah tah-REH-ah
While your child is studying, the television should be turned off and any other distractions (e.g., e-mail, the Internet, calls from friends) should not be allowed.	**Mientras su hijo/hija estudia, el televisor debe estar apagado y no se debe permitir ninguna otra distracción (e.g., el correo electrónico, el internet, las llamadas de amigos).**
	MYEHN-trahs soo EE-hoh/EE-hah ehs-TOO-dyah, ehl teh-leh-bee-SOHR DEH-beh ehs-TAHR ah-pah-GAH-doh ee noh seh DEH-beh pehr-mee-TEER neen-GOO-nah OH-trah dees-trahk-SYOHN (e.g., ehl koh-RREH-oh eh-lehk-TROH-nee-koh, ehl een-tehr-NEHT, lahs yah-MAH-dahs deh ah-MEE-gohs)
If possible, make sure that your child has a quiet, comfortable, well-lit study area to study and do homework.	**Si es posible, asegúrese de que su hijo/hija tenga un área de estudio tranquila y cómoda, con buena luz para estudiar y hacer la tarea.**
	see ehs poh-SEE-bleh, ah-seh-GOO-reh-seh deh keh soo EE-hoh/EE-hah TEHN-gah oon AH-reh-ah deh ehs-TOO-dyoh trahn-KEE-lah ee KOH-moh-dah, kohn BWEH-nah loos PAH-rah ehs-too-DYAHR ee ah-SEHR lah tah-REH-ah

Make sure that your child has the school supplies he/she needs to do assignments.	**Asegúrese de que su hijo/hija tenga los materiales que necesita para hacer las tareas.** ah-seh-GOO-reh-seh deh keh soo EE-hoh/EE-hah TEHN-gah lohs mah-teh-RYAH-lehs keh neh-seh-SEE-tah PAH-rah ah-SEHR lahs tah-REH-ahs

Preparing for Exams
Para prepararse para los exámenes

Increased accountability has moved many school districts and schools to increase the number of classroom tests, as well as standardized tests. Success on these tests depends not only on good instruction but also on parental support and hard work by students. In Chapter 7, pages 275–277, you will find information about the most common tests that you may need to explain to parents.

Children need help finding methods for study and review that work best for them as they prepare for exams (**prepararse para los exámenes** [preh-pah-RAHR-seh PAH-rah lohs ehk-SAH-meh-nehs]). For younger students, some recommendations for parents could be the following.

Give your child practice tests.	**Haga exámenes de práctica con su hijo/hija.** AH-gah ehk-SAH-meh-nehs deh PRAHK-tee-kah kohn soo EE-hoh/EE-hah
Help your child correct his/her work using the word list.	**Ayude a su hijo/hija a corregir su trabajo usando la lista de palabras.** ah-YOO-deh ah soo EE-hoh/EE-hah ah koh-rreh-HEER soo trah-BAH-hoh oo-SAHN-doh lah LEES-tah deh pah-LAH-brahs

The following recommendations are appropriate for children of all ages.

Encourage your child …	**Anime a su hijo/hija a…** ah-NEE-meh ah soo EE-hoh/EE-hah ah
to not leave studying for the last minute	**no dejar el estudio para el último momento** noh deh-HAHR ehl ehs-TOO-dyoh PAH-rah ehl OOL-tee-moh moh-MEHN-toh
to prepare an exam study schedule	**preparar un horario de repaso para los exámenes** preh-pah-RAHR oon oh-RAH-ryoh deh rreh-PAH-soh PAH-rah lohs ehk-SAH-meh-nehs

Encourage your child ...	**Anime a su hijo/hija a...**
	ah-NEE-meh ah soo EE-hoh/EE-hah ah
to read the instructions carefully	**leer las instrucciones con cuidado**
	leh-EHR lahs eens-trook-SYOH-nehs kohn kwee-DAH-doh
to answer the easiest questions first	**contestar a las preguntas más fáciles primero**
	kohn-tehs-TAHR ah lahs preh-GOON-tahs mahs FAH-see-lehs pree-MEH-roh
to avoid spending too much time on one question	**evitar el pasar mucho tiempo en una pregunta**
	eh-bee-TAHR ehl pah-SAHR MOO-choh TYEHM-poh ehn oo-nah preh-GOON-tah

Being prepared for a test also includes many physical aspects. Here are some suggestions for parents.

Make sure that your child ...	**Asegúrese de que su hijo/hija...**
	ah-seh-GOO-reh-seh deh keh soo EE-hoh/EE-hah
gets a good night's rest the night before a test	**duerma bastante la noche antes**
	DWEHR-mah bahs-TAHN-teh lah NOH-cheh AHN-tehs
eats a good breakfast	**se desayune bien**
	seh deh-sah-YOO-neh byehn
relaxes mentally	**se relaje mentalmente**
	seh rreh-LAH-heh mehn-tahl-MEHN-teh

Evaluating Students' Work

Para evaluar el trabajo de los estudiantes

As you work with students and parents, you will constantly be in the position of evaluating students' work (**evaluar el trabajo de los estudiantes** [eh-bah-LWAHR ehl trah-BAH-hoh deh lohs ehs-too-DYAHN-tehs]). To communicate about this with students and parents, you will need to be able to describe the student and his/her work.

By now you are familiar with many adjectives in Spanish. Some adjectives can be used with the verb **ser** [sehr], and others must be used with **estar** [ehs-TAHR]. If you remember that **estar** is used with an adjective to describe a condition or state, and **ser** is used with an adjective to describe a characteristic or inherent quality, you should have no problem making yourself understood.

The Successful Student
El estudiante que tiene éxito

There are many qualities that can be used to describe a successful student (**el estudiante que tiene éxito** [ehl ehs-too-DYAHN-teh keh TYEH-neh EHK-see-toh]). A parent may ask you about the student as follows.

What is my child like in class?	**¿Cómo es mi hijo/hija en clase?**
	KOH-moh ehs mee EE-hoh/EE-hah ehn KLAH-seh

You may answer using one or more of the following descriptions.

Your child is …	**Su hijo/hija es…**
	SOO EE-hoh/EE-hah ehs
artistic	**artístico**
	ahr-TEES-tee-koh
athletic	**atlético**
	ah-TLEH-tee-koh
careful	**cuidadoso**
	kwee-dah-DOH-soh
creative	**creativo**
	kreh-ah-TEE-boh
hardworking	**trabajador / trabajadora**
	trah-bah-hah-DOHR / trah-bah-hah-DOH-rah
honest	**honesto**
	oh-NEHS-toh
independent	**independiente**
	een-deh-pehn-DYEHN-teh
inquisitive	**curioso**
	koo-RYOH-soh
intelligent	**inteligente**
	een-teh-lee-HEHN-teh
obedient	**obediente**
	oh-beh-DYEHN-teh
organized	**organizado**
	ohr-gah-nee-SAH-doh
punctual	**puntual**
	poon-TWAHL
respectful	**respetuoso**
	rrehs-peh-TWOH-soh

Your child is ...	**Su hijo/hija es...**
	soo EE-hoh/EE-hah ehs
studious	**estudioso / aplicado**
	ehs-too-DYOH-soh / ah-plee-KAH-doh
Your child is always ...	**Su hijo/hija siempre está...**
	soo EE-hoh/EE-hah SYEHM-preh ehs-TAH
ready for class	**listo para la clase**
	LEES-toh PAH-rah lah KLAH-seh
well prepared	**bien preparado**
	byehn preh-pah-RAH-doh
His/Her homework is always ...	**Su tarea siempre está...**
	soo tah-REH-ah SYEHM-preh ehs-TAH
complete	**completa**
	kohm-PLEH-tah
well done	**bien hecha**
	byehn EH-chah

Remember that the ending of any adjective you use must agree in gender and number with the noun it is describing.

The Student at Risk of Failing a Subject / the School Year
El estudiante en riesgo de suspender una asignatura / el año escolar

Many signals can indicate that a student is at risk academically, that he/she might be at risk of failing a subject or the school year (**en riesgo de suspender una asignatura o el año escolar** [ehn RRYEHS-goh deh soos-pehn-DEHR oo-nah ah-seeg-nah-TOO-rah oh ehl AH-nyoh ehs-koh-LAHR]). Here are some of the signals to discuss with parents.

Your child ...	**Su hijo/hija...**
	soo EE-hoh/EE-hah
arrives late to school / to class	**llega tarde a la escuela / a la clase**
	YEH-gah TAHR-deh ah lah
	ehs-KWEH-lah / ah lah KLAH-seh
misses school often	**falta a la escuela a menudo**
	FAHL-tah ah lah ehs-KWEH-lah ah
	meh-NOO-doh
is not attentive in class	**no presta atención en la clase**
	noh PREHS-tah ah-tehn-SYOHN ehn
	lah KLAH-seh

does not participate in class	**no participa en la clase** noh pahr-tee-SEE-pah ehn lah KLAH-seh
misbehaves in school	**se porta mal en la escuela** seh POHR-tah mahl ehn lah ehs-KWEH-lah
talks to his/her classmates during class	**habla con sus compañeros durante la clase** AH-blah kohn soos kohm-pah-NYEH-rohs doo-RAHN-teh lah KLAH-seh
does not concentrate	**no se concentra** noh seh kohn-SEHN-trah

If you want to address the student directly, just add an **-s** at the end of the verb. For those sentences where **se** appears, you add the **-s** and also change **se** [seh] to **te** [teh].

You ...	**Tú...** too
arrive late to school	**llegas tarde a la escuela** YEH-gahs TAHR-deh ah lah ehs-KWEH-lah
misbehave in school	**te portas mal en la escuela** teh POHR-tahs mahl ehn lah ehs-KWEH-lah

Other concerns you may want to share with parents are the following.

Your child's homework is ...	**La tarea de su hijo/hija está...** lah tah-REH-ah deh soo EE-hoh/EE-hah ehs-TAH
incomplete	**incompleta** een-kohm-PLEH-tah
late	**atrasada** ah-trah-SAH-dah
done carelessly	**hecha sin cuidado** EH-chah seen kwee-DAH-doh
His/Her test grades are low.	**Su nota en los exámenes es baja.** soo NOH-tah ehn lohs ehk-SAH-meh-nehs ehs BAH-hah

To do well or not on a test or in a class is expressed in Spanish with **salir bien** [sah-LEER byehn] or **salir mal** [sah-LEER mahl].

You did not do well on the test.	**No saliste bien en el examen.**
	noh sah-LEES-teh byehn ehn ehl ehk-SAH-mehn

To receive good or bad grades in Spanish is expressed as follows.

to get good grades	**sacar buenas notas**
	sah-KAHR BWEH-nahs NOH-tahs
to get bad grades	**sacar malas notas**
	sah-KAHR MAH-lahs NOH-tahs
He/She does not get good grades in (geography).	**Él/Ella no saca buenas notas en (geografía).**
	ehl/EH-yah noh SAH-kah BWEH-nahs NOH-tahs ehn (heh-oh-grah-FEE-ah)
All the students in the class got bad grades.	**Todos los estudiantes de la clase sacaron malas notas.**
	TOH-dohs lohs ehs-too-DYAHN-tehs deh lah KLAH-seh sah-KAH-rohn MAH-lahs NOH-tahs

Note that the first example above uses the present tense, and the second example uses the preterite. It is important for you to become familiar with both tenses. In the Introduction, pages 9–15, and in Chapter 6, pages 230–232, you will find information about the formation and use of these two tenses. You may also refer to the Appendix, where you will find many common verbs fully conjugated.

Students who are at risk often exhibit frustration at home. The parents can be on the alert for signs of frustration.

Does your child say that …?	**¿Dice su hijo/hija que…?**
	DEE-seh soo EE-hoh/EE-hah keh
the homework is too hard	**la tarea es demasiado difícil**
	lah tah-REH-ah ehs deh-mah-SYAH-doh dee-FEE-seel
he/she does not understand the instructions	**no comprende las instrucciones**
	noh kohm-PREHN-deh lahs eens-trook-SYOH-nehs
the homework takes too much time	**la tarea toma demasiado tiempo**
	lah tah-REH-ah TOH-mah deh-mah-SYAH-doh TYEHM-poh

Getting Academic Help

Para recibir ayuda académica

It's not easy to speak to parents of children who are at risk, whether it is regarding academics or behavior. They are often very upset and at a loss as to what they can do. You may find that you need to help them calm down before you can begin to share your concerns and recommendations. Some expressions that may be helpful are the following.

Calm down.	**Tranquilícese.**
	trahn-kee-LEE-seh-seh
Don't worry.	**No se preocupe.**
	noh seh preh-oh-KOO-peh
There are several ways in which you can help your child.	**Hay varias maneras en que Ud. puede ayudar a su hijo/hija.**
	AH-ee BAH-ryahs mah-NEH-rahs ehn keh OOS-TEHD PWEH-deh ah-yoo-DAHR ah soo EE-hoh/EE-hah

Once the parents have calmed down, you will be able to suggest strategies for solving or lessening the problem, and for informing them of help that is available. The suggestions will depend on what the problem is, how severe it is, and what the needs of a particular child are. Some possibilities are the following.

The school can provide help with the subject matter or the assignments.	**La escuela puede proporcionar ayuda con la materia o las tareas.**
	lah ehs-KWEH-lah PWEH-deh proh-pohr-syoh-NAHR ah-yoo-dah kohn lah mah-TEH-ryah oh lahs tah-REH-ahs
If your child cannot do the homework, he/she can receive help by telephone.	**Si su hijo/hija no comprende la tarea, puede recibir ayuda por teléfono.**
	see soo EE-hoh/EE-hah noh kohm-PREHN-deh lah tah-REH-ah, PWEH-deh rreh-see-BEER ah-YOO-dah pohr teh-LEH-foh-noh
The telephone number is (*phone number*).	**El número de teléfono es** (*phone number*).
	ehl NOO-meh-roh deh teh-LEH-foh-noh ehs

Your child can go to the library and ask the librarian for suggestions.	**Su hijo/hija puede ir a la biblioteca y pedirle sugerencias al bibliotecario / a la bibliotecaria.** soo EE-hoh/EE-hah PWEH-deh eer ah lah bee-blyoh-TEH-kah ee peh-DEER-leh soo-heh-REHN-syahs ahl bee-blyoh-teh-KAH-ryoh / ah lah bee-blyoh-teh-KAH-ryah

You may also want to add a few suggestions such as the following.

Keep in touch with me.	**Manténgase en contacto conmigo.** mahn-TEHN-gah-seh ehn kohn-TAHK-toh kohn-MEE-goh
If you have any concerns, call me at (*phone number*) between (*time*) and (*time*).	**Si tiene alguna preocupación, llámeme al (*phone number*) entre (*time*) y (*time*).** see TYEH-neh ahl-GOO-nah preh-oh-koo-pah-SYOHN, YAH-meh-meh ahl… EHN-treh… ee…
Make an appointment to see me.	**Haga una cita para hablar conmigo.** AH-gah OO-nah SEE-tah PAH-rah ah-BLAHR kohn-MEE-goh
Come to see me during Parents' Night.	**Venga a verme durante la noche de la Reunión de Padres.** BEHN-gah ah BEHR-meh doo-RAHN-teh lah NOH-cheh deh lah rreh-oo-NYOHN deh PAH-drehs

When sensitive issues are involved, it is important to have an interpreter attend any meetings you have with a parent or member of the family who doesn't understand English. Students with serious personal or social problems are usually referred to a counselor. For more on this, see Chapter 7, "In the Counselor's Office."

Summary Practice

Express the following sentences in Spanish. You may want to review the chapter before doing the exercise. You may also need to consult the English-Spanish Glossary at the end of the book.

1. Upon returning to school, your child must bring a note signed by you.

   _____

2. It is important to pay attention.

   _____

3. In order to do well, you (**tú**) must ask questions when you do not understand.

   _____

4. It is forbidden to yell in the hallways.

   _____

5. You (**tú**) have to take the exam again.

   _____

6. You (**Uds.**) are going to have a test next week.

   _____

7. If she behaves badly, she cannot participate in sports.

   _____

8. What wonderful homework!

   _____

9. I hope that you study a lot.

   _____

10. It is important that he sleep at least eight hours a night.

    _____

6

Health, Medical Problems, and Emergencies

La salud, los problemas médicos y las emergencias

Before entering school, children must have all their vaccinations (**las vacunas** [lahs bah-KOO-nahs]) at a doctor's office (**la consulta del médico / de la médica** [lah kohn-SOOL-tah dehl MEH-dee-koh / deh lah MEH-dee-kah]) or at a clinic (**la clínica** [lah KLEE-nee-kah]).

The parent or guardian must also provide information about the child's general health (**la salud** [lah sah-LOOD]), as well as contact information in case of illness. For more about the information that may be required, see Chapter 1.

In the Nurse's Office

En la oficina del enfermero / de la enfermera

Most medical emergencies (**las emergencias** [lahs eh-mehr-HEHN-syahs]) that take place in school, whether major or minor, will probably be dealt with first in the nurse's office (**en la oficina del enfermero / de la enfermera** [ehn lah oh-fee-SEE-nah dehl ehn-fehr-MEH-roh / deh lah ehn-fehr-MEH-rah]). There a student may rest in bed (**la cama** [lah KAH-mah]), have his/her temperature taken with a thermometer (**el termómetro** [ehl tehr-MOH-meh-troh]), and be evaluated by the nurse.

If a student needs to go to the nurse's office, you may say the following to him/her.

Go to the nurse's office.	**Ve a la oficina del enfermero / de la enfermera.** beh ah lah oh-fee-SEE-nah dehl ehn-fehr-MEH-roh / deh lah ehn-fehr-MEH-rah

Describing Symptoms

Para describir los síntomas

One way to find out what a sick child is feeling is to ask him/her to describe symptoms (**describir los síntomas** [dehs-kree-BEER lohs SEEN-toh-mahs]).

What's wrong?	**¿Qué tienes? / ¿Qué te pasa?** keh TYEH-nehs / keh teh PAH-sah

The child will likely describe his/her symptoms using an expression with **tener** [teh-NEHR], as shown in the following pattern: "I have" + (*ailment*) (**Tengo** [TEHN-goh] + (*ailment*)).

I have a headache.	**Tengo dolor de cabeza.** TEHN-goh doh-LOHR deh kah-BEH-sah

I have a cough.	**Tengo tos.** TEHN-goh tohs

Here are some of the illnesses or conditions that may bring a student to the nurse's office.

acne	**el acné** ehl ahk-NEH
backache	**el dolor de espalda** ehl doh-LOHR deh ehs-PAHL-dah
chills	**los escalofríos** lohs ehs-kah-loh-FREE-ohs
constipation	**el estreñimiento** ehl ehs-treh-nyee-MYEHN-toh
cough	**la tos** lah tohs
cramps	**los calambres** lohs kah-LAHM-brehs
diarrhea	**la diarrea** lah dyah-RREH-ah
dizziness	**los mareos** lohs mah-REH-ohs
earache	**el dolor de oído** ehl doh-LOHR deh oh-EE-doh
fever	**la fiebre** lah FYEH-breh
gas	**los gases** los GAH-sehs
headache	**el dolor de cabeza** ehl doh-LOHR deh kah-BEH-sah
hiccup(s)	**el hipo** ehl EE-poh
indigestion	**la indigestión** lah een-dee-hehs-TYOHN
infection	**la infección** lah een-fehk-SYOHN
insect bite	**la picadura** lah pee-kah-DOO-rah
itch	**la picazón** lah pee-kah-SOHN
lice	**los piojos** lohs PYOH-hohs

menstrual period	**el período / la regla**
	ehl peh-REE-oh-doh / la RREH-glah
mucus	**la flema**
	lah FLEH-mah
nausea	**la náusea**
	lah NAH-oo-seh-ah
rash	**la erupción**
	lah eh-roop-SYOHN
seizure	**la convulsión**
	lah kohn-bool-SYOHN
sore throat	**el dolor de garganta**
	ehl doh-LOHR deh gahr-GAHN-tah
stomachache	**el dolor de estómago**
	doh-LOHR deh ehs-TOH-mah-goh
toothache	**el dolor de muelas**
	ehl doh-LOHR deh MWEH-lahs

Another way to find out how a child is feeling is to ask the following question.

How are you?	**¿Cómo estás? / ¿Cómo te sientes?**
	KOH-moh ehs-TAHS /
	KOH-moh teh SYEHN-tehs

In addition to answering your question with **tengo** [TEHN-goh] + (*ailment*), a child may describe his/her symptoms using **estoy** [ehs-TOH-ee], meaning "I am," + an adjective or **me siento** [meh SYEHN-toh], meaning "I feel," + an adjective.

I am sick.	**Estoy enfermo.**
	ehs-TOH-ee ehn-FEHR-moh
I feel sick.	**Me siento enfermo.**
	meh SYEHN-toh ehn-FEHR-moh

For more information about describing a state of being, see Chapter 5, pages 203–204.

Remember that the verb **estar** [ehs-TAHR] is used with an adjective to indicate the physical or emotional condition of someone, and that for adjectives in the feminine form, the **-o** ending changes to **-a**.

| Elena is sick. | **Elena está enferma.** |
| | eh-LEH-nah ehs-TAH ehn-FEHR-mah |

When making a determination about the nature and seriousness of an illness or injury, a nurse may ask the child to do the following.

Breathe deeply.	**Respire profundamente.**
	rrehs-PEE-reh proh-foon-dah-MEHN-teh
Exhale.	**Exhale.**
	ehk-SAH-leh
Inhale.	**Inhale.**
	ee-NAH-leh
Open your mouth.	**Abra la boca.**
	AH-brah lah BOH-kah
Stick out your tongue.	**Saque la lengua.**
	SAH-keh lah LEHN-gwah
Swallow.	**Trague.**
	TRAH-geh

For an explanation of how to form commands, see the Introduction, pages 16–18, 20, and 21.

Some situations will require a visit to the doctor (**el médico / la médica** [ehl MEH-dee-koh / lah MEH-dee-kah]), the dentist (**el/la dentista** [ehl/lah dehn-TEES-tah]), or even to the hospital emergency room (**la sala de emergencia del hospital** [lah SAH-lah deh eh-mehr-HEHN-syah dehl ohs-pee-TAHL]).

Accidents

Los accidentes

No matter how hard parents and teachers try to prevent them, accidents (**los accidentes** [lohs ahk-see-DEHN-tehs]) happen both at home and at school. You will need to use the preterite tense to talk about what happened in the past.

What happened to him/her?	**¿Qué le pasó?**
	keh leh pah-SOH
He/She fell.	**Él/Ella se cayó.**
	ehl/EH-yah seh kah-YOH

Practice 6-1

Find the words in the list below within the grid of letters. Words can appear horizontally, vertically, and backward, but not diagonally.

agotado
débil
el dolor
el hipo
el oído
la erupción
la espalda
la fiebre
la flema
la garganta
la regla
la tos
los mareos
los piojos

```
U N M N L O S M A R E O S S E
Z Q R K S Z X X L O P C G H B
N G K D E A L G E R A L A L K
L H A D L A P S E A L C J A U
E L J O R S I I Y R C T D F T
R A D D E L D O L O R Z Y L W
B F N A L A T O S P P B D E G
E K U T L C E L H I P O L M U
I B M O Y A T N A G R A G A L
F O U G D Y E Z F K S D L Q P
A N L A N G L I B E D S N Q Y
L N Q C D E O D I O L E A K R
A D X R B V S O J O I P S O L
W D K K L A E R U P C I O N J
I L X O X P O X L R Z F K S W
```

GRAMMAR · The Preterite Tense

The preterite tense can be used to talk about something that happened in the past. Regular Spanish verbs form the preterite tense by dropping the infinitive endings (**-ar**, **-er**, **-ir**) and adding a set of endings to the stem as follows.

- For verbs ending in **-ar**

   Add **-é, -aste, -ó, -amos, -asteis, -aron.**

   repasar [rreh-pah-SAHR] to review

I reviewed	**yo repasé**	yoh rreh-pah-SEH
you reviewed	**tú repasaste**	too rreh-pah-SAHS-teh
he reviewed	**él repasó**	ehl rreh-pah-SOH
she reviewed	**ella repasó**	EH-yah rreh-pah-SOH
you reviewed	**Ud. repasó**	oos-TEHD rreh-pah-SOH
we reviewed	**nosotros repasamos**	noh-SOH-trohs rreh-pah-SAH-mohs
we reviewed	**nosotras repasamos**	noh-SOH-trahs rreh-pah-SAH-mohs
they reviewed	**ellos repasaron**	EH-yohs rreh-pah-SAH-rohn
they reviewed	**ellas repasaron**	EH-yahs rreh-pah-SAH-rohn
you (*plural*) reviewed	**Uds. repasaron**	oos-TEH-dehs rreh-pah-SAH-rohn

- For verbs ending in **-er** or **-ir**

  Add **-í, -iste, -ió, -imos, -isteis, -ieron**.

  toser [toh-SEHR] to cough

I coughed	**yo tosí**	yoh toh-SEE
you coughed	**tú tosiste**	too toh-SEES-teh
he coughed	**él tosió**	ehl toh-SYOH
she coughed	**ella tosió**	EH-yah toh-SYOH
you coughed	**Ud. tosió**	OOS-TEHD toh-SYOH
we coughed	**nosotros tosimos**	noh-SOH-trohs toh-SEE-mohs
we coughed	**nosotras tosimos**	noh-SOH-trahs toh-SEE-mohs
they coughed	**ellos tosieron**	EH-yohs toh-SYEH-rohn
they coughed	**ellas tosieron**	EH-yahs toh-SYEH-rohn
you (*plural*) coughed	**Uds. tosieron**	OOS-TEH-dehs toh-SYEH-rohn

  abrir [ah-BREER] to open

I opened	**yo abrí**	yoh ah-BREE
you opened	**tú abriste**	too ah-BREES-teh
he opened	**él abrió**	ehl ah-BRYOH
she opened	**ella abrió**	EH-yah ah-BRYOH
you opened	**Ud. abrió**	OOS-TEHD ah-BRYOH
we opened	**nosotros abrimos**	noh-SOH-trohs ah-BREE-mohs
we opened	**nosotras abrimos**	noh-SOH-trahs ah-BREE-mohs
they opened	**ellos abrieron**	EH-yohs ah-BRYEH-rohn
they opened	**ellas abrieron**	EH-yahs ah-BRYEH-rohn
you (*plural*) opened	**Uds. abrieron**	OOS-TEH-dehs ah-BRYEH-rohn

You may find the following words and expressions useful when talking about the past.

yesterday	**ayer** ah-YEHR
yesterday morning	**ayer por la mañana** ah-YEHR pohr lah mah-NYAH-nah
yesterday afternoon	**ayer por la tarde** ah-YEHR pohr lah TAHR-deh
last night	**anoche** ah-NOH-cheh
the day before yesterday	**anteayer** ahn-teh-ah-YEHR
the night before last	**anteanoche** ahn-teh-ah-NOH-cheh

last Tuesday	**el martes pasado**
	ehl MAHR-tehs pah-SAH-doh
last week	**la semana pasada**
	lah seh-MAH-nah pah-SAH-dah
last weekend	**el fin de semana pasado**
	ehl feen deh seh-MAH-nah pah-SAH-doh
last month	**el mes pasado**
	ehl mehs pah-SAH-doh
last summer	**el verano pasado**
	ehl beh-RAH-noh pah-SAH-doh
last year	**el año pasado**
	ehl AH-nyoh pah-SAH-doh

GRAMMAR · Reflexive Verbs II

Many of the verbs used to talk about accidents are reflexive verbs. You will recognize reflexive verbs by the **-se** which is attached to the infinitive. Some of the reflexive verbs that are most commonly used when talking about accidents are listed here.

to break	**romperse**	rrohm-PEHR-seh
to burn	**quemarse**	keh-MAHR-seh
to cut	**cortarse**	kohr-TAHR-seh
to fall	**caerse** (*irreg.*)	kah-EHR-seh
to hit	**golpearse**	gohl-peh-AHR-seh
to sprain	**torcerse**	tohr-SEHR-seh

Remember that reflexive verbs are conjugated like nonreflexive verbs except that the appropriate reflexive pronoun (**me** [meh], **te** [teh], **se** [seh], **nos** [nohs], **se** [seh]) must be placed immediately before the conjugated form of the reflexive verb. Affirmative commands formed with reflexive verbs are the only exception to this pattern. For a further explanation of reflexive verbs, see Chapter 3, pages 129–131.

Injuries
Las heridas

You will sometimes need to talk about injuries (**las heridas** [lahs eh-REE-dahs]) to specific parts of the body. The Spanish pattern for this is different from the English pattern with which you are familiar. English uses a nonreflexive verb and precedes the part of the body with a possessive adjective. Spanish uses a reflexive verb with the definite article before the named part of the body in the following pattern: reflexive verb + definite article + (*part of the body*).

| He broke his leg. | **Se rompió la pierna.** |
| | seh rrohm-PYOH lah PYEHR-nah |

She burned her hand. | **Se quemó la mano.**
seh keh-MOH lah MAH-noh

He cut his finger. | **Se cortó el dedo.**
seh kohr-TOH ehl DEH-doh

She hit her leg. | **Se golpeó la pierna.**
seh gohl-peh-OH lah PYEHR-nah

She sprained her ankle. | **Se torció el tobillo.**
seh tohr-SYOH ehl toh-BEE-yoh

When using an adjective to describe the injury, you use a pattern with **tener** [teh-NEHR] as follows: **tener** + definite article + (*part of the body*) + adjective.

He/She has a … (ankle). | **Tiene (el tobillo)….**
TYEH-neh (ehl toh-BEE-yoh)

broken | **roto**
RROH-toh

burned | **quemado**
keh-MAH-doh

infected | **infectado**
een-fehk-TAH-doh

swollen | **hinchado**
een-CHAH-doh

twisted | **torcido**
tohr-SEE-doh

He has a broken leg. | **Tiene la pierna rota.**
TYEH-neh lah PYEHR-nah RROH-tah

She has an infected foot. | **Tiene el pie infectado.**
TYEH-neh ehl pyeh een-fehk-TAH-doh

Remember that for the feminine form of adjectives that end in **-o**, the **-o** changes to **-a**. When you have a plural adjective, add **-s**.

For a list of the parts of the body, see pages 237–238 in this chapter.
Other terms having to do with injuries that may be helpful to you are the following.

He/She has … | **Tiene…**
TYEH-neh

a blister | **una ampolla**
OO-nah ahm-POH-yah

He/She has ...	Tiene...
	TYEH-neh
a bruise	un moretón
	oon moh-reh-TOHN
a burn	una quemadura
	oo-nah keh-mah-DOO-rah
a cut	una herida
	oo-nah eh-REE-dah
a scratch/scrape	un arañazo
	oon ah-rah-NYAH-soh
a sprain	una torcedura
	oo-nah tohr-seh-DOO-rah
a wound	una herida
	oo-nah eh-REE-dah
He has a blister.	Tiene una ampolla.
	TYEH-neh oo-nah ahm-POH-yah
She has a burn.	Tiene una quemadura.
	TYEH-neh oo-nah keh-mah-DOO-rah

For more on these and other types of emergencies that have to be dealt with right away, see pages 243–247 in this chapter.

Practice 6-2

A *Complete the following sentences with the correct preterite form of the verb in parentheses.*

1. Antonio _____ (correr) en el parque.

2. ¿Qué le _____ (pasar) a Teresa?

3. Yo _____ (respirar) profundamente.

4. Tú no _____ (abrir) la boca.

5. Nosotros _____ (aprender) mucho.

6. Ellos _____ (salir) bien en el examen.

7. El maestro _____ (calificar) las composiciones.

8. Yo no _____ (asistir) a clase.

9. Ellos no _____ (comprender) nada.

10. Nosotros _____ (tomar) apuntes.

B *Write the word or phrase that expresses each of the following in a past context.*

MODELO   este año   *el año pasado*

1. hoy _____

2. esta tarde _____

3. esta noche _____

4. este verano _____

5. hoy por la mañana _____

6. este lunes _____

C *Complete the following sentences by writing the correct form of the verb in parentheses in the first blank, then writing the Spanish equivalent of the English phrase in parentheses in the second blank.*

1. Ellos _____ (toser) mucho _____
(*the day before yesterday*).

2. Ella _____ (visitar) al dentista _____
(*last Friday*).

3. La enfermera _____ (dar) información a los padres

_____ (*last Tuesday*).

4. Nosotros _____ (asistir) a la conferencia

_____ (*the night before last*).

5. Tú _____ (salir) de la escuela con Juan

_____ (*yesterday*).

Contagious Illnesses

Las enfermedades contagiosas

You may need to know about the following contagious illnesses (**las enfermedades contagiosas** [lahs ehn-fehr-meh-DAH-dehs kohn-tah-HYOH-sahs]).

bronchitis	**la bronquitis** lah brohn-KEE-tees
chicken pox	**la varicela** lah bah-ree-SEH-lah
cold (common cold)	**el resfriado / el catarro** ehl rrehs-FRYAH-doh / ehl kah-TAH-rroh

diphtheria	**la difteria**	
	lah deef-ᴛᴇʜ-ryah	
flu	**la gripe**	
	lah ɢʀᴇᴇ-peh	
hepatitis	**la hepatitis**	
	lah eh-pah-ᴛᴇᴇ-tees	
measles	**el sarampión**	
	ehl sah-rahm-ᴘʏᴏʜɴ	
meningitis	**la meningitis**	
	lah meh-neen-ʜᴇᴇ-tees	
mononucleosis	**la mononucleosis**	
	lah moh-noh-noo-kleh-ᴏʜ-sees	
mumps	**las paperas**	
	lahs pah-ᴘᴇʜ-rahs	
pneumonia	**la pulmonía**	
	lah pool-moh-ɴᴇᴇ-ah	
rubella	**la rubéola**	
	lah rroo-ʙᴇʜ-oh-lah	
scarlet fever	**la escarlatina**	
	lah ehs-kahr-lah-ᴛᴇᴇ-nah	
tuberculosis	**la tuberculosis**	
	lah too-behr-koo-ʟᴏʜ-sees	

Verbs

to cough	**toser**	toh-sᴇʜʀ
to faint	**desmayarse**	dehs-mah-ʏᴀʜʀ-seh
to get better	**mejorarse**	meh-hoh-ʀᴀʜʀ-seh
to get dizzy	**marearse**	mah-reh-ᴀʜʀ-seh
to get sick	**enfermarse**	ehn-fehr-ᴍᴀʜʀ-seh
to sneeze	**estornudar**	ehs-tohr-noo-ᴅᴀʜʀ
to stay in bed	**guardar cama**	gwahr-ᴅᴀʜʀ ᴋᴀʜ-mah
to take care of yourself	**cuidarse**	kwee-ᴅᴀʜʀ-seh
to vomit	**vomitar**	boh-mee-ᴛᴀʜʀ

To avoid several of the illnesses, get vaccinated!

Para evitar varias de las enfermedades, ¡vacúnese!

ᴘᴀʜ-rah eh-bee-ᴛᴀʜʀ ʙᴀʜ-ryahs deh lahs ehn-fehr-meh-ᴅᴀʜ-dehs, bah-ᴋᴏᴏ-neh-seh

Parts of the Body

Las partes del cuerpo

ankle	el tobillo	ehl toh-BEE-yoh
arm	el brazo	ehl BRAH-soh
back	la espalda	lah ehs-PAHL-dah
blood	la sangre	lah SAHN-greh
brain	el cerebro	ehl seh-REH-broh
cheek	la mejilla	lah meh-HEE-yah
chest	el pecho	ehl PEH-choh
chin	la barbilla	lah bahr-BEE-yah
ear (inner)	el oído	ehl oh-EE-doh
ear (outer)	la oreja	lah oh-REH-hah
elbow	el codo	ehl KOH-doh
eye	el ojo	ehl OH-hoh
face	la cara	lah KAH-rah
finger	el dedo	ehl DEH-doh
foot	el pie	ehl pyeh
forehead	la frente	lah FREHN-teh
hair	el pelo / el cabello	ehl PEH-loh / ehl kah-BEH-yoh
hand	la mano	lah MAH-noh
head	la cabeza	lah kah-BEH-sah
heart	el corazón	ehl koh-rah-SOHN
hip	la cadera	lah kah-DEH-rah
knee	la rodilla	lah rroh-DEE-yah
leg	la pierna	lah PYEHR-nah
lip	el labio	ehl LAH-byoh
lung	el pulmón	ehl pool-MOHN
mouth	la boca	lah BOH-kah
nail	la uña	lah OO-nyah
neck	el cuello	ehl KWEH-yoh
nose	la nariz	lah nah-REES
shoulder	el hombro	ehl OHM-broh
skin	la piel	lah pyehl
stomach	el estómago	ehl ehs-TOH-mah-goh

thigh	**el muslo**	ehl MOOS-loh
throat	**la garganta**	lah gahr-GAHN-tah
toe	**el dedo del pie**	ehl DEH-doh dehl pyeh
tongue	**la lengua**	lah LEHN-gwah
tooth	**el diente**	ehl DYEHN-teh
waist	**la cintura**	lah seen-TOO-rah
wrist	**la muñeca**	lah moo-NYEH-kah

GRAMMAR · Talking About What Hurts or Aches

When a Spanish-speaking child talks about a part of the body that hurts, he or she is likely to use the verb **doler** [doh-LEHR], meaning "to hurt or ache," according to the following pattern: "my/his/her/our/their" + (*part of the body*) + "hurts" (**me/le/nos/les** [meh/leh/nohs/lehs] + **duele** [DWEH-leh] + definite article + (*part of the body*)).

My (head) hurts.	**Me duele (la cabeza).**
	meh DWEH-leh (lah kah-BEH-sah)
His/Her (head) hurts.	**Le duele (la cabeza).**
	leh DWEH-leh (lah kah-BEH-sah)
Our (heads) hurt.	**Nos duele (la cabeza).**
	nohs DWEH-leh (lah kah-BEH-sah)
Their (heads) hurt.	**Les duele (la cabeza).**
	lehs DWEH-leh (lah kah-BEH-sah)

Note that in Spanish, unlike English, when the subject is plural, you still use a singular noun for parts of the body. It is assumed that each person has only one—one "head" (**la cabeza** [lah kah-BEH-sah]) in the example above.

If you want to know what part of the body is hurting, ask the question "What hurts?" (**¿Qué te/le/les duele?** [keh teh/leh/lehs DWEH-leh]).

What hurts (you [*plural*])?	**¿Qué les duele?**
	keh lehs DWEH-leh
Does your (stomach) hurt?	**¿Te duele (el estómago)?**
	teh DWEH-leh (ehl ehs-TOH-mah-goh)

In a situation where the child may be too young or too sick to verbalize what he or she is feeling, but may be able to point to where it hurts, ask him/her *where* it hurts.

| Where does it hurt? | **¿Dónde te duele?** |
| | DOHN-deh teh DWEH-leh |

When more than one part of the body hurts, **duele** [DWEH-leh] changes to **duelen** [DWEH-lehn].

Do your arms hurt?	**¿Te duelen los brazos?**
	teh DWEH-lehn lohs BRAH-sohs
No, my legs hurt.	**No, me duelen las piernas.**
	noh, meh DWEH-lehn lahs PYEHR-nahs

Practice 6-3

Use the cue in parentheses to express who is hurting.

1. _____ duele el brazo. (nosotros)

2. _____ duele la cabeza. (yo)

3. Juan, ¿_____ duele el muslo? (tú)

4. _____ duelen los dedos. (ella)

5. _____ duele la garganta. (ellos)

6. _____ duelen las rodillas. (él)

Medical Equipment

Los aparatos médicos

Minor accidents require only a Band-Aid® (**una curita**®/**una tirita**® [oo-nah koo-REE-tah/oo-nah tee-REE-tah]), but often something more is required. Here is a list of some common medical equipment (**los aparatos médicos** [lohs ah-pah-RAH-tohs MEH-dee-kohs]).

bandage	**la venda**
	lah BEHN-dah
cane	**el bastón**
	ehl bahs-TOHN
cast	**el yeso**
	ehl YEH-soh
crutches	**las muletas**
	lahs moo-LEH-tahs
stitches	**los puntos**
	lohs POON-tohs
wheelchair	**la silla de ruedas**
	lah SEE-yah deh RRWEH-dahs

Verbs

to bandage the wound	**vendar la herida** behn-DAHR lah eh-REE-dah
to clean the wound	**limpiar la herida** leem-PYAHR lah eh-REE-dah
to give a shot (injection)	**inyectar / ponerle una inyección** een-yehk-TAHR / poh-NEHR-leh oo-nah een-yehk-SYOHN
to put a cast on	**enyesar** ehn-yeh-SAHR
to stitch (close with stitches)	**poner puntos** poh-NEHR POON-tohs
to take (one's) blood pressure	**tomarle la presión arterial** toh-MAHR-leh lah preh-SYOHN ahr-teh-RYAHL
to take (one's) pulse	**tomarle el pulso** toh-MAHR-leh ehl POOL-soh
to take (one's) temperature	**tomarle la temperatura** toh-MAHR-leh lah tehm-peh-rah-TOO-rah

For additional vocabulary having to do with students with special needs, see Chapter 7, pages 278–281.

Communications from the Nurse's Office

Los mensajes de la oficina del enfermero / de la enfermera

After the nurse examines a child, he/she may have to call the parent at home or at work. Here are some things that he/she may say in a message (**el mensaje** [ehl mehn-SAH-heh]).

Your (*male*) child is sick.	**Su hijo está enfermo.** soo EE-hoh ehs-TAH ehn-FEHR-moh
Your (*female*) child is sick.	**Su hija está enferma.** soo EE-hah ehs-TAH ehn-FEHR-mah
He/She is …	**Está…** ehs-TAH
bleeding	**sangrando** sahn-GRAHN-doh

dehydrated	**deshidratado/deshidratada** dehs-ee-drah-TAH-doh/ dehs-ee-drah-TAH-dah
dizzy	**mareado/mareada** mah-reh-AH-doh/mah-reh-AH-dah
vomiting	**vomitando** boh-mee-TAHN-doh
wounded	**herido/herida** eh-REE-doh/eh-REE-dah
He/She has …	**Tiene…** TYEH-neh
a burn	**una quemadura** oo-nah keh-mah-DOO-rah
convulsions	**convulsiones** kohn-bool-SYOH-nehs
a rash	**una erupción** oo-nah eh-roop-SYOHN
sunstroke	**una insolación** oo-nah een-soh-lah-SYOHN
His/Her (stomach) hurts.	**Le duele (el estómago).** leh DWEH-leh (ehl ehs-TOH-mah-goh)
You have to pick him/her up immediately.	**Tiene que recogerlo/recogerla inmediatamente.** TYEH-neh keh rreh-koh-HEHR-loh/ rreh-koh-HEHR-lah een-meh-dyah-tah-MEHN-teh
You need to call the doctor.	**Necesita llamar al médico.** neh-seh-SEE-tah yah-MAHR ahl MEH-dee-koh
You need to take your child to the doctor.	**Necesita llevar a su hijo/hija al médico.** neh-seh-SEE-tah yeh-BAHR ah soo EE-hoh/EE-hah ahl MEH-dee-koh
You need to take your child to the pediatrician.	**Necesita llevar a su hijo/hija al pediatra.** neh-seh-SEE-tah yeh-BAHR ah soo EE-hoh/EE-hah ahl peh-DYAH-trah
You need to take your child to the hospital.	**Necesita llevar a su hijo/hija al hospital.** neh-seh-SEE-tah yeh-BAHR ah soo EE-hoh/EE-hah ahl ohs-pee-TAHL

Medications

Las medicinas

Some medications (**las medicinas** [lahs meh-dee-SEE-nahs]) that may be recommended by a doctor are the following.

antacids	**los antiácidos**
	lohs ahn-TYAH-see-dohs
antibiotics	**los antibióticos**
	lohs ahn-tee-BYOH-tee-kohs
antihistamines	**los antihistamínicos**
	lohs ahn-tees-tah-MEE-nee-kohs
antiseptic	**el antiséptico**
	ehl ahn-tee-SEHP-tee-koh
aspirin	**la aspirina**
	lah ahs-pee-REE-nah
cough syrup	**el jarabe para la tos**
	ehl hah-RAH-beh PAH-rah lah tohs
cream	**la pomada**
	lah poh-MAH-dah
iodine	**el yodo**
	ehl YOH-doh
liniment	**el linimento**
	ehl lee-nee-MEHN-toh
lotion	**la loción**
	lah loh-SYOHN
penicillin	**la penicilina**
	lah peh-nee-see-LEE-nah
powder	**el polvo**
	ehl POHL-boh
tablets (lozenges)	**las pastillas**
	lahs pahs-TEE-yahs
vitamins	**las vitaminas**
	lahs bee-tah-MEE-nahs

In an Emergency

En una emergencia

It is impossible to know what on-site emergencies or disasters may occur while school is in session. Careful preparation and a plan of action are required in order to deal with the unforeseen as effectively as possible.

Medical Emergencies

Las emergencias médicas

In certain situations, for example, if the child can't breathe (**no puede respirar** [noh PWEH-deh rrehs-pee-RAHR]), is choking or suffocating (**está asfixiándose** [ehs-TAH ahs-feek-SYAHN-doh-seh]), or is unconscious (**está sin conocimiento** [ehs-TAH seen koh-noh-see-MYEHN-toh]), the nurse would most likely call 9-1-1 (**nueve-uno-uno** [NWEH-beh oo-noh oo-noh]) before calling the parent. For more information about describing symptoms, see pages 226–228 in this chapter.

Call 9-1-1.	**Llame al 9-1-1.**
	YAH-meh ahl NWEH-beh oo-noh oo-noh
I need an ambulance.	**Necesito una ambulancia.**
	neh-seh-SEE-toh oo-nah
	ahm-boo-LAHN-syah

Other Emergencies

Otras emergencias

While medical emergencies usually generate a call to 9-1-1, other types of emergencies may require a call to the fire department (**el cuerpo de bomberos** [ehl KWEHR-poh deh bohm-BEH-rohs]), the police department (**el cuerpo de policía** [ehl KWEHR-poh deh poh-lee-SEE-ah]), or another government agency.
Some emergencies in this category might be the following.

bomb scare	**la amenaza de bomba**
	lah ah-meh-NAH-sah deh BOHM-bah
chemical spill	**el derrame de sustancia química**
	ehl deh-RRAH-meh deh soos-TAHN-syah
	KEE-mee-kah
explosion	**la explosión / el estallido**
	lah ehs-PLOH-syohn /
	ehl ehs-tah-YEE-doh
gas leak	**el escape de gas**
	ehl ehs-KAH-peh deh gahs

riot	**el motín**
	ehl moh-TEEN
robbery	**el robo**
	ehl RROH-boh
shooting	**el tiroteo**
	ehl tee-roh-TEH-oh
traffic accident	**el accidente de tráfico**
	ehl ahk-see-DEHN-teh deh TRAH-fee-koh

Here are some other useful words and expressions.

Call the fire department.	**Llame a los bomberos.**
	YAH-meh ah lohs bohm-BEH-rohs
fire	**el fuego / el incendio**
	ehl FWEH-goh / ehl een-SEHN-dyoh
fire alarm	**la alarma de incendios**
	lah ah-LAHR-mah deh een-SEHN-dyohs
fire door	**la puerta contra incendios**
	lah PWEHR-tah KOHN-trah
	een-SEHN-dyohs
fire drill	**el simulacro de incendio**
	ehl see-moo-LAH-kroh deh
	een-SEHN-dyoh
fire escape	**la escalera de emergencia**
	lah ehs-kah-LEH-rah deh
	eh-mehr-HEHN-syah
fire exit	**la salida de emergencia**
	lah sah-LEE-dah deh
	eh-mehr-HEHN-syah
fire extinguisher	**el extintor**
	ehl ehs-teen-TOHR
firefighter	**el bombero**
	ehl bohm-BEH-roh
flames	**las llamas**
	lahs YAH-mahs
siren	**la sirena**
	lah see-REH-nah
smoke	**el humo**
	ehl OO-moh
smoke detector	**el detector de humo**
	ehl deh-tehk-TOHR deh OO-moh

Call the police.	**Llame a la policía.** YAH-meh ah lah poh-lee-SEE-ah
(in) police custody	**(bajo) custodia policial** (BAH-hoh) koos-TOH-dyah poh-lee-SYAHL
police record	**los antecedentes penales** lohs ahn-teh-seh-DEHN-tehs peh-NAH-lehs
police station	**la comisaría** lah koh-mee-sah-REE-ah
policeman	**el policía** ehl poh-lee-SEE-ah
policewoman	**la mujer policía** lah moo-HEHR poh-lee-SEE-ah

Safety (**la seguridad** [lah seh-goo-ree-DAHD]) is a major concern, and threats (**las amenazas** [lahs ah-meh-NAH-zahs]) must be taken seriously. A safe and orderly school usually includes its own security personnel (**el personal de seguridad** [ehl pehr-soh-NAHL deh seh-goo-ree-DAHD]).

You may also need the following key vocabulary.

danger	**el peligro** ehl peh-LEE-groh
evacuation	**la evacuación** lah eh-bah-kwah-SYOHN
rescue	**el rescate** ehl rrehs-KAH-teh
shelter	**el refugio** ehl rreh-FOO-hyoh
threat	**la amenaza** lah ah-meh-NAH-sah
warning	**la advertencia** lah ahd-behr-TEHN-syah

You may need to order the students to take certain actions in case of an emergency. Here are some phrases you should learn.

Don't yell!	**¡No griten!** noh GREE-tehn
Don't run!	**¡No corran!** noh KOH-rrahn
Don't go near the window / the door!	**¡No se acerquen a la ventana / la puerta!** noh seh ah-SEHR-kehn ah lah behn-TAH-nah / lah PWEHR-tah

Walk quietly!	**¡Caminen tranquilamente!** kah-MEE-nehn trahn-kee-lah-MEHN-teh
Walk toward _____!	**¡Caminen hacia _____!** kah-MEE-nehn AH-syah
Run toward _____!	**¡Corran hacia _____!** KOH-rrahn AH-syah
Danger!	**¡Peligro!** peh-LEE-groh
Fire!	**¡Fuego!** FWEH-goh
Help!	**¡Socorro! / ¡Auxilio!** soh-KOH-rroh / ah-ook-SEE-lyoh
Hurry up!	**¡Dense prisa!** DEHN-seh PREE-sah
Listen!	**¡Escuchen!** ehs-KOO-chehn
Look!	**¡Miren!** MEE-rehn
Police!	**¡Policía!** poh-lee-SEE-ah
Silence!	**¡Silencio!** see-LEHN-syoh
Watch out!	**¡Cuidado!** kwee-DAH-doh
Get under the desk!	**¡Pónganse debajo del pupitre!** POHN-gahn-seh deh-BAH-hoh dehl poo-PEE-treh
Cover your head!	**¡Cúbranse la cabeza!** KOO-brahn-seh lah kah-BEH-sah
Cover your mouth!	**¡Cúbranse la boca!** KOO-brahn-seh lah BOH-kah

Natural Disasters
Los desastres naturales

Depending on the part of the country in which you live, the following natural disasters (**los desastres naturales** [lohs deh-SAHS-trehs nah-too-RAH-lehs]) may or may not be common occurrences.

blackout	**el apagón** ehl ah-pah-GOHN
earthquake	**el terremoto** ehl teh-rreh-MOH-toh

epidemic	**la epidemia**
	lah eh-pee-DEH-myah
flood	**la inundación**
	lah ee-noon-dah-SYOHN
hailstorm	**la granizada**
	lah grah-nee-SAH-dah
hurricane	**el huracán**
	ehl oo-rah-KAHN
landslide	**el desprendimiento de tierra**
	ehl dehs-prehn-dee-MYEHN-toh deh
	TYEH-rrah
snowstorm	**la nevada**
	lah neh-BAH-dah
thunderstorm	**la tormenta**
	lah tohr-MEHN-tah
tornado	**el tornado**
	ehl tohr-NAH-doh
tsunami	**el maremoto**
	ehl mah-reh-MOH-toh

Practice 6-4

Write what you would say in Spanish as a response to the following situations.

1. There is an emergency in your school.

    _____

2. There is a fire in the science lab.

    _____

3. The students are yelling in the hallways.

    _____

4. There is a hole in the sidewalk.

    _____

5. You want the students to hurry.

    _____

6. You want all the students to get under their desks.

    _____

7. You want the students to walk quietly.

_____

8. Everyone must cover his or her head.

_____

Summary Practice

Express the following sentences in Spanish.

1. You (**tú**) need to go to the nurse's office.

_____

2. Do you (**tú**) have a sore throat?

_____

3. She feels dizzy.

_____

4. What happened to her?

_____

5. He broke his foot.

_____

6. You (**tú**) have to stay in bed.

_____

7. Does your (**tú**) neck hurt?

_____

8. I have a toothache.

_____

9. There is smoke in the hallways.

_____

10. Cover (**Uds.**) your mouth!

_____

In the Counselor's Office

7

En la oficina del consejero

Although counselors do different things in different schools, their work with students often begins with registration (**la matrícula** [lah mah-TREE-koo-lah]) and does not end until transfer (**la transferencia** [lah trahns-feh-REHN-syah]) or graduation (**la graduación** [lah grah-dwah-SYOHN]). In the following sections, you will find vocabulary and expressions that will prove useful in many of the situations in which a counselor (**el consejero / la consejera** [ehl kohn-seh-HEH-roh / lah kohn-seh-HEH-rah]) may be involved.

For information about enrolling students in school, see Chapter 1.

Scheduling Classes

Para establecer el horario de clases

Counselors sometimes advise students on which courses are best suited for them and which ones they should not take. The following phrases will help both the teacher and the counselor communicate about scheduling classes (**establecer el horario de clases** [ehs-tah-bleh-SEHR ehl oh-RAH-ryoh deh KLAH-sehs]).

You can't take that class.	**No puedes tomar esa clase.** noh PWEH-dehs toh-MAHR EH-sah KLAH-seh
It is too advanced.	**Es demasiado avanzada.** ehs deh-mah-SYAH-doh ah-bahn-SAH-dah
It is too elementary.	**Es demasiado elemental.** ehs deh-mah-SYAH-doh eh-leh-mehn-TAHL
You do not have the prerequisites.	**Tú no tienes los requisitos.** too noh TYEH-nehs lohs rreh-kee-SEE-tohs
You already took that class.	**Ya tú tomaste esa clase.** yah too toh-MAHS-teh EH-sah KLAH-seh
This class is at the same time as _____.	**Esta clase es a la misma hora que** _____. EHS-tah KLAH-seh ehs ah lah MEES-mah OH-rah keh
You already have a full program.	**Tú ya tienes un programa completo.** too yah TYEH-nehs oon proh-GRAH-mah kohm-PLEH-toh

If you need to discuss specific issues dealing with scheduling, such as the time a class meets, you will find some helpful information in Chapter 3.

Bilingual Programs

Los programas bilingües

In many instances, students who come to this country not knowing English need to be placed in bilingual programs (**los programas bilingües** [lohs proh-GRAH-mahs bee-LEEN-gwehs]) or classes.

Your child is going to participate in the bilingual program.	**Su hijo/hija va a participar en el programa bilingüe.** SOO EE-hoh/EE-hah bah ah pahr-tee-see-PAHR ehn ehl proh-GRAH-mah bee-LEEN-gweh
All the classes are in English and Spanish.	**Todas las clases son en inglés y en español.** TOH-dahs lahs KLAH-sehs sohn ehn een-GLEHS ee ehn ehs-pah-NYOHL
The morning classes are in (English).	**Las clases de la mañana son en (inglés).** lahs KLAH-sehs deh lah mah-NYAH-nah sohn ehn (een-GLEHS)
In the afternoon, / After lunch, the classes are in (Spanish).	**Por la tarde / Después del almuerzo las clases son en (español).** pohr lah TAHR-deh / dehs-PWEHS dehl ahl-MWEHR-soh lahs KLAH-sehs sohn ehn (ehs-pah-NYOHL)
Your child is also going to attend the English as a Second Language classes.	**Su hijo/hija también va a asistir a clases de inglés como segunda lengua.** SOO EE-hoh/EE-hah tahm-BYEHN bah ah ah-sees-TEER ah KLAH-sehs deh een-GLEHS KOH-moh seh-GOON-dah LEHN-gwah
After (*number*) years, your child is going to attend all his/her classes in English.	**Después de (*number*) años, su hijo/hija va a asistir a todas las clases en inglés.** dehs-PWEHS deh… AH-nyohs, SOO EE-hoh/EE-hah bah ah ah-sees-TEER ah TOH-dahs lahs KLAH-sehs ehn een-GLEHS
Your child may feel more at ease in this program.	**Es posible que su hijo/hija se sienta más a gusto en este programa.** ehs poh-SEE-bleh keh SOO EE-hoh/EE-hah seh SYEHN-tah mahs ah GOOS-toh ehn EHS-teh proh-GRAH-mah

Emotional Problems and Feelings

Los problemas emocionales y las emociones

In many instances, it is the job of the counselor to deal with the students' emotional problems (**los problemas emocionales** [lohs proh-BLEH-mahs eh-moh-syoh-NAH-lehs]). Talking about emotional problems or feelings (**las emociones** [lahs eh-moh-SYOH-nehs]) is difficult for anyone. Here are some questions that may be useful in opening such a conversation.

How do you feel?	**¿Cómo te sientes?** KOH-moh teh SYEHN-tehs
What's wrong?	**¿Qué te pasa?** keh teh PAH-sah

Following is a list of some of the feelings that may come up.

afraid	**asustado** ah-soos-TAH-doh
angry	**enojado/enfadado** eh-noh-HAH-doh/ehn-fah-DAH-doh
anxious	**ansioso** ahn-SYOH-soh
ashamed	**avergonzado** ah-behr-gohn-SAH-doh
bitter	**amargado** ah-mahr-GAH-doh
depressed	**deprimido** deh-pree-MEE-doh
embarrassed	**avergonzado** ah-behr-gohn-SAH-doh
exhausted	**agotado** ah-goh-TAH-doh
fed up	**harto** AHR-toh
frustrated	**frustrado** froos-TRAH-doh
furious	**furioso** foo-RYOH-soh
insecure	**inseguro** een-seh-GOO-roh
jealous	**celoso** seh-LOH-soh

lost	**perdido** pehr-DEE-doh
nervous	**nervioso** nehr-BYOH-soh
resentful	**resentido** reh-sehn-TEE-doh
restless	**inquieto** een-KYEH-toh
sad	**triste** TREES-teh
sensitive	**sensible** sehn-SEE-bleh
tense	**tenso** TEHN-soh
tired	**cansado** kahn-SAH-doh
uncomfortable	**incómodo** een-KOH-moh-doh
unhappy	**descontento/infeliz** dehs-kohn-TEHN-toh/een-feh-LEES
worried	**preocupado** preh-oh-koo-PAH-doh

Remember that when you are talking about how a person feels, you must use the verb **estar** [ehs-TAHR]. For more discussion on using the verb **estar** to express emotions or feelings, see Chapter 5, pages 203–204.

Financial Problems
Los problemas financieros

Sometimes a student expresses feelings that are the consequence of financial problems (**los problemas financieros** [lohs proh-BLEH-mahs fee-nahn-SYEH-rohs]) at home. Depending on the circumstances, there are many programs to which parents can be referred, some of which are listed here.

Salvation Army	**el Ejército de Salvación** ehl eh-HEHR-see-toh deh sahl-bah-SYOHN
Social Security office	**la Oficina de Seguro Social** lah oh-fee-SEE-nah deh seh-GOO-roh soh-SYAHL
Unemployment Office	**la Oficina de Desempleo** lah oh-fee-SEE-nah deh deh-sehm-PLEH-oh

Veteran's Administration office	**la Oficina de la Administración para Veteranos** lah oh-fee-SEE-nah deh lah ahd-mee-nees-trah-SYOHN PAH-rah beh-teh-RAH-nohs
Welfare office	**la Oficina de Asistencia Social** lah oh-fee-SEE-nah deh ah-sees-TEHN-syah soh-SYAHL

GRAMMAR · Adverbs

Many Spanish adverbs are formed from Spanish adjectives. To form adverbs in this way, you begin with the feminine singular form of the adjective and add **-mente**.

ENGLISH ADJECTIVE	ENGLISH ADVERB	SPANISH ADJECTIVE MASCULINE	SPANISH ADJECTIVE FEMININE	SPANISH ADVERB
slow	slowly	**lento**	**lenta**	**lentamente**
intelligent	intelligently	**inteligente**	**inteligente**	**inteligentemente**
easy	easily	**fácil**	**fácil**	**fácilmente**

He/She reads slowly.	**Él/Ella lee lentamente.** ehl/EH-yah leh-eh lehn-tah-MEHN-teh
Your son/daughter learns easily.	**Su hijo/hija aprende fácilmente.** SOO EE-hoh/EE-hah ah-PREHN-deh FAH-seel-MEHN-teh

You have already learned to use **¿Cómo?** [KOH-moh], meaning "How?," to ask how someone is (**¿Cómo estás?** [KOH-moh ehs-TAHS]). **¿Cómo?** can also be used to find out how someone does something. Here are some examples.

How does he/she act at home?	**¿Cómo actúa él/ella en casa?** KOH-moh ahk-TOO-ah ehl/EH-yah ehn KAH-sah
He/She behaves very restlessly.	**Él/Ella se porta muy intranquilamente.** ehl/EH-yah seh POHR-tah MOO-ee een-trahn-kee-lah-MEHN-teh

The following list of adverbs will help you describe how your students do their work or how they do different activities in class.

a little	**un poco**
	oon POH-koh
a lot	**mucho**
	MOO-choh
badly	**mal**
	mahl
better	**mejor**
	meh-HOHR
less	**menos**
	MEH-nohs
more	**más**
	mahs
quickly	**de prisa / rápidamente**
	deh PREE-sah / RRAH-pee-dah-MEHN-teh
slowly	**despacio**
	dehs-PAH-syoh
so-so	**regular**
	rreh-goo-LAHR
well	**bien**
	byehn
worse	**peor**
	peh-OHR

The following adverbs can be used to express how often someone does something.

frequently	**frecuentemente**
	freh-kwehn-teh-MEHN-teh
from time to time	**de vez en cuando**
	deh behs ehn KWAHN-doh
many times	**muchas veces**
	MOO-chahs BEH-sehs
once	**una vez**
	oo-nah behs
rarely	**rara vez**
	RRAH-rah behs
sometimes	**a veces**
	ah BEH-sehs

then	entonces
	ehn-TOHN-sehs
(four) times	(cuatro) veces
	(KWAH-troh) BEH-sehs
twice	dos veces
	dohs BEH-sehs

Practice 7-1

A *Complete the following sentences with the Spanish equivalent of the words in parentheses.*

1. Yo estoy muy _____ (*well*).

2. Salí _____ (*better*) en el examen de hoy.

3. Ahora tenemos _____ (*a lot*) trabajo.

4. Por favor, camina más _____ (*slowly*).

5. Juan, ayúdame _____ (*a little*).

6. Ahora se comporta _____ (*worse*).

B *Complete the following sentences with the Spanish equivalent of the words in parentheses.*

1. ¿Cuándo visitas a Hugo? Visito a Hugo _____ (*from time to time*).

2. ¿Vas al teatro frecuentemente? No, voy al teatro _____ (*rarely*).

3. ¿Cuántas veces llamas a tu padre? Yo llamo a mi padre

   _____ (*once*) al día.

4. ¿Asistes a los conciertos de rock? Sí, asisto a los conciertos

   _____ (*many times*).

5. ¿Haces los experimentos una vez? No, hago los experimentos

   _____ (*twice*).

6. ¿Viajas a otro estado regularmente? No, viajo a otro estado

   _____ (*sometimes*).

Dealing with Personal Problems

Para hacerles frente a los problemas personales

Students often talk to counselors about personal problems that are bothering them. Because you may need to discuss some of these with your students, many of the issues that students have to face nowadays are listed below.

abuse (emotional)	**el abuso mental** ehl ah-BOO-soh mehn-TAHL
abuse (physical)	**el abuso físico** ehl ah-BOO-soh FEE-see-koh
abuse (sexual)	**el abuso sexual** ehl ah-BOO-soh sehk-SWAHL
alcoholism	**el alcoholismo** ehl ahl-koh-LEES-moh
arson	**el incendio premeditado** ehl een-SEHN-dyoh preh-meh-dee-TAH-doh
attempted murder	**el intento de asesinato** ehl een-TEHN-toh deh ah-seh-see-NAH-toh
battery	**el maltrato** ehl mahl-TRAH-toh
bullying	**la intimidación** lah een-tee-mee-dah-SYOHN
child abuse	**el maltrato de niños** ehl mahl-TRAH-toh deh NEE-nyohs
clothing style	**el estilo de ropa** ehl ehs-TEE-loh deh RROH-pah
discrimination	**la discriminación** lah dees-kree-mee-nah-SYOHN
domestic violence	**la violencia doméstica** lah byoh-LEHN-syah doh-MEHS-tee-kah
drug abuse	**el abuso de drogas** ehl ah-BOO-soh deh DROH-gahs
drug overdose	**la sobredosis (de drogas)** lah soh-breh-DOH-sees (deh DROH-gahs)
emotional instability	**la falta de estabilidad emocional** lah FAHL-tah deh ehs-tah-bee-lee-DAHD eh-moh-syoh-NAHL

gambling	**las apuestas / el juego** lahs ah-PWEHS-tahs / ehl HWEH-goh
gang	**la pandilla** lah pahn-DEE-yah
harassment	**el acoso** ehl ah-KOH-soh
homelessness	**el estar sin hogar/vivienda** ehl ehs-TAHR seen oh-GAHR/ bee-BYEHN-dah
hunger	**el hambre** ehl AHM-breh
incest	**el incesto** ehl een-SEHS-toh
juvenile delinquency	**la delincuencia juvenil** lah deh-leen-KWEHN-syah hoo-beh-NEEL
kidnapping	**el secuestro** ehl seh-KWEHS-troh
manslaughter	**el homicidio involuntario** ehl oh-mee-SEE-dyoh een-boh-loon-TAH-ryoh
molestation	**el asalto sexual** ehl ah-SAHL-toh sehk-SWAHL
murder	**el homicidio** ehl oh-mee-SEE-dyoh
poverty	**la pobreza** lah poh-BREH-sah
pregnancy (unwanted)	**el embarazo (no deseado)** ehl ehm-bah-RAH-soh (noh deh-seh-AH-doh)
racism	**el racismo** ehl rrah-SEES-moh
rape	**la violación** lah byoh-lah-SYOHN
runaway child	**el niño / la niña que huyó de casa** ehl NEE-nyoh / lah NEE-nyah keh oo-YOH deh KAH-sah
sexual harassment	**el acoso sexual** ehl ah-KOH-soh sehk-SWAHL
sexual relations	**las relaciones sexuales** lahs rreh-lah-SYOH-nehs sehk-SWAH-lehs
suicide	**el suicidio** ehl swee-SEE-dyoh

theft	**el robo**
	ehl RROH-boh
threat	**la amenaza**
	lah ah-meh-NAH-sah
unemployment	**el desempleo**
	ehl deh-sehm-PLEH-oh
unwanted child	**el hijo no deseado**
	ehl EE-hoh noh deh-seh-AH-doh
	la hija no deseada
	lah EE-hah noh deh-seh-AH-dah
vandalism	**el vandalismo**
	ehl bahn-dah-LEES-moh
venereal disease	**la enfermedad venérea**
	lah ehn-fehr-meh-DAHD beh-NEH-reh-ah
violence	**la violencia**
	lah byoh-LEHN-syah
violent behavior	**el comportamiento violento**
	ehl kohm-pohr-tah-MYEHN-toh
	byoh-LEHN-toh

Advice

Los consejos

Here are some expressions that may be useful when giving advice (**los consejos** [lohs kohn-SEH-hohs]) to students.

You should not ...	**Tú no debes...**
	too noh DEH-behs
drink alcoholic beverages	**beber bebidas alcohólicas**
	beh-BEHR beh-BEE-dahs
	ahl-KOH-lee-kahs
get together with those students	**juntarte con esos estudiantes**
	hoon-TAHR-teh kohn EH-sohs
	ehs-too-DYAHN-tehs
smoke cigarettes	**fumar cigarrillos**
	foo-MAHR see-gah-RREE-yohs
smoke marijuana	**fumar marihuana**
	foo-MAHR mah-ree-WAH-nah
use drugs	**usar drogas**
	oo-SAHR DROH-gahs

You can also use an impersonal expression + infinitive pattern.

It is important not to …	**Es importante no…**
	ehs eem-pohr-TAHN-teh noh
drink alcohol	**beber alcohol**
	beh-BEHR ahl-KOHL
drink and drive	**beber y conducir**
	beh-BEHR ee kohn-doo-SEER

GRAMMAR · Negative Sentences

Remember that to make a sentence negative in Spanish, you place **no** [noh] *before* the verb.

I do not go to school on weekends.	**No voy a la escuela los fines de semana.**
	noh BOH-ee ah lah ehs-KWEH-lah lohs
	FEE-nehs deh seh-MAH-nah

Other negative words that can be placed *before* the verb are the following.

nothing	**nada**
	NAH-dah
no one, nobody	**nadie**
	NAH-dyeh
none, no one, no	**ninguno/ninguna**
	neen-GOO-noh/neen-GOO-nah
never	**nunca**
	NOON-kah
neither	**tampoco**
	tahm-POH-koh

The negative words above can also be placed *after* the verb. However, this pattern requires that an additional negative word, usually **no** [noh], be placed *before* the verb. The meaning is exactly the same.

Nobody does the homework.	**Nadie hace la tarea.**
	NAH-dyeh AH-seh lah tah-REH-ah
	No hace la tarea nadie.
	noh AH-seh lah tah-REH-ah NAH-dyeh

The affirmative counterparts of these negative words are shown here.

NEGATIVE		AFFIRMATIVE	
nothing	**nada** NAH-dah	something	**algo** AHL-goh
no one, nobody	**nadie** NAH-dyeh	someone, anybody	**alguien** AHL-gyehn
none, no one, no	**ninguno/ninguna** neen-GOO-noh/ neen-GOO-nah	some, someone	**alguno/alguna** ahl-GOO-noh/ ahl-GOO-nah
		some, any	**algunos/algunas** ahl-GOO-nohs/ ahl-GOO-nahs
never	**nunca** NOON-kah	always	**siempre** SYEHM-preh
neither	**tampoco** tahm-POH-koh	also	**también** tahm-BYEHN

When used before a masculine singular noun, **ninguno** [neen-GOO-noh] changes to **ningún** [neen-GOON] and **alguno** [ahl-GOO-noh] changes to **algún** [ahl-GOON].

Compare the following pairs of sentences.

I don't understand anything.	**No comprendo nada.** noh kohm-PREHN-doh NAH-dah
I understand something.	**Comprendo algo.** kohm-PREHN-doh AHL-goh
No one is going.	**Nadie va.** NAH-dyeh bah
Someone is going.	**Alguien va.** AHL-gyehn bah
I have no money. / I don't have any money.	**No tengo ningún dinero.** noh TEHN-goh neen-GOON dee-NEH-roh
I have some money.	**Tengo algún dinero.** TEHN-goh ahl-GOON dee-NEH-roh
We don't read any poems.	**No leemos ningún poema.** noh leh-EH-mohs neen-GOON poh-EH-mah
We read some poems.	**Leemos algunos poemas.** leh-EH-mohs ahl-GOO-nohs poh-EH-mahs

I never arrive late.	**Nunca llego tarde.**
	NOON-kah YEH-goh TAHR-deh
I always arrive early.	**Siempre llego temprano.**
	SYEHM-preh YEH-goh tehm-PRAH-noh
I know how to sing also.	**Yo sé cantar también.**
	yoh seh kahn-TAHR tahm-BYEHN
I don't know how to sing either.	**Yo no sé cantar tampoco.**
	yoh noh seh kahn-TAHR tahm-POH-koh

Practice 7-2

A *Change the following sentences to negative sentences.*

1. Siempre estudio.

   _____

2. Nosotros comemos en la cafetería.

   _____

3. Alguien corre en el parque.

   _____

4. ¿Lees algunas novelas?

   _____

5. Ellos caminan en el parque también.

   _____

6. Alguien va a la fiesta.

   _____

B *Answer the following questions with as many negative words as possible.*

1. ¿Estás nervioso?

   _____

2. ¿Tienes mucho trabajo hoy?

   _____

3. ¿Visitas a tus tíos todos los días?

   _____

4. ¿Compras mucha ropa en la tienda?

   _____

5. ¿Comes el almuerzo en la escuela siempre?

6. ¿Hay alguien en el pasillo?

7. ¿Quieres beber algo?

8. ¿Vas a la escuela los sábados también?

Disciplinary Action

Las medidas de disciplina

You may have to inform students and their parents of disciplinary action (**las medidas de disciplina** [lahs meh-DEE-dahs deh dee-see-PLEE-nah]) taken by the school when their child breaks the school's rules.

You need to come to school immediately and pick up your child.	**Ud. tiene que venir a la escuela inmediatamente y recoger a su hijo/hija.** oohs-TEHD TYEH-neh keh beh-NEER ah lah ehs-KWEH-lah een-meh-dyah-tah-MEHN-teh ee rreh-koh-HEHR ah soo EE-hoh/EE-hah
Your (*male*) child is suspended for (*number*) days/weeks.	**Su hijo está suspendido de la escuela por (*number*) días/semanas.** soo EE-hoh ehs-TAH soos-pehn-DEE-doh deh lah ehs-KWEH-lah pohr... DEE-ahs/seh-MAH-nahs
Your (*female*) child is suspended for (*number*) days/weeks.	**Su hija está suspendida de la escuela por (*number*) días/semanas.** soo EE-hah ehs-TAH soos-pehn-DEE-dah deh lah ehs-KWEH-lah pohr... DEE-ahs/seh-MAH-nahs
Your child cannot return to school for (*number*) days/weeks.	**Su hijo/hija no puede regresar a la escuela por (*number*) días/semanas.** soo EE-hoh/EE-hah noh PWEH-deh rreh-greh-SAHR ah lah ehs-KWEH-lah pohr... DEE-ahs/seh-MAH-nahs

Your child has to spend all his/her free periods in the principal's office.	**Su hijo/hija tiene que pasar todos sus períodos libres en la oficina del director.** soo EE-hoh/EE-hah TYEH-neh keh pah-SAHR TOH-dohs soos peh-REE-oh-dohs LEE-brehs ehn lah oh-fee-SEE-nah dehl dee-rehk-TOHR
Your child has to participate in an anger management program.	**Su hijo/hija tiene que asistir a un programa para el control de la cólera.** soo EE-hoh/EE-hah TYEH-neh keh ah-sees-TEER ah oon proh-GRAH-mah PAH-rah ehl kohn-TROHL deh lah KOH-leh-rah
Your child has to attend a stop-smoking program.	**Su hijo/hija tiene que asistir a un programa para dejar de fumar.** soo EE-hoh/EE-hah TYEH-neh keh ah-sees-TEER ah oon proh-GRAH-mah PAH-rah deh-HAHR deh foo-MAHR
Your child is not allowed to return to this school.	**Su hijo/hija no puede regresar a esta escuela.** soo EE-hoh/EE-hah noh PWEH-deh rreh-greh-SAHR ah EHS-tah ehs-KWEH-lah
You must transfer your child to another school.	**Ud. tiene que trasladar a su hijo/hija a otra escuela.** oos-TEHD TYEH-neh keh trahs-lah-DAHR ah soo EE-hoh/EE-hah ah OH-trah ehs-KWEH-lah

Listed here are some of the programs available to help students deal with disciplinary problems.

after school program	**el programa que ofrece diferentes actividades educacionales o recreativas después de las clases** ehl proh-GRAH-mah keh oh-FREH-seh dee-feh-REHN-tehs ahk-tee-bee-DAH-dehs eh-doo-kah-syoh-NAH-lehs oh rreh-kreh-ah-TEE-bahs dehs-PWEHS deh lahs KLAH-sehs
anger management program	**el programa para controlar la cólera** ehl proh-GRAH-mah PAH-rah kohn-troh-LAHR lah KOH-leh-rah
conflict resolution program	**el programa para resolver conflictos** ehl proh-GRAH-mah PAH-rah rreh-sohl-BEHR kohn-FLEEK-tohs

counseling	**el asesoramiento** ehl ah-seh-soh-rah-MYEHN-toh
peer mediation program	**el programa que usa a otros jóvenes como intermediarios en conflictos** ehl proh-GRAH-mah keh oo-sah ah OH-trohs HOH-beh-nehs KOH-moh een-tehr-meh-DYAH-ryohs ehn kohn-FLEEK-tohs

Other helpful information can be found in the section dealing with Rules of Behavior in Chapter 5, pages 192–193.

After School Jobs

Los trabajos después de las clases

Although in some Spanish-speaking countries students work while they are attending school, you may need to explain to the student and to his/her parents what is involved in getting an after school job (**el trabajo después de las clases** [ehl trah-BAH-hoh dehs-PWEHS deh lahs KLAH-sehs]).

Students can only work part-time.	**Los estudiantes sólo pueden trabajar a tiempo parcial.** lohs ehs-too-DYAHN-tehs SOH-loh PWEH-dehn trah-bah-HAHR ah TYEHM-poh pahr-SYAHL
There are many opportunities in the neighborhood.	**Hay muchas oportunidades en el barrio.** AH-ee MOO-chahs oh-pohr-too-nee-DAH-dehs ehn ehl BAH-rryoh
It is important that he/she keep up with his/her work/homework for school.	**Es importante que él/ella se mantenga al tanto de su trabajo/tarea para la escuela.** ehs eem-pohr-TAHN-teh keh ehl/EH-yah seh mahn-TEHN-gah ahl TAHN-toh deh soo trah-BAH-hoh/tah-REH-ah PAH-rah lah ehs-KWEH-lah

In the first set of examples that follow, the comments are addressed to the parents. A second set of examples provides the phrasing you will need if you are addressing the student.

Your child needs …	**Su hijo/hija necesita…** soo EE-hoh/EE-hah neh-seh-SEE-tah
to get a work permit	**obtener un permiso de trabajo** ohb-teh-NEHR oon pehr-MEE-soh deh trah-BAH-hoh

Your child needs …	**Su hijo/hija necesita…**
	soo EE-hoh/EE-hah neh-seh-SEE-tah
to prepare a résumé	**preparar un resumen de su educación y su experiencia de trabajo**
	preh-pah-RAHR oon rreh-soo-mehn deh soo eh-doo-kah-SYOHN ee soo ehs-peh-RYEHN-syah deh trah-BAH-hoh
to request references from one of his/her teachers	**pedir referencias de uno de sus maestros**
	peh-DEER rreh-feh-REHN-syahs deh oo-noh deh soos mah-EHS-trohs
to request an appointment	**pedir una cita**
	peh-DEER oo-nah SEE-tah
to request an interview	**pedir una entrevista**
	peh-DEER oo-nah ehn-treh-BEES-tah
to fill out a job application	**llenar una solicitud de empleo**
	yeh-NAHR oo-nah soh-lee-see-TOOD deh ehm-PLEH-oh
to have a driver's license	**tener una licencia de conducir**
	teh-NEHR oo-nah lee-SEHN-syah deh kohn-doo-SEER
to go through training	**pasar por un entrenamiento**
	pah-SAHR pohr oon ehn-treh-nah-MYEHN-toh
You need …	**Tú necesitas…**
	too neh-seh-SEE-tahs
to get a work permit	**obtener un permiso de trabajo**
	ohb-teh-NEHR oon pehr-MEE-soh deh trah-BAH-hoh
to prepare a résumé	**preparar un resumen de tu educación y tu experiencia de trabajo**
	preh-pah-RAHR oon rreh-soo-mehn deh too eh-doo-kah-SYOHN ee too ehs-peh-RYEHN-syah deh trah-BAH-hoh
to request references from one of your teachers	**pedir referencias de uno de tus maestros**
	peh-DEER rreh-feh-REHN-syahs deh oo-noh deh toos mah-EHS-trohs
to request an appointment	**pedir una cita**
	peh-DEER oo-nah SEE-tah
to request an interview	**pedir una entrevista**
	peh-DEER oo-nah ehn-treh-BEES-tah

to fill out a job application	**llenar una solicitud de empleo**
	yeh-NAHR OO-nah soh-lee-see-TOOD deh ehm-PLEH-oh
to have a driver's license	**tener una licencia de conducir**
	teh-NEHR OO-nah lee-SEHN-syah deh kohn-doo-SEER
to go through training	**pasar por un entrenamiento**
	pah-SAHR pohr oon ehn-treh-nah-MYEHN-toh

Practice 7-3

Complete the following sentences with the Spanish equivalent of the phrase in parentheses.

1. Su hija _____ (*is suspended*) por tres días.

2. Ella necesita _____ (*to fill out a job application*).

3. Su hijo sólo puede trabajar _____ (*part-time*).

4. Todos los estudiantes participan en _____ (*an anger management program*).

5. Si quieres trabajar, tienes que _____ (*go through training*).

6. En la oficina puedes obtener _____ (*a work permit*).

7. Cuando vas a buscar un trabajo, tienes que estar preparada para _____ (*an interview*).

8. Es necesario _____ (*to keep up with your school work*).

Career Plans

Los planes para una carrera

Students often need guidance on the different career opportunities available to them. The following questions will help you open a conversation about career plans (**los planes para una carrera** [lohs PLAH-nehs PAH-rah OO-nah kah-RREH-rah]) with the student. There are many other questions you can ask to assess the student's interests; these are just a few to begin the dialogue.

What would you like to do after finishing high school?	**¿Qué quisieras / te gustaría hacer después de terminar la escuela secundaria?**
	keh kee-SYEH-rahs / teh goos-tah-REE-ah ah-SEHR dehs-PWEHS deh tehr-mee-NAHR lah ehs-KWEH-lah seh-koon-DAH-ryah
Is it more important for you to be happy or to make lots of money?	**¿Es más importante para ti ser feliz o ganar mucho dinero?**
	ehs mahs eem-pohr-TAHN-teh PAH-rah tee sehr feh-LEES oh gah-NAHR MOO-choh dee-NEH-roh

Occupations and Professions
Las ocupaciones y las profesiones

The following is a list of some of the most common occupations and professions (**las ocupaciones y las profesiones** [lahs oh-koo-pah-SYOH-nehs ee lahs proh-feh-SYOH-nehs]) you may want to discuss with your students and their parents.

accountant	**el contador / la contadora** ehl kohn-tah-DOHR / lah kohn-tah-DOH-rah
actor	**el actor** ehl ahk-TOHR
actress	**la actriz** lah ahk-TREES
architect	**el arquitecto / la arquitecta** ehl ahr-kee-TEHK-toh / lah ahr-kee-TEHK-tah
author	**el autor / la autora** ehl ah-oo-TOHR / lah ah-oo-TOH-rah
businessman	**el hombre de negocios** ehl OHM-breh deh neh-GOH-syohs
businesswoman	**la mujer de negocios** lah moo-HEHR deh neh-GOH-syohs
carpenter	**el carpintero / la carpintera** ehl kahr-peen-TEH-roh / lah kahr-peen-TEH-rah
cashier	**el cajero / la cajera** ehl kah-HEH-roh / lah kah-HEH-rah
cook	**el cocinero / la cocinera** ehl koh-see-NEH-roh / lah koh-see-NEH-rah

dentist	**el/la dentista**
	ehl/lah dehn-TEES-tah
doctor	**el doctor / la doctora**
	ehl dohk-TOHR / lah dohk-TOH-rah
	el médico / la médica
	ehl MEH-dee-koh / lah MEH-dee-kah
driver	**el conductor / la conductora**
	ehl kohn-dook-TOHR / lah kohn-dook-TOH-rah
engineer	**el ingeniero / la ingeniera**
	ehl een-heh-NYEH-roh / lah een-heh-NYEH-rah
firefighter	**el bombero / la bombera**
	ehl bohm-BEH-roh / lah bohm-BEH-rah
flight attendant	**el/la asistente de vuelo**
	ehl/lah ah-sees-TEHN-teh deh BWEH-loh
gardener	**el jardinero / la jardinera**
	ehl hahr-dee-NEH-roh / lah hahr-dee-NEH-rah
hairdresser	**el peluquero / la peluquera**
	ehl peh-loo-KEH-roh / lah peh-loo-KEH-rah
interpreter	**el/la intérprete**
	ehl/lah een-TEHR-preh-teh
journalist	**el reportero / la reportera**
	ehl rreh-pohr-TEH-roh / lah rreh-pohr-TEH-rah
lawyer	**el abogado / la abogada**
	ehl ah-boh-GAH-doh / lah ah-boh-GAH-dah
mechanic	**el mecánico / la mecánica**
	ehl meh-KAH-nee-koh / lah meh-KAH-nee-kah
nurse	**el enfermero / la enfermera**
	ehl ehn-fehr-MEH-roh / lah ehn-fehr-MEH-rah
painter	**el pintor / la pintora**
	ehl peen-TOHR / lah peen-TOH-rah
photographer	**el fotógrafo / la fotógrafa**
	ehl foh-TOH-grah-foh / lah foh-TOH-grah-fah
plumber	**el plomero / la plomera**
	ehl ploh-MEH-roh / lah ploh-MEH-rah

police officer	**el policía / la mujer policía**
	ehl poh-lee-SEE-ah /
	lah moo-HEHR poh-lee-SEE-ah
programmer	**el programador / la programadora**
	ehl proh-grah-mah-DOHR /
	lah proh-grah-mah-DOH-rah
salesperson	**el vendedor / la vendedora**
	ehl behn-deh-DOHR /
	lah behn-deh-DOH-rah
secretary	**el secretario / la secretaria**
	ehl seh-kreh-TAH-ryoh /
	lah seh-kreh-TAH-ryah
singer	**el/la cantante**
	ehl/lah kahn-TAHN-teh
surgeon	**el cirujano / la cirujana**
	ehl see-roo-HAH-noh /
	lah see-roo-HAH-nah
teacher	**el maestro / la maestra**
	ehl mah-EHS-troh / lah mah-EHS-trah
trainer	**el entrenador / la entrenadora**
	ehl ehn-treh-nah-DOHR /
	lah ehn-treh-nah-DOH-rah
writer	**el escritor / la escritora**
	ehl ehs-kree-TOHR / lah ehs-kree-TOH-rah

The Army (**las fuerzas armadas** [lahs FWEHR-sahs ahr-MAH-dahs]), the Air Force (**las fuerzas aéreas** [lahs FWEHR-sahs ah-EH-reh-ahs]), and the Navy (**la marina de guerra** [lah mah-REE-nah deh GEH-rrah]) may also be viable options for your students. In most recruiting stations (**las oficinas de reclutamiento** [lahs oh-fee-SEE-nahs deh rreh-kloo-tah-MYEHN-toh]) they have Spanish-speaking personnel (**el personal hispanohablante** [ehl pehr-soh-NAHL ees-pah-noh-ah-BLAHN-teh]).

In Chapter 2, pages 66–68, you will find a list of professions and occupations found in the school setting.

GRAMMAR · Demonstrative Adjectives

Demonstrative adjectives point out specific people and things. In Spanish, they precede the noun they are pointing out and agree with it in gender and number.

The demonstrative adjective "this" has four forms in Spanish.

- **este** [EHS-teh]   **este reportero** ("this journalist")
  (*masculine singular*)   EHS-teh rreh-pohr-TEH-roh

- **esta** [EHS-tah]
  (*feminine singular*)

  esta reportera ("this journalist")
  EHS-tah rreh-pohr-TEH-rah

- **estos** [EHS-tohs]
  (*masculine plural*)

  estos reporteros ("these journalists")
  EHS-tohs rreh-pohr-TEH-rohs

- **estas** [EHS-tahs]
  (*feminine plural*)

  estas reporteras ("these journalists")
  EHS-tahs rreh-pohr-TEH-rahs

This photographer is my favorite.	**Este fotógrafo es mi favorito.** EHS-teh foh-TOH-grah-foh ehs mee fah-boh-REE-toh
These secretaries are very hardworking.	**Estas secretarias son muy trabajadoras.** EHS-tahs seh-kreh-TAH-ryahs sohn MOO-ee trah-bah-hah-DOH-rahs

There are two words for the demonstrative adjective "that" in Spanish.

When referring to something or someone far from you, but near the person to whom you are speaking, use **ese** [EH-seh].

When referring to something or someone far from you, and also far from the person with whom you are speaking, use **aquel** [ah-KEHL].

Ese and **aquel** both have four forms.

- **ese** [EH-seh]
  (*masculine singular*)

  ese arquitecto ("that architect")
  EH-seh ahr-kee-TEHK-toh

- **esa** [EH-sah]
  (*feminine singular*)

  esa arquitecta ("that architect")
  EH-sah ahr-kee-TEHK-tah

- **esos** [EH-sohs]
  (*masculine plural*)

  esos arquitectos ("those architects")
  EH-sohs ahr-kee-TEHK-tohs

- **esas** [EH-sahs]
  (*feminine plural*)

  esas arquitectas ("those architects")
  EH-sahs ahr-kee-TEHK-tahs

- **aquel** [ah-KEHL]
  (*masculine singular*)

  aquel ingeniero ("that engineer")
  ah-KEHL een-heh-NYEH-roh

- **aquella** [ah-KEH-yah]
  (*feminine singular*)

  aquella ingeniera ("that engineer")
  ah-KEH-yah een-heh-NYEH-rah

- **aquellos** [ah-KEH-yohs]
  (*masculine plural*)

  aquellos ingenieros ("those engineers")
  ah-KEH-yohs een-heh-NYEH-rohs

- **aquellas** [ah-KEH-yahs]
  (*feminine plural*)

  aquellas ingenieras ("those engineers")
  ah-KEH-yahs een-heh-NYEH-rahs

That woman is an excellent dentist.	**Esa mujer es una dentista excelente.** EH-sah moo-HEHR ehs OO-nah dehn-TEES-tah ehk-seh-LEHN-teh

| Those firefighters are very brave. | **Esos bomberos son muy valientes.**
EH-sohs bohm-BEH-rohs sohn MOO-ee bah-LYEHN-tehs |
| That mechanic is honest. | **Aquel mecánico es honesto.**
ah-KEHL meh-KAH-nee-koh ehs oh-NEHS-toh |

Practice 7-4

A *You are talking to one of your students about his/her interests. Using ¿Te gusta...?, ask him/her a question related to each of the following professions.*

MODELO   maestro   *¿Te gusta trabajar con niños?*

1. cocinero

   _____

2. actriz

   _____

3. fotógrafo

   _____

4. jardinera

   _____

5. mujer de negocios

   _____

B *Complete each sentence with the Spanish equivalent of the word in parentheses.*

1. _____ (This) libro es nuevo.

2. Quiero _____ (those—far from you and from the person you are talking to) mochilas.

3. _____ (This) cajera es muy eficiente.

4. _____ (That) chica es mi mejor amiga.

5. Me gustan mucho _____ (these) pantalones.

6. El libro es de _____ (that—far from you and from the person you are talking to) autor.

7. _____ (Those) mujeres son médicas.

8. _____ (Those) restaurantes son mexicanos.

College Planning

Los planes para la universidad

Planning for college is a daunting experience for any student. It is even more daunting for students and parents who may not be familiar with the application process, admissions, and financial aid. There is an enormous amount of information that needs to be conveyed to the parent with regard to college planning (**los planes para la universidad** [lohs PLAH-nehs PAH-rah lah oo-nee-behr-see-DAHD]). We have included here some of the important issues you may need to relate to the parents, but this is not a complete list.

Important Issues to Consider

Algunos asuntos importantes que se deben considerar

Finding out what the student and his/her parents are interested in with regard to college, as well as what options are available, are very important topics to explore. Here are a few questions that will allow you to start the dialogue. Since it is often the parents who come to talk with the counselor about their child's college plans, the questions are addressed to the parents. The verb form you need to use if you are addressing the student directly is in parentheses.

Is your child (Are you) planning to attend a university?	**¿Piensa su hijo/hija (Piensas) asistir a una universidad?** PYEHN-sah soo EE-hoh/EE-hah (PYEHN-sahs) ah-sees-TEER an oo-nah oo-nee-behr-see-DAHD
What university is he/she (are you) considering?	**¿Qué universidad está (estás) considerando?** keh oo-nee-behr-see-DAHD ehs-TAH (ehs-TAHS) kohn-see-deh-RAHN-doh
Do you want your child (Do you want) to attend a university near your home?	**¿Quiere que su hijo/su hija asista (Quieres asistir) a una universidad cerca de casa?** KYEH-reh keh soo EE-hoh/EE-hah ah-SEES-tah (KYEH-rehs ah-sees-TEER) ah oo-nah oo-nee-behr-see-DAHD SEHR-kah deh KAH-sah
You can take a virtual tour of the university using your computer.	**Se puede hacer una visita virtual a la universidad usando la computadora.** seh PWEH-deh ah-SEHR oo-nah bee-SEE-tah beer-TWAHL ah lah oo-nee-behr-see-DAHD oo-SAHN-doh lah kohm-poo-tah-DOH-rah

Many universities have programs to attract minorities.	**Muchas universidades tienen programas para atraer minorías.** moo-chahs oo-nee-behr-see-DAH-dehs TYEH-nehn proh-GRAH-mahs PAH-rah ah-trah-EHR mee-noh-REE-ahs
The requirements for admission vary at each university.	**Los requisitos para el ingreso varían en cada universidad.** lohs rreh-kee-SEE-tohs PAH-rah ehl een-GREH-soh bah-REE-ahn ehn KAH-dah oo-nee-behr-see-DAHD

General Requirements
Los requisitos generales

Following is a list of words and phrases that will be helpful as you discuss many of the issues dealing with the general requirements (**los requisitos generales** [lohs rreh-kee-SEE-tohs heh-neh-RAH-lehs]) of college admissions.

academic prize	**el premio académico** ehl PREH-myoh ah-kah-DEH-mee-koh
admission exams	**los exámenes de ingreso** lohs ehk-SAH-meh-nehs deh een-GREH-soh
application	**la solicitud** lah soh-lee-see-TOOD
catalogue	**el catálogo** ehl kah-TAH-loh-goh
deadline	**la fecha límite** lah FEH-chah LEE-mee-teh
experience outside school	**la experiencia fuera de la escuela** lah ehs-peh-RYEHN-syah FWEH-rah deh lah ehs-KWEH-lah
financial aid	**la ayuda financiera** lah ah-YOO-dah fee-nahn-SYEH-rah
financial aid application	**la solicitud de ayuda financiera** lah soh-lee-see-TOOD deh ah-YOO-dah fee-nahn-SYEH-rah
form	**el formulario** ehl fohr-moo-LAH-ryoh
hobby	**el pasatiempo favorito** ehl pah-sah-TYEHM-poh fah-boh-REE-toh
interview	**la entrevista** lah ehn-treh-BEES-tah

letters of recommendation	**las cartas de recomendación** lahs KAHR-tahs deh rreh-koh-mehn-dah-SYOHN
personal essay	**el ensayo personal** ehl ehn-SAH-yoh pehr-soh-NAHL
success	**el éxito** ehl EHK-see-toh
summer jobs	**los trabajos de verano** lohs trah-BAH-hohs deh beh-RAH-noh
transcript	**la relación de notas** lah rreh-lah-SYOHN deh NOH-tahs
volunteer work	**el trabajo voluntario** ehl trah-BAH-hoh boh-loon-TAH-ryoh

Standardized Testing
Las pruebas uniformes

Most universities require students to take standardized tests so that the institution has an assessment of the student that is independent of the student's high school testing.

A standardized test is a test administered according to standardized procedures that assesses a student's aptitude compared to a standard.

Una prueba uniforme es una prueba que se administra bajo procedimientos uniformes y que asesora la capacidad de un estudiante comparándola con una norma.
oo-nah PRWEH-bah oo-nee-FOHR-meh ehs oo-nah PRWEH-bah keh seh ahd-mee-NEES-trah BAH-hoh proh-seh-dee-MYEHN-tohs oo-nee-FOHR-mehs ee keh ah-seh-SOH-rah lah kah-pah-see-DAHD deh oon ehs-too-DYAHN-teh kohm-pah-RAHN-doh-lah kohn oo-nah NOHR-mah

It is typical for colleges and universities to require students to take the SAT exams. These exams do not exist in the Spanish-speaking world, so you may have to explain what they are.

SAT test (Scholastic Aptitude Test)

el examen de SAT / de aptitud escolar
ehl ehk-SAH-mehn deh ehs EH-ee tee / deh ahp-tee-TOOD ehs-koh-LAHR

The Scholastic Aptitude Test is a test used to predict the degree of success in college.

El examen de aptitud escolar es un examen que se usa para predecir el grado de éxito en la universidad.
ehl ehk-SAH-mehn deh ahp-tee-TOOD ehs-koh-LAHR ehs oon ehk-SAH-mehn keh seh OO-sah PAH-rah preh-deh-SEER ehl GRAH-doh deh EHK-see-toh ehn lah OO-nee-behr-see-DAHD

There are also SAT tests on specific subjects.

También hay exámenes de SAT (de aptitud) en asignaturas específicas.
tahm-BYEHN AH-ee ehk-SAH-meh-nehs deh ehs EH-ee tee (deh ahp-tee-TOOD) ehn ah-seeg-nah-TOO-rahs ehs-peh-SEE-fee-kahs

To take the exam, one needs to register by (date).

Para hacer el examen tiene que matricularse para el (date).
PAH-rah ah-SEHR ehl ehk-SAH-mehn TYEH-neh keh mah-tree-koo-LAHR-seh PAH-rah ehl

The maximum score a student can receive is (number).

La nota más alta que un estudiante puede recibir es (number).
lah NOH-tah mahs AHL-tah keh oon ehs-too-DYAHN-teh PWEH-deh rreh-see-BEER ehs

(number) is a very good score.

(number) es una nota muy buena.
ehs OO-nah NOH-tah MOO-ee BWEH-nah

(number) is a low score.

(number) es una nota baja.
ehs OO-nah NOH-tah BAH-hah

Your child should take the test again.

Su hijo/hija debe hacer el examen de nuevo.
soo EE-hoh/EE-hah DEH-beh ah-SEHR ehl ehk-SAH-mehn deh NWEH-boh

There are places that offer courses to prepare oneself for the test.

Hay lugares que ofrecen cursos para prepararse para el examen.
AH-ee loo-GAH-rehs keh oh-FREH-sehn KOOR-sohs PAH-rah preh-pah-RAHR-seh PAH-rah ehl ehk-SAH-mehn

Students can also take advanced courses while still in high school. The Advanced Placement courses and exams, sometimes called AP courses and exams, will also need to be explained.

The AP courses are advanced courses in a number of subjects.	**Los cursos de AP son cursos avanzados en varias asignaturas.** lohs KOOR-sohs deh EH-ee pee sohn KOOR-sohs ah-bahn-SAH-dohs ehn BAH-ryahs ah-seeg-nah-TOO-rahs
The courses are very demanding.	**Los cursos son muy exigentes.** lohs KOOR-sohs sohn MOO-ee ehk-see-HEHN-tehs
Universities like applicants who have taken these courses.	**A las universidades les gustan los candidatos que han tomado estos cursos.** ah lahs oo-nee-behr-see-DAH-dehs lehs GOOS-tahn lohs kahn-dee-DAH-tohs keh ahn toh-MAH-doh EHS-tohs KOOR-sohs
Some universities will give credit to students who do well on an AP exam.	**Algunas universidades les dan crédito a los estudiantes que salen bien en un examen de AP.** ahl-GOO-nahs oo-nee-behr-see-DAH-dehs lehs dahn KREH-dee-toh ah lohs ehs-too-DYAHN-tehs keh SAH-lehn byehn ehn oon ehk-SAH-mehn deh EH-ee pee

Paying for College
Para pagar por la universidad

Parents are generally very concerned about how to pay for their child's college education (**pagar por la universidad** [pah-GAHR pohr lah oo-nee-behr-see-DAHD]). You can reassure them that there are good possibilities for financial aid.

How do you plan to pay for college?	**¿Cómo piensan Uds. pagar por los estudios?** KOH-moh PYEHN-sahn OOS-TEH-dehs pah-GAHR pohr lohs ehs-TOO-dyohs
Do you know the different organizations that offer scholarships?	**¿Conoce Ud. las diferentes organizaciones que ofrecen becas?** koh-NOH-seh OOS-TEHD lahs dee-feh-REHN-tehs ohr-gah-nee-sah-SYOH-nehs keh oh-FREH-sehn BEH-kahs
Often the unions offer scholarships.	**Muchas veces los sindicatos ofrecen becas.** MOO-chahs BEH-sehs lohs seen-dee-KAH-tohs oh-FREH-sehn BEH-kahs
The government offers grants and loans.	**El gobierno ofrece becas y préstamos.** ehl goh-BYEHR-noh oh-FREH-seh BEH-kahs ee PREHS-tah-mohs

Financial aid depends on your income and your need.	**La ayuda financiera depende de sus ingresos y de su necesidad.** lah ah-YOO-dah fee-nahn-SYEH-rah deh-PEHN-deh deh soos een-GREH-sohs ee deh soo neh-seh-see-DAHD

GRAMMAR · Talking About What Just Happened

When talking about something that just happened, such as something that you just did, you use the present tense of the verb **acabar de** [ah-kah-BAHR deh] + an infinitive.

He has just taken the test.	**Él acaba de hacer el examen.** ehl ah-KAH-bah deh ah-SEHR ehl ehk-SAH-mehn
They have just started their studies.	**Ellos acaban de empezar sus estudios.** EH-yohs ah-KAH-bahn deh ehm-peh-SAHR soos ehs-TOO-dyohs

Practice 7-5

Complete the following sentences with the Spanish equivalent of the phrase in parentheses.

1. _____ (*We have just*) recibir una beca.

2. _____ (*He has just*) pedir una solicitud para la universidad.

3. _____ (*She has just*) tener una entrevista.

4. _____ (*They have just*) hacer el examen de SAT.

5. _____ (*I have just*) recibir una nota excelente.

Students with Special Needs

Los estudiantes con necesidades especiales

The counselor, together with the school nurse, is usually the person in school who is most familiar with students who have special needs (**los estudiantes con necesidades especiales** [lohs ehs-too-DYAHN-tehs kohn neh-seh-see-DAH-dehs ehs-peh-SYAH-lehs]). The counselor helps to inform the teachers and, together with the teachers and the family, helps to accommodate the student in order to make it possible for him/her to achieve his/her full potential. Students with special needs may suffer from a variety of different illnesses and birth defects, including the following.

AIDS
el SIDA
ehl SEE-dah

asthma
el asma
ehl AHS-mah

attention deficit disorder
el desorden deficitario de la atención
ehl dehs-OHR-dehn deh-fee-see-TAH-ryoh
deh ah-tehn-SYOHN

autism
el autismo / el trastorno generalizado del desarrollo
ehl ah-oo-TEES-moh / ehl trahs-TOHR-noh
heh-neh-rah-lee-SAH-doh dehl
deh-sah-RROH-yoh

blindness
la ceguera
lah seh-GEH-rah

cancer
el cáncer
ehl KAHN-sehr

cerebral palsy
la parálisis cerebral
lah pah-RAH-lee-sees seh-reh-BRAHL

diabetes
la diabetes
lah dyah-BEH-tehs

Down's syndrome
el síndrome de Down
ehl SEEN-droh-meh deh DAH-oon

dyslexia
la dislexia
lah dees-LEHK-syah

emotional problems
los problemas emocionales
lohs proh-BLEH-mahs
eh-moh-syoh-NAH-lehs

epilepsy
la epilepsia
lah eh-pee-LEHP-syah

fainting spells
los desmayos
lohs dehs-MAH-yohs

hearing problems
la sordera / la pérdida de capacidad auditiva
lah sohr-DEH-rah / lah PEHR-dee-dah deh
kah-pah-see-DAHD ah-oo-dee-TEE-bah

high blood pressure
la presión (arterial) alta
lah preh-SYOHN (ahr-teh-RYAHL) AHL-tah

infectious disease
la enfermedad infecciosa
lah ehn-fehr-meh-DAHD
een-fehk-SYOH-sah

learning disability	la discapacidad de aprendizaje
	lah dees-kah-pah-see-DAHD deh ah-prehn-dee-SAH-heh
leukemia	la leucemia
	lah leh-oo-SEH-myah
low blood pressure	la presión (arterial) baja
	lah preh-SYOHN (ahr-teh-RYAHL) BAH-hah
mental retardation	el retraso mental
	ehl rreh-TRAH-soh mehn-TAHL
migraine	la jaqueca
	lah hah-KEH-kah
multiple sclerosis	la esclerosis múltiple
	lah ehs-kleh-ROH-sees MOOL-tee-pleh
muscular dystrophy	la distrofia muscular
	lah dees-TROH-fyah moos-koo-LAHR
obesity	la obesidad
	lah oh-beh-see-DAHD
paralysis	la parálisis
	lah pah-RAH-lee-sees
rheumatism	el reumatismo
	ehl rreh-oo-mah-TEES-moh
speaking problems	los trastornos del habla y el lenguaje
	lohs trahs-TOHR-nohs dehl AH-blah ee ehl lehn-GWAH-heh
spina bifida	la espina bífida
	lah ehs-PEE-nah BEE-fee-dah
visual impediments	los impedimentos visuales
	lohs eem-peh-dee-MEHN-tohs bee-SWAH-lehs

Special Needs
Las necesidades especiales

When talking to parents about any special need (**la necesidad especial** [lah neh-seh-see-DAHD ehs-peh-SYAHL]) that the child might have, you will need to find out what extra accommodations or attention he/she might need during the school day.

Does your child need …?	¿Necesita su hijo/hija…?
	neh-seh-SEE-tah soo EE-hoh/EE-hah
to take medicines regularly	tomar medicinas regularmente
	toh-MAHR meh-dee-SEE-nahs rreh-goo-lahr-MEHN-teh

to sit in the front of the class	**sentarse al frente de la clase** sehn-TAHR-seh ahl FREHN-teh deh lah KLAH-seh
to go to the bathroom frequently	**ir al baño frecuentemente** eer ahl BAH-nyoh freh-kwehn-teh-MEHN-teh
to use a hearing aid	**usar un audífono / aparato de oído** OO-SAHR oon ah-oo-DEE-foh-noh / ah-pah-RAH-toh deh oh-EE-doh
to use a wheelchair	**usar una silla de ruedas** OO-SAHR OO-nah SEE-yah deh RRWEH-dahs
more time for tests	**más tiempo para los exámenes** mahs TYEHM-poh PAH-rah lohs ehk-SAH-meh-nehs

Learning Disability
La discapacidad de aprendizaje

If a child shows a number of problems with learning, then the parents and teacher will need to consider the possibility that the child has a learning disability (**la discapacidad de aprendizaje** [lah dees-kah-pah-see-DAHD deh ah-prehn-dee-SAH-heh]). Indications of such problems that you may want to share with the parents are the following.

Your child …	**Su hijo/hija...** SOO EE-hoh/EE-hah
has trouble connecting letters to their sound	**tiene problemas en relacionar las letras con su sonido** TYEH-neh proh-BLEH-mahs ehn rreh-lah-syoh-NAHR lahs LEH-trahs kohn SOO soh-NEE-doh
does not understand what he/she reads	**no comprende lo que él/ella lee** noh kohm-PREHN-deh loh keh ehl/EH-yah LEH-eh
has a great deal of trouble with spelling	**tiene gran dificultad con el deletreo** TYEH-neh grahn dee-fee-kool-TAHD kohn ehl deh-leh-TREH-oh
confuses math symbols	**confunde los signos de matemáticas** kohn-FOON-deh lohs SEEG-nohs deh mah-teh-MAH-tee-kahs
misreads numbers	**interpreta mal los números** een-tehr-PREH-tah mahl lohs NOO-meh-rohs

If a child has unexpected problems learning to read, write, listen, speak, or do math, then you may want to suggest that the child be evaluated to see if he or she has a learning disability.

Your child needs to be evaluated to see if he/she has a learning disability.	**Su hijo/hija debe pasar una evaluación para determinar si él/ella tiene una discapacidad de aprendizaje.** soo EE-hoh/EE-hah DEH-beh pah-SAHR oo-nah eh-bah-lwah-SYOHN PAH-rah deh-tehr-mee-NAHR see ehl/EH-yah TYEH-neh oo-nah dees-kah-pah-see-DAHD deh ah-prehn-dee-SAH-heh

Although the information is not in Spanish, the National Center for Learning Disabilities is a good place for parents to start learning about this topic. Its Web address is **www.ncld.org**. In addition, several governmental agencies have information in Spanish.

Homeschooling

La escuela en casa

Some parents may not be familiar with the concept of homeschooling (**la escuela en casa** [lah ehs-KWEH-lah ehn KAH-sah]). The following phrases will help you explain it to them.

When your child cannot come to school for a long period of time, he/she can receive instruction at home.	**Cuando su hijo/hija no puede venir a la escuela por un período largo de tiempo, él/ella puede recibir instrucción en casa.** KWAHN-doh soo EE-hoh/EE-hah noh PWEH-deh beh-NEER ah lah ehs-KWEH-lah pohr oon peh-REE-oh-doh LAHR-goh deh TYEHM-poh, ehl/EH-yah PWEH-deh rreh-see-BEER eens-trook-SYOHN ehn KAH-sah
The state can provide an instructor free of charge.	**El estado puede proveer un instructor / una instructora gratis.** ehl ehs-TAH-doh PWEH-deh proh-beh-EHR oon eens-trook-TOHR / oo-nah eens-trook-TOH-rah GRAH-tees

| Your child can take all the tests at home, too. | **Su hijo/hija puede hacer los exámenes en casa también.** |
| | soo EE-hoh/EE-hah PWEH-deh ah-SEHR lohs ehk-SAH-meh-nehs ehn KAH-sah tahm-BYEHN |

| If your child receives instruction at home, he/she is not going to lose the year. | **Si su hijo/hija recibe instrucción en casa no va a perder el año.** |
| | see soo EE-hoh/EE-hah rreh-SEE-beh eens-trook-SYOHN ehn KAH-sah noh bah ah pehr-DEHR ehl AH-nyoh |

Summer School

La escuela de verano

For some students, summer school (**la escuela de verano** [lah ehs-KWEH-lah deh beh-RAH-noh]) is a necessity. Parents need to understand what it entails.

| Students need to go to summer school when they fail a course. | **Los estudiantes tienen que ir a la escuela de verano cuando suspenden una asignatura.** |
| | lohs ehs-too-DYAHN-tehs TYEH-nehn keh eer ah lah ehs-KWEH-lah deh beh-RAH-noh KWAHN-doh soos-PEHN-dehn oo-nah ah-seeg-nah-TOO-rah |

| Your child needs to take (*number*) courses in summer school. | **Su hijo/hija necesita tomar** (*number*) **cursos en la escuela de verano.** |
| | soo EE-hoh/EE-hah neh-seh-SEE-tah toh-MAHR… KOOR-sohs ehn lah ehs-KWEH-lah deh beh-RAH-noh |

| Summer school lasts (*number*) weeks. | **La escuela de verano dura** (*number*) **semanas.** |
| | lah ehs-KWEH-lah deh beh-RAH-noh DOO-rah… seh-MAH-nahs |

| If he/she passes summer school, he/she can go on to the next grade. | **Si él/ella aprueba los cursos de la escuela de verano, puede avanzar al próximo grado.** |
| | see ehl/EH-yah ah-PRWEH-bah lohs KOOR-sohs deh lah ehs-KWEH-lah deh beh-RAH-noh, PWEH-deh ah-bahn-SAHR ahl PROHK-see-moh GRAH-doh |

He/She needs to pass/take that course to graduate.	**Él/Ella necesita aprobar/tomar ese curso para graduarse.** ehl/EH-yah neh-seh-SEE-tah ah-proh-BAHR/toh-MAHR EH-seh KOOR-soh PAH-rah grah-DWAHR-seh

General Education Diploma
El diploma de educación general

The General Education Diploma (**el diploma de educación general** [ehl dee-PLOH-mah deh eh-doo-kah-SYOHN heh-neh-RAHL]), also known as the GED [yee ee dee], could be an alternative for those students who cannot complete their high school education in a regular school. This concept may be new to some parents.

Your child can study and take the GED exam.	**Su hijo/hija puede estudiar y hacer el examen de GED.** SOO EE-hoh/EE-hah PWEH-deh ehs-too-DYAHR ee ah-SEHR ehl ehk-SAH-mehn deh yee ee dee
If your child passes the GED exam, he/she will receive the General Education Diploma / the GED.	**Si su hijo/hija aprueba el examen de GED, él/ella va a recibir el diploma de educación general / el GED.** see SOO EE-hoh/EE-hah ah-PRWEH-bah ehl ehk-SAH-men deh yee ee dee, ehl/EH-yah bah ah rreh-see-BEER ehl dee-PLOH-mah deh eh-doo-kah-SYOHN heh-neh-RAHL / ehl yee ee dee
The GED diploma is considered equal to a high school diploma.	**El diploma de GED se considera equivalente a un diploma de escuela secundaria.** ehl dee-PLOH-mah deh yee ee dee seh kohn-see-DEH-rah eh-kee-bah-LEHN-teh ah oon dee-PLOH-mah de ehs-KWEH-lah seh-koon-DAH-ryah

Practice 7-6

Write a complete sentence in Spanish to explain the following phrases.

1. summer school

_____

2. GED exam

   _____

3. learning disability

   _____

4. visual impediments

   _____

5. hearing aid

   _____

6. attention deficit disorder

   _____

Graduation

La graduación

In some schools it is the responsibility of the counselor to handle matters related to graduation (**la graduación** [lah grah-dwah-SYOHN]). Following is a list of many of the terms related to the graduation ceremony and other elements typical of American schools.

cap and gown	**el birrete y la toga que llevan los estudiantes durante la ceremonia de graduación** ehl bee-RREH-teh ee lah TOH-gah keh YEH-bahn lohs ehs-too-DYAHN-tehs doo-RAHN-teh lah seh-reh-MOH-nyah deh grah-dwah-SYOHN
class photos	**las fotos de la clase de su hijo/hija** lahs FOH-tohs deh lah KLAH-seh deh soo EE-hoh/EE-hah
class ring	**el anillo de la clase (un anillo que simboliza la graduación de una escuela en particular)** ehl ah-NEE-yoh deh lah KLAH-seh (oon ah-NEE-yoh keh seem-boh-LEE-sah lah grah-dwah-SYOHN deh oo-nah ehs-KWEH-lah ehn pahr-tee-koo-LAHR)
commencement exercises	**la ceremonia de graduación** lah seh-reh-MOH-nyah deh grah-dwah-SYOHN

diploma	**el diploma** ehl dee-PLOH-mah
graduation fees	**el dinero que se usa para pagar por varias actividades de graduación** ehl dee-NEH-roh keh seh OO-sah PAH-rah pah-GAHR pohr BAH-ryahs ahk-tee-bee-DAH-dehs deh grah-dwah-SYOHN
graduation speech	**el discurso de graduación** ehl dees-KOOR-soh deh grah-dwah-SYOHN
homecoming	**el regreso a la escuela de estudiantes que se han graduado en años anteriores** ehl rreh-GREH-soh ah lah ehs-KWEH-lah deh ehs-too-DYAHN-tehs keh seh ahn grah-DWAH-doh ehn AH-nyohs ahn-teh-RYOH-rehs
prom	**la fiesta donde los estudiantes celebran su graduación** lah FYEHS-tah DOHN-deh lohs ehs-too-DYAHN-tehs seh-LEH-brahn soo grah-dwah-SYOHN
valedictorian	**el estudiante que da la oración de despedida a los estudiantes que se gradúan** ehl ehs-too-DYAHN-teh keh dah lah oh-rah-SYOHN deh dehs-peh-DEE-dah ah lohs ehs-too-DYAHN-tehs keh seh grah-DOO-ahn
yearbook	**el anuario (un libro con fotos y recuerdos de los años en la escuela)** ehl ah-NWAH-ryoh (oon LEE-broh kohn FOH-tohs ee rreh-KWEHR-dohs deh lohs AH-nyohs ehn lah ehs-KWEH-lah)

GRAMMAR · Summary: *ser* and *estar*

The verb "to be" can be translated two ways in Spanish: **ser** [sehr] and **estar** [ehs-TAHR]. These two Spanish verbs are not interchangeable. Each one is used in very specific situations.

The verb **ser** is used in the following ways.

- To find out or state the identity of people, places, and things

What is he/she/it?	**¿Qué es?** keh ehs

It's a diploma.   **Es un diploma.**
ehs oon dee-PLOH-mah

Who is he/she/it?   **¿Quién es?**
kyehn ehs

It is the dance teacher.   **Es el maestro de baile.**
ehs ehl mah-EHS-troh deh BAH-ee-leh

- To find out or state ownership

Whose is it?   **¿De quién es?**
deh kyehn ehs

It is my classmate's.   **Es de mi compañero de clase.**
ehs deh mee kohm-pah-NYEH-roh deh
KLAH-seh

- To find out or state the origin of someone or something

Where is he/she/it from?   **¿De dónde es?**
deh DOHN-deh ehs

He/She/It is from Venezuela.   **Es de Venezuela.**
ehs deh beh-neh-SWEH-lah

- To find out or state the nationality of someone or something

What nationality is he/she/it?   **¿De qué nacionalidad es?**
deh keh nah-syoh-nah-lee-DAHD ehs

He/She/It is Peruvian.   **Es peruano/peruana.**
ehs peh-RWAH-noh/peh-RWAH-nah

- To find out or state of what material something is made

What is it made of?   **¿De qué es?**
deh keh ehs

It's made of silver.   **Es de plata.**
ehs deh PLAH-tah

- To find out or state the characteristics of someone or something

What is he/she/it like?   **¿Cómo es?**
KOH-moh ehs

It's very exciting.   **Es muy emocionante.**
ehs MOO-ee eh-moh-syoh-NAHN-teh

For a list of adjectives that can be used with the verb **ser**, see Chapter 5, pages 217–218.

The verb **estar** is used in the following ways.

- To find out or state where someone or something is located

Where is he/she/it?	**¿Dónde está?** DOHN-deh ehs-TAH
He/She/It is in the counselor's office.	**Está en la oficina del consejero.** ehs-TAH ehn lah oh-fee-SEE-nah dehl kohn-seh-HEH-roh

- To find out or state the physical or emotional condition of a person or thing

How are they?	**¿Cómo están?** KOH-moh ehs-TAHN
They are tired.	**Están cansados.** ehs-TAHN kahn-SAH-dohs
How's lunch today?	**¿Cómo está el almuerzo hoy?** KOH-moh ehs-TAH ehl ahl-MWEHR-soh OH-ee
It's delicious.	**Está delicioso.** ehs-TAH deh-lee-SYOH-soh

For a list of adjectives that can be used with the verb **estar**, see Chapter 5, pages 203–204 and also pages 252–253 in this chapter.

Summary Practice

A *Match the words on the left with their meaning on the right.*

1. _____ una vez   a. *clothing*

2. _____ el secuestro   b. *gang*

3. _____ el robo   c. *neither*

4. _____ a veces   d. *someone*

5. _____ la amenaza   e. *kidnapping*

6. _____ tampoco   f. *unemployment*

7. _____ la fecha límite   g. *sometimes*

8. _____ la pandilla   h. *theft*

9. _____ el desempleo   i. *threat*

10. _____ la jaqueca   j. *once*

11. _____ alguien   k. *deadline*

12. _____ la ropa   l. *migraine*

B *Express the following sentences in Spanish.*

1. That class is too advanced and you do not have the prerequisites.

   _____

2. The bilingual program is a transitional program.

   _____

3. Your child has to go to summer school.

   _____

4. Your child misreads the words when she reads.

   _____

5. The students should not smoke in the schoolyard.

   _____

C *Use the verb* **estar** *and one of the adjectives from the list below to express how each person is feeling. There are more adjectives than you need, and there may be more than one possible answer.*

cansado	perdido
inquieto	preocupado
frustrado	incómodo
asustado	

1. Juan tiene miedo. Él _____.

2. Gilberto no sabe donde ir. Él _____.

3. Nosotros trabajamos mucho hoy. Nosotros _____.

4. María, tú no estudiaste para el examen. Tú _____.

5. Ellas no comprenden el problema. Ellas _____.

D *Complete the following sentences with the correct form of* **ser** *or* **estar**.

1. Yo acabo de hacer un examen, _____ nervioso.

2. Y tú, ¿de dónde _____?

3. Los bomberos _____ muy valientes.

4. Ellos _____ de Honduras.

5. María y Marco _____ en la oficina del enfermero.

6. La graduación _____ muy emocionante.

7. Ese hombre _____ el director de la escuela.

8. ¿Dónde _____ el gimnasio?

Appendix

VERB CONJUGATION CHARTS

Regular Verbs

		ENDINGS				
	STEM	FIRST-PERSON SING.	SECOND-PERSON SING.	THIRD-PERSON SING.	FIRST-PERSON PLURAL	THIRD-PERSON PLURAL

-ar Verbs

hablar *to speak*

	STEM					
PRESENT	habl-	o	as	a	amos	an
PRETERITE	habl-	é	aste	ó	amos	aron
PRES. SUBJUNCTIVE	habl-	e	es	e	emos	en
COMMAND	habl-		a	e		en

-er Verbs

comer *to eat*

	STEM					
PRESENT	com-	o	es	e	emos	en
PRETERITE	com-	í	iste	ió	imos	ieron
PRES. SUBJUNCTIVE	com-	a	as	a	amos	an
COMMAND	com-		e	a		an

-ir Verbs

vivir *to live*

	STEM					
PRESENT	viv-	o	es	e	imos	en
PRETERITE	viv-	í	iste	ió	imos	ieron
PRES. SUBJUNCTIVE	viv-	a	as	a	amos	an
COMMAND	viv-		e	a		an

Verbs with Stem Changes

e > *ie* (-*ar* and -*er* Verbs)

INFINITIVE	**cerrar** *to close*
PRESENT	cierro, cierras, cierra, cerramos, cierran
PRES. SUBJUNCTIVE	cierre, cierres, cierre, cerremos, cierren

INFINITIVE	**perder** *to lose*
PRESENT	pierdo, pierdes, pierde, perdemos, pierden
PRES. SUBJUNCTIVE	pierda, pierdas, pierda, perdamos, pierdan

Also atender, comenzar, despertar(se), empezar, entender, negar, pensar, recomendar, sentar(se)

e > *ie*, *e* > *i* (-*ir* Verbs)

INFINITIVE	**sentir** *to feel*
PRESENT	siento, sientes, siente, sentimos, sienten
PRETERITE	sentí, sentiste, sintió, sentimos, sintieron
PRES. SUBJUNCTIVE	sienta, sientas, sienta, sintamos, sientan

Also herir, mentir, preferir, requerir

e > *i* (-*ir* Verbs)

INFINITIVE	**pedir** *to request*
PRESENT	pido, pides, pide, pedimos, piden
PRETERITE	pedí, pediste, pidió, pedimos, pidieron
PRES. SUBJUNCTIVE	pida, pidas, pida, pidamos, pidan

Also conseguir, corregir, desvestir(se), repetir, seguir, servir, vestir(se)

INFINITIVE	**reír** *to laugh*
PRESENT	río, ríes, ríe, reímos, ríen
PRETERITE	reí, reíste, rió, reímos, rieron
PRES. SUBJUNCTIVE	ría, rías, ría, riamos, rían

Also reírse, sonreír(se)

o > ue (-ar and -er Verbs)

INFINITIVE	**contar** *to count, tell*
PRESENT	cuento, cuentas, cuenta, contamos, cuentan
PRES. SUBJUNCTIVE	cuente, cuentes, cuente, contemos, cuenten

INFINITIVE	**volver** *to return*
PRESENT	vuelvo, vuelves, vuelve, volvemos, vuelven
PRES. SUBJUNCTIVE	vuelva, vuelvas, vuelva, volvamos, vuelvan

Also acostar(se), almorzar, aprobar, costar, demostrar, devolver, doler, encontrar, morder, mostrar, probar(se), recordar, soñar

o > ue, o > u (-ir Verbs)

INFINITIVE	**dormir** *to sleep*
PRESENT	duermo, duermes, duerme, dormimos, duermen
PRETERITE	dormí, dormiste, durmió, dormimos, durmieron
PRES. SUBJUNCTIVE	duerma, duermas, duerma, durmamos, duerman

Also dormirse, morir

u > ue (-ar Verbs)

INFINITIVE	**jugar** *to play*
PRESENT	juego, juegas, juega, jugamos, juegan
PRES. SUBJUNCTIVE	juegue, juegues, juegue, juguemos, jueguen

Irregular Verbs

caer *to fall*

PRESENT	caigo, caes, cae, caemos, caen
PRETERITE	caí, caíste, cayó, caímos, cayeron
PRES. SUBJUNCTIVE	caiga, caigas, caiga, caigamos, caigan

Also caerse

coger *to catch*

PRESENT	cojo, coges, coge, cogemos, cogen
PRES. SUBJUNCTIVE	coja, cojas, coja, cojamos, cojan

Also recoger

conducir *to drive*

PRESENT	conduzco, conduces, conduce, conducimos, conducen
PRETERITE	conduje, condujiste, condujo, condujimos, condujeron
PRES. SUBJUNCTIVE	conduzca, conduzcas, conduzca, conduzcamos, conduzcan

Also traducir

conocer *to know, be acquainted with*

PRESENT	conozco, conoces, conoce, conocemos, conocen
PRES. SUBJUNCTIVE	conozca, conozcas, conozca, conozcamos, conozcan

Also desobedecer, establecer, lucir, obedecer

construir *to build*

PRESENT	construyo, construyes, construye, construimos, construyen
PRETERITE	construí, construiste, construyó, construimos, construyeron
PRES. SUBJUNCTIVE	construya, construyas, construya, construyamos, construyan

continuar *to continue*

PRESENT	continúo, continúas, continúa, continuamos, continúan
PRES. SUBJUNCTIVE	continúe, continúes, continúe, continuemos, continúen

dar *to give*

PRESENT	doy, das, da, damos, dan
PRETERITE	di, diste, dio, dimos, dieron
PRES. SUBJUNCTIVE	dé, des, dé, demos, den

decir *to say*

PRESENT	digo, dices, dice, decimos, dicen
PRETERITE	dije, dijiste, dijo, dijimos, dijeron
PRES. SUBJUNCTIVE	diga, digas, diga, digamos, digan
tú COMMAND	di

estar *to be*

PRESENT	estoy, estás, está, estamos, están
PRETERITE	estuve, estuviste, estuvo, estuvimos, estuvieron
PRES. SUBJUNCTIVE	esté, estés, esté, estemos, estén

hacer *to do, make*

PRESENT	hago, haces, hace, hacemos, hacen
PRETERITE	hice, hiciste, hizo, hicimos, hicieron
PRES. SUBJUNCTIVE	haga, hagas, haga, hagamos, hagan
tú COMMAND	haz

ir *to go*

PRESENT	voy, vas, va, vamos, van
PRETERITE	fui, fuiste, fue, fuimos, fueron
PRES. SUBJUNCTIVE	vaya, vayas, vaya, vayamos, vayan
tú COMMAND	ve

leer *to read*

PRETERITE	leí, leíste, leyó, leímos, leyeron

Also creer

oír *to hear*

PRESENT	oigo, oyes, oye, oímos, oyen
PRETERITE	oí, oíste, oyó, oímos, oyeron
PRES. SUBJUNCTIVE	oiga, oigas, oiga, oigamos, oigan

poder *to be able, can*

PRESENT	puedo, puedes, puede, podemos, pueden
PRETERITE	pude, pudiste, pudo, pudimos, pudieron
PRES. SUBJUNCTIVE	pueda, puedas, pueda, podamos, puedan

poner *to put, place*

PRESENT	pongo, pones, pone, ponemos, ponen
PRETERITE	puse, pusiste, puso, pusimos, pusieron
PRES. SUBJUNCTIVE	ponga, pongas, ponga, pongamos, pongan
tú COMMAND	pon

Also ponerse

querer *to want*

PRESENT	quiero, quieres, quiere, queremos, quieren
PRETERITE	quise, quisiste, quiso, quisimos, quisieron
PRES. SUBJUNCTIVE	quiera, quieras, quiera, queramos, quieran

saber *to know (facts)*

PRESENT	sé, sabes, sabe, sabemos, saben
PRETERITE	supe, supiste, supo, supimos, supieron
PRES. SUBJUNCTIVE	sepa, sepas, sepa, sepamos, sepan

salir *to leave*

PRESENT	salgo, sales, sale, salimos, salen
PRES. SUBJUNCTIVE	salga, salgas, salga, salgamos, salgan
tú COMMAND	sal

ser *to be*

PRESENT	soy, eres, es, somos, son
PRETERITE	fui, fuiste, fue, fuimos, fueron
PRES. SUBJUNCTIVE	sea, seas, sea, seamos, sean
tú COMMAND	sé

tener *to have*

PRESENT	tengo, tienes, tiene, tenemos, tienen
PRETERITE	tuve, tuviste, tuvo, tuvimos, tuvieron
PRES. SUBJUNCTIVE	tenga, tengas, tenga, tengamos, tengan
tú COMMAND	ten

Also obtener

traer *to bring*

PRESENT	traigo, traes, trae, traemos, traen
PRETERITE	traje, trajiste, trajo, trajimos, trajeron
PRES. SUBJUNCTIVE	traiga, traigas, traiga, traigamos, traigan

venir *to come*

PRESENT	vengo, vienes, viene, venimos, vienen
PRETERITE	vine, viniste, vino, vinimos, vinieron
PRES. SUBJUNCTIVE	venga, vengas, venga, vengamos, vengan
tú COMMAND	ven

ver *to see*

PRESENT	veo, ves, ve, vemos, ven
PRETERITE	vi, viste, vio, vimos, vieron
PRES. SUBJUNCTIVE	vea, veas, vea, veamos, vean

Answer Key

Introduction

Practice I-1

1. Este es el señor / Esta es la señora / la señorita (*student teacher's last name*). / Quisiera presentarle al señor / a la señora / a la señorita (*student teacher's last name*).
2. Mucho gusto. / Es un placer conocerlo.
3. Buenas noches. / Hasta pronto.
4. Soy el señor / la señora / la señorita (*your last name*).
5. Hasta el lunes.
6. Hasta la semana próxima.
7. ¿Cómo estás? / ¿Cómo te va? / ¿Qué tal?
8. Regular. / Así, así, gracias.
9. Estoy bien, gracias. ¿Y tú?
10. ¡Que te vaya bien!

Practice I-2

A
1. nosotros/nosotras
2. él/ella/Ud.
3. ellos/ellas/Uds.
4. tú
5. yo
6. ellos/ellas/Uds.

B
1. comprenden, comprendo, comprendemos
2. recibes, reciben, recibe
3. termino, termina, terminamos

C
1. they understand, I understand, we understand
2. you receive, you receive, she receives
3. I finish, you finish, we finish

D
1. I write a novel. / I do write a novel. / I am writing a novel.
2. Do you study very little? / Are you studying very little?
3. We are running in the park tomorrow. / We'll run in the park tomorrow.

Practice I-3

A
1. cierran
2. volvemos
3. vistes
4. sirvo
5. dormimos
6. piensa
7. encuentran
8. juega
9. pedimos
10. comienzo

B
1. cierras
2. duermen
3. servimos
4. repite
5. entiendo
6. devolvemos
7. cuesta
8. comenzamos
9. Juegan
10. vuelvo

Practice I-4

A
1. camine, caminen
2. lea, lean
3. vaya, vayan
4. asista, asistan
5. dé, den
6. sepa, sepan
7. esté, estén
8. escuche, escuchen
9. sea, sean
10. beba, beban
11. traduzca, traduzcan
12. traiga, traigan

B Put **no** before the commands in Exercise A. The verb does not change.

C
1. Camine
2. Sean
3. Dé
4. Vayan
5. Asista
6. Escuchen
7. Lean
8. Borre
9. Corra
10. Estén

D
1. No camine
2. No sean
3. No dé
4. No vayan
5. No asista
6. No escuchen
7. No lean
8. No borre
9. No corra
10. No estén

Practice I-5

1. Haz
2. Sal
3. Sé
4. Pon
5. Ven
6. Di
7. Ve

Practice I-6

A
1. escucha, no escuches
2. sal, no salgas
3. haz, no hagas
4. escribe, no escribas
5. sé, no seas
6. come, no comas
7. pon, no pongas
8. ve, no vayas

B
1. Come
2. Habla
3. corras
4. Ven
5. escuches
6. Copia
7. Aprende
8. Trae
9. borres
10. abras
11. Repite
12. estés

Practice I-7

A
1. (Tú) hablas español, ¿verdad?
2. ¿Asisten (Uds.) a la clase de física?
3. ¿(Ellos) corren en el parque?
4. ¿(Nosotros) terminamos la tarea?
5. ¿(Ella) no aprende mucho en la clase?

B 1. Sí, hablo español. / No, no hablo español.
2. No, no asistimos a la clase de física. / Sí, asistimos a la clase de física.
3. Sí, ellos corren en el parque. / No, ellos no corren en el parque.
4. Sí, Uds. terminan la tarea. / Sí, nosotros terminamos la tarea. /
No, Uds. no terminan la tarea. / No, nosotros no terminamos la tarea.
5. No, no aprende mucho en la clase. / Sí, aprende mucho en clase.

Practice I-8

A

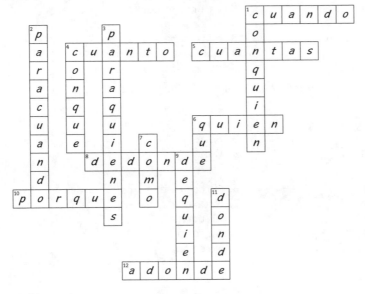

B 1. Quiénes
2. Qué
3. Por qué
4. Dónde
5. De dónde
6. Cuánto
7. Quién
8. Cuándo
9. Cómo
10. Con quiénes

Summary Practice

1. Este es el señor / Esta es la señora / Esta es la señorita (*principal's last name*).
2. ¡Qué le vaya bien!
3. Hasta la semana próxima.
4. Firme, por favor.
5. Escribe en la pizarra.
6. No corras en los pasillos.
7. ¿Dónde está el señor Smith?
8. ¿De quién es el libro?

Chapter 1
Practice 1-1

1. `t e n e m o s` `f r í o`
2. `t i e n e n` `s u e ñ o`
3. `t e n g o` `s u e r t e`
4. `t i e n e s` `p r i s a`
5. `t i e n e` `h a m b r e`
6. `t e n e m o s` `s e d`
7. `t e n g o` `m i e d o`
8. `t i e n e` `d i e z` `a ñ o s`

Practice 1-2

1. ¿Cuántos años tiene el niño / la niña / (*name of student*)?
2. ¿Cuál es su dirección?
3. ¿Tiene el niño / la niña hermanos?
4. ¿Cuál es la fecha de nacimiento del niño / de la niña?
5. ¿Quién está a cargo del niño / de la niña?
6. ¿Cuál es el número de teléfono del trabajo?

Practice 1-3

A

```
T B H E R M A N A S T R A X V
M A V G O R M G N O V I O W P
L Z E V O L E U B A E V F S A
W Y E R M O D O N I R D A P D
S E U V D D V T A U D S U O R
U R N F F A A O A O A B V M A
E N F M I U P M J H M J Z C S
G O T L A C K M I I D M E E T
R T A T H D A U O R H G S T R
A P T I D I R N H C P L P N O
R G X Y Y I Q I A L R W O E S
T W W L B J Y C N M L L S I Q
B V J E J E O B H A R Q A R R
A D A J I H A A L D U E M A K
D L X T C U Y K C W D K H P B
```

B
1. tío
2. cuñada
3. abuela
4. sobrino
5. hijo
6. prima
7. nieta
8. novia

Practice 1-4

A

```
T O D O P A N A M E Ñ O S S O
M D O M I N I C A N A O S A M
O C E T L A M E T A U G E R I
O C A N O S E W D K A G Q N P
N F A N A I B M O L O C C A E
A R S C E E M W X D R X C Z R
L F O N A C I X E M X I H A U
O X F H B W N K N W D Y I N A
Z X F Q X Q R P V L H R L I N
E V O N A I R O T A U C E T O
N Z V V T Z G H E K L M N N S
E A O Y H C U B A N O X A E N
V X K Q B E P Y L W G D D G Y
H P B J R B E B D L T O K R B
P U E R T O R R I Q U E Ñ A P
```

$\underline{T O D O S} \quad \underline{S O M O S} \quad \underline{A M E R I C A N O S}$

B

A	B	C	D	E	F	G	H	I	J	K	L	M	N	O	P	Q	R	S	T	U	V	W	X	Y	Z
N			L	R	E						Y	O	T	S			D			I	A	U			

¿$\underline{D E}$ $\underline{D O N D E}$ $\underline{E R E S}$? $\underline{S O Y}$ $\underline{D E}$ $\underline{L O S}$
   R F   R J A R F   F E F L   L J I   R F   D J L

$\underline{E S T A D O S}$ $\underline{U N I D O S}$.
  F L K W R J L   X A V R J L

C 1. ¿De dónde es (Ud.)?
     2. ¿Eres (tú) de Colombia?
     3. ¿De qué nacionalidad es (él)?
     4. (Nosotras) somos españolas.
     5. (Yo) soy de Nicaragua.

Practice 1-5

A 1. la chica mexicana
     2. los papeles blancos
     3. los estudiantes inteligentes
     4. la doctora guatemalteca
     5. las pizarras grandes
     6. el hombre cubano

B 1. las chicas mexicanas
     2. el papel blanco
     3. el estudiante inteligente
     4. las doctoras guatemaltecas
     5. la pizarra grande
     6. los hombres cubanos

Practice 1-6

A 1. ¿Tiene Ud. otros ingresos?
     2. ¿Tiene problemas con el oído?
     3. ¿Está tomando su hijo alguna medicina?
     4. En caso de emergencia, ¿a quién debemos llamar?
     5. ¿Tiene Ud. seguro médico?

6. Para comprobar su dirección, <u>Ud. puede traer</u> la licencia de conducir.
7. Necesita traer <u>el reporte de todas las vacunas</u>.

B

| l | a | v | i | s | t | a |

| l | a | e | n | f | e | r | m | e | d | a | d |

| e | l | p | o | l | v | o |

| l | o | s | m | a | r | i | s | c | o | s |

| l | a | h | i | e | r | b | a |

| e | l | p | e | s | o |

| l | a | m | o | r | d | e | d | u | r | a | d | e | a | b | e | j | a | s |

¿ $\underset{1}{T}\underset{2}{i}\underset{3}{e}\underset{4}{n}\underset{5}{e}$ $\underset{6}{s}\underset{7}{u}$ $\underset{8}{h}\underset{9}{i}\underset{10}{j}\underset{11}{o}$ $\underset{12}{a}\underset{13}{l}$ g u n $\underset{14}{a}$ $\underset{15}{a}\underset{16}{l}\underset{17}{e}\underset{18}{r}$ g $\underset{19}{i}\underset{20}{a}$?

Practice 1-7

A

```
L Y X Z B P J C U I G X F Q X
F S C S W J O I C I F I D E V
U A C E R A A E B N K Y P R N
E A W E I E C V E A N S A E K
N R R I M T T M E J U B W W T
T D N A D L K N I N A V D M J
E A V O S Y S J E E I I G G J
D U I A J C Y V A U H D G G E
E C T X K E A S D N P S A V L
F D R U C H L C N W I B W U L
D S I J D U N L I G P U D N A
C U N O C Z H B A E S H O G C
K J A B K C M N J C L I Y S X
A N A Z N A M J C C Y O U N E
H O Q C I M G O W M K Y S D T
```

B

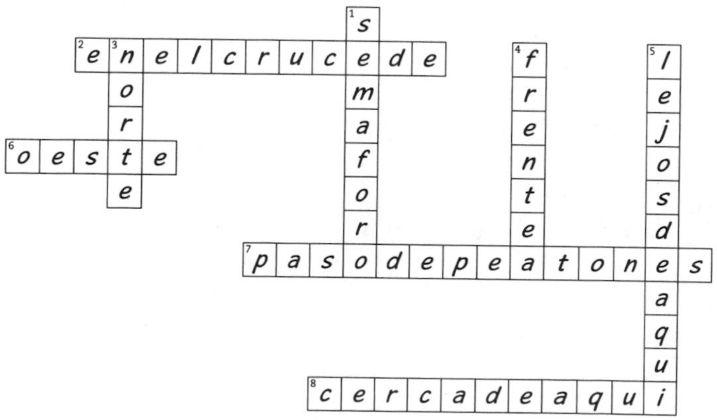

Across/Down crossword answers:

1. s m a f o r (down)
2. e n e l c r u c e d e (across) / e o r e (down)
4. f r e n t e (down)
5. l e j o s d e a q u i (down)
6. o e s t e (across)
7. p a s o d e p e a t o n e s (across)
8. c e r c a d e a q u i (across)

C 1. Esperen la luz verde.
2. Suban al autobús.
3. No empujen.
4. Caminen, no corran.
5. No griten.

Practice 1-8

1. Juan, (tú) <u>tienes</u> que <u>cruzar la calle</u>.
2. Nosotros <u>tenemos</u> que <u>esperar la luz verde</u>.
3. Ellos <u>tienen</u> que <u>llegar a tiempo a la parada</u>.
4. Ella <u>tiene</u> que <u>ir hasta la esquina</u>.
5. Yo <u>tengo</u> que <u>doblar a la derecha</u>.

Summary Practice

1. ¿Tiene su hijo/hija alguna condición que requiere atención especial?
2. ¿Cuántas personas viven en su casa?
3. (Yo) tengo mucha prisa.
4. ¿Cuántos años tiene (ella)?
5. La oficina está a dos cuadras.
6. ¿De dónde es (usted)?
7. (Usted) tiene que seguir derecho.
8. ¿Cómo llega su hija a la escuela?
9. Ud. tiene que esperar la llegada del autobús en la parada indicada.
10. Estoy perdido/perdida.
11. Espere la señal del chofer antes de cruzar.

Chapter 2

Practice 2-1

1. el bibliotecario / la bibliotecaria
2. el guardián / la guardiana
3. el/la conserje
4. el traductor / la traductora
5. la persona encargada de ayudar a los niños a cruzar la calle
6. el/la recepcionista
7. el/la guardia de seguridad
8. el cocinero / la cocinera
9. el entrenador / la entrenadora
10. el conductor / la conductora de autobús

Practice 2-2

1. Es una calculadora.
2. Es un lápiz.
3. Es una mochila.
4. Son unas tijeras.
5. Es un cuaderno.
6. Son cinco libros.

Practice 2-3

A

| e | l | c | u | a | r | t | o | d | e | b | a | ñ | o |

| l | a | s | a | l | a | d | e | m | a | e | s | t | r | o | s |

| e | l | s | ó | t | a | n | o |

| e | l | s | a | l | ó | n | d | e | c | l | a | s | e | s |

| l | a | b | i | b | l | i | o | t | e | c | a |

| e | l | a | u | d | i | t | o | r | i | o |

| e | l | c | u | a | r | t | o | d | e | c | o | r | r | e | o |

| e | l | g | i | m | n | a | s | i | o |

| e | l | v | e | s | t | u | a | r | i | o |

| l | a | o | f | i | c | i | n | a | d | e | l | c | o | n | s | e | j | e | r | o |

<u>l o s</u>   <u>c u a r t o s</u>   <u>d e</u>   <u>l a</u>   <u>e s c u e l a</u>
1 2 3   4 5 6 7 8 9 10   11 12   13 14   15 16 17 18 19 20 21

B

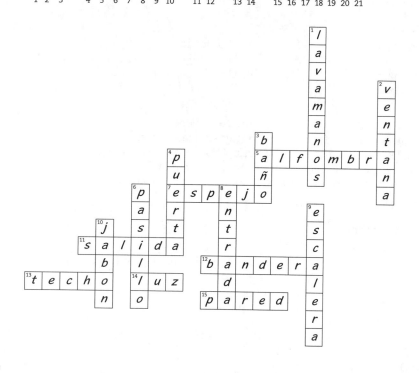

C 1. Está en el sótano.
2. Están allí.
3. Están en el cajón.
4. Está enfrente del auditorio / salón de actos.
5. Está al lado de la impresora.
6. Está en el rincón.
7. Están en la pared.
8. Está al lado del enfermero / de la enfermera.
9. Está enfrente de los pupitres.
10. Están detrás de la copiadora.

D 1. gymnasium
2. water fountains
3. paper towels
4. principal's office
5. stapler
6. trash can
7. posters
8. counselor
9. desk
10. bookcases

Practice 2-4

1. el boletín
2. la taquilla
3. la butaca
4. la multa
5. el recreo
6. la tarea
7. el periódico
8. el examen / la prueba
9. el horario
10. la nota

Practice 2-5

A 1. la carne
2. la sopa
3. el maíz
4. el arroz
5. traer
6. el pescado
7. la naranja
8. el pollo
9. limpiar
10. jamón

B 1. Sí, me gusta beber té. / No, no me gusta beber té.
2. Sí, le gustan las fresas. / No, no le gustan las fresas.
3. Sí, les gusta comer en la cafetería. / No, no les gusta comer en la cafetería.
4. Sí, me gustan los postres. / No, no me gustan los postres.
5. Sí, le gusta el melocotón. / No, no le gusta el melocotón.

C ¿Qué les gusta?

Summary Practice

Answers will vary.
1. ¿Quiénes son Uds.? / ¿Quiénes son los estudiantes en el pasillo?
2. ¿Te gusta compartir el/tu almuerzo?
3. ¿Hay ensalada (para el almuerzo)?
4. ¿Dónde está el cuarto de baño para damas?
5. ¿Cuál es el postre?
6. ¿No les gusta traer el almuerzo de casa?
7. ¿Dónde está el sacapuntas?
8. ¿Qué son esos papeles?
9. ¿Está la oficina del director / de la directora a la derecha de la entrada?
10. ¿Hay una luz en el estacionamiento?

Chapter 3

Practice 3-1

A
1. el quince de septiembre de mil novecientos noventa
2. el veinte y cinco de octubre del dos mil uno
3. el primero de julio del dos mil seis
4. el treinta y uno de enero de mil novecientos ochenta y cuatro

B lunes, miércoles, viernes, domingo

C
1. Son las nueve y diez de la mañana.
2. Es (el) mediodía.
3. Son las tres menos veinte y cinco de la tarde.
4. Son las cinco de la tarde.
5. Es (la) medianoche.
6. Son las siete y media de la noche.
7. Son las once y cuarto de la mañana.

D
1. todos los días
2. a principios de
3. ahora mismo
4. a partir de
5. a mediados de

E
1. ¿Qué hora es?
2. ¿Cuál es la fecha de hoy? / ¿A cómo estamos hoy?
3. ¿Cuándo es?
4. ¿A qué hora es la clase de español?

Practice 3-2

1. ¿Qué tiempo hizo ayer?
2. Hace frío y está nublado.
3. Hace mal tiempo.
4. Va a hacer buen tiempo mañana.
5. Está nevando.

Practice 3-3

A *Answers will vary.*
1. pantalones cortos / una camiseta / una blusa de algodón
2. un suéter / un sombrero
3. una gabardina / un impermeable
4. un abrigo / una bufanda / guantes
5. una chaqueta / pantalones largos

B
1. (La camiseta) es de Juan.
2. (Los calcetines) son de Alberto y Pedro.
3. (La falda) es de Graciela.
4. (Los calzoncillos) son de David.
5. (Las chaquetas) son de Diego y Tina.

C
1. Mi, azul
2. Nuestros, negros
3. Su, amarilla
4. Tus, blancos
5. Sus, rojos

Practice 3-4

1. Sí, sé deletrear en español. / No, no sé deletrear en español.
2. Sí, traigo un sacapuntas a la escuela. / No, no traigo un sacapuntas a la escuela.
3. Salgo de la escuela a la(s) (*number*).
4. Sí, conozco a todos los estudiantes. / No, no conozco a todos los estudiantes.
5. Sí, doy mucha tarea. / No, no doy mucha tarea.
6. Sí, hago mucho trabajo en la escuela. / No, no hago mucho trabajo en la escuela.

Practice 3-5

A

d	u	é	r	m	e	t	e		

n	o	l	l	o	r	e	s		

l	e	v	á	n	t	a	t	e	

n	o	p	e	l	e	e	s		

n	o	c	o	r	r	a	s		

n	o	t	e	p	o	r	t	e	s	m	a	l

a	c	u	é	s	t	a	t	e	

p	ó	r	t	a	t	e	b	i	e	n

B
1. me
2. se
3. nos
4. te
5. se

C
1. lo
2. las
3. te
4. la
5. los

D
1. a
2. X
3. X
4. a
5. X
6. a

Summary Practice

1. ¿Conoces al director / a la directora?
2. ¿Cuándo es la reunión? / ¿A qué hora es la reunión?
3. ¿Qué tiempo va a hacer mañana?
4. Está lloviendo.
5. Mi bufanda es blanca y negra.
6. ¿De quién es el abrigo?
7. El vestido está de moda.
8. ¿De qué color es la camisa?
9. Escríbelo en la pizarra.
10. No las pongas en tu mochila.
11. Guarden los juguetes.
12. Pórtense bien.

Chapter 4

Practice 4-1

1. conozco
2. sabemos
3. saben
4. Conoces
5. sabe
6. sé
7. conocen
8. conoce

Practice 4-2

A *Answers will vary. Possible answers:* una subasta, un concurso, una fiesta, un baile, una rifa, un sorteo, una función.

B
1. el museo
2. el parque zoológico / la granja / el acuario
3. el parque de atracciones
4. el ayuntamiento
5. la casa de bomberos
6. la biblioteca

C *Answers will vary. Possible answers:*
1. Los padres tienen que firmar la carta.
2. Uds. tienen que traer el almuerzo.
3. Avíseme si Ud. está dispuesto a acompañarnos.

D
1. Toma a tu / Tomen a su compañero de la mano.
2. Súbete/Súbanse al autobús.
3. Ponte/Pónganse en fila.

Chapter 5

Practice 5-1

Answers will vary.
1. Es aconsejable traer una nota de tu/su padre.
2. Es mejor llamar a un compañero de clase.
3. Es necesario prestar atención.
4. Es bueno hacer la tarea todos los días.
5. Hay que estudiar regularmente.

Practice 5-2

1. Podemos
2. puedes
3. pueden
4. puede
5. puedo
6. pueden

Practice 5-3

Answers will vary.
1. No, (ellos) no pueden pelear en el patio. Se prohíbe pelear en la escuela.
2. No, (yo) no puedo llegar tarde. Se prohíbe llegar tarde a la escuela.
3. No, (tú) no puedes comer fuera de la cafetería. Se prohíbe comer fuera de la cafetería en la escuela.
4. No, (ella) no puede salir sin permiso. Se prohíbe salir de la escuela sin permiso.
5. No, (Uds.) no pueden / (nosotros) no podemos jugar en los pasillos. Se prohíbe jugar en los pasillos de la escuela.

Practice 5-4

A
1. (Tú) tienes que estudiar ahora.
2. (Uds.) tienen que / (Nosotros) tenemos que asistir a clases de repaso.
3. (Yo) tengo que trabajar con un profesor / una profesora particular.
4. (Ellos) tienen que quedarse en la escuela después de las clases.

B
1. Nosotros vamos a estudiar en la biblioteca más tarde.
2. Ellos van a asistir a las clases de repaso mañana por la tarde.
3. Tú vas a hacer el examen la semana próxima.
4. Yo voy a hacer la tarea mañana por la mañana.
5. Ud. va a llamar al director pasado mañana.

C
1. peleas, vas
2. asistimos, vamos
3. usa, va
4. salen, va
5. hablo, van

Practice 5-5

1. cansado
2. ansiosos/furiosos
3. sorprendidos
4. avergonzado/avergonzada / ansioso/ansiosa
5. aburridos
6. ocupada/furiosa
7. sorprendido/sorprendida / avergonzado/avergonzada / ansioso/ansiosa / furioso/furiosa

Practice 5-6

A
1. vengan
2. leas
3. coman
4. entregues
5. sea
6. sepan
7. hable
8. repasemos

B
1. estudies temprano
2. vengan a tiempo
3. estudies en la biblioteca
4. no vayan al parque hoy
5. sepa cuando (tú) estás / (Ud.) está ausente / (Uds.) están ausentes
6. coman en los pasillos
7. participe más en clase
8. hable con Ud. / contigo
9. copien la tarea de otro estudiante
10. salgas bien en el examen

Summary Practice

1. Al regresar a la escuela, su hijo/hija tiene que traer una nota firmada por Ud.
2. Es importante prestar atención.
3. Para salir bien, (tú) tienes que hacer preguntas cuando no comprendes.
4. Se prohíbe gritar en los pasillos.
5. Tienes que hacer el examen otra vez.
6. Uds. van a tener un examen la semana próxima / que viene.
7. Si se porta mal, (ella) no puede participar en los deportes.
8. ¡Qué tarea más/tan estupenda!

9. (Yo) espero que / Ojalá que estudies mucho.
10. Es importante que (él) duerma por lo menos ocho horas cada noche.

Chapter 6
Practice 6-1

```
U N M N L O S M A R E O S S E
Z Q R K S Z X X L O P C G H B
N G K D E A L G E R A L A L K
L H A D L A P S E A L C J A U
E L J O R S I I Y R C T D F T
R A D D E L D O L O R Z Y L W
B F N A L A T O S P P B D E G
E K U T L C E L H I P O L M U
I B M O Y A T N A G R A G A L
F O U G D Y E Z F K S D L Q P
A N L A N G L I B E D S N Q Y
L N Q C D E O D I O L E A K R
A D X R B V S O J O I P S O L
W D K K L A E R U P C I O N J
I L X O X P O X L R Z F K S W
```

Practice 6-2

A
1. corrió
2. pasó
3. respiré
4. abriste
5. aprendimos
6. salieron
7. calificó
8. asistí
9. comprendieron
10. tomamos

B
1. ayer
2. ayer por la tarde
3. anoche
4. el verano pasado
5. ayer por la mañana
6. el lunes pasado

C
1. tosieron, anteayer
2. visitó, el viernes pasado
3. dio, el martes pasado
4. asistimos, anteanoche
5. saliste, ayer

Practice 6-3

1. Nos
2. Me
3. te
4. Le
5. Les
6. Le

Practice 6-4

1. ¡Socorro!
2. ¡Fuego!
3. ¡No griten!
4. ¡Cuidado!
5. ¡Dense prisa!
6. ¡Pónganse debajo del pupitre!
7. ¡Caminen tranquilamente!
8. ¡Cúbranse la cabeza!

Summary Practice

1. Tienes que ir a la oficina del enfermero / de la enfermera.
2. ¿Tienes dolor de garganta?
3. Se siente / Está mareada.
4. ¿Qué le pasó?
5. Él se rompió el pie.
6. Tienes que guardar cama.
7. ¿Te duele el cuello?
8. Tengo dolor de muelas.
9. Hay humo en los pasillos.
10. ¡Cúbranse la boca!

Chapter 7

Practice 7-1

A   1. bien
2. mejor
3. mucho
4. despacio
5. un poco
6. peor

B   1. de vez en cuando
2. rara vez
3. una vez
4. muchas veces
5. dos veces
6. a veces

Practice 7-2

A   1. Nunca estudio. / No estudio nunca.
2. Nosotros no comemos en la cafetería.
3. Nadie corre en el parque.
4. ¿No lees ninguna novela?
5. Ellos no caminan en el parque tampoco.
6. Nadie va a la fiesta.

B   1. No, no estoy nervioso nunca.
2. No, no tengo ningún trabajo nunca.
3. No, no visito a mis tíos nunca.
4. No, no compro ninguna ropa en la tienda nunca.
5. No, no como el almuerzo en la escuela nunca.
6. No, no hay nadie en el pasillo nunca.
7. No, no quiero beber nada nunca.
8. No, no voy a la escuela los sábados tampoco.

Practice 7-3

1. está suspendida
2. llenar una solicitud de empleo
3. a tiempo parcial
4. un programa para controlar la cólera
5. pasar por un entrenamiento
6. un permiso de trabajo
7. una entrevista
8. mantenerte al tanto de tu trabajo / tus tareas para la escuela

Practice 7-4

A *Answers will vary.*
1. ¿Te gusta cocinar?
2. ¿Te gusta actuar?
3. ¿Te gusta sacar fotos?
4. ¿Te gusta trabajar al aire libre?
5. ¿Te gusta trabajar con computadoras?

B
1. Este
2. aquellas
3. Esta
4. Esa
5. estos
6. aquel
7. Esas
8. Esos

Practice 7-5

1. Acabamos de
2. (Él) acaba de
3. (Ella) acaba de
4. (Ellos) acaban de
5. (Yo) acabo de

Practice 7-6

Answers will vary.
1. Los estudiantes tienen que ir a la escuela de verano cuando suspenden una asignatura. Si el estudiante aprueba los cursos de la escuela de verano, puede avanzar al próximo grado.
2. El examen de GED incluye escritura, lectura, estudios sociales, ciencia y matemáticas. Si un estudiante aprueba el examen de GED, él/ella va a recibir un diploma equivalente a un diploma de escuela secundaria.
3. Si un estudiante tiene mucha dificultad para aprender a leer, escribir, escuchar, hablar o con las matemáticas, es posible que tenga una discapacidad de aprendizaje.
4. Un impedimento visual no permite que un estudiante vea todo lo que necesita ver y puede impedir que aprenda.
5. Un audífono / aparato de oído ayuda a las personas que no oyen bien a oír mejor.
6. Cuando un estudiante no puede estar sentado, enfocar su atención en el trabajo ni controlar sus impulsos es posible que tenga un desorden deficitario de la atención.

Summary Practice

A
1. j
2. e
3. h
4. g
5. i
6. c
7. k
8. b
9. f
10. l
11. d
12. a

B
1. Esa clase es demasiado avanzada y tú no tienes los requisitos.
2. El programa bilingüe es un programa de transición.
3. Su hijo/hija tiene que asistir a la escuela de verano.
4. Su hijo/hija interpreta mal las palabras cuando lee.
5. Los estudiantes no deben fumar en el patio de la escuela.

C   1. está inquieto / está asustado
2. está perdido / está frustrado
3. estamos cansados
4. estás asustada / estás inquieta / estás preocupada
5. están frustradas / están perdidas

D   1. estoy
2. eres
3. son
4. son
5. están
6. es
7. es
8. está

English-Spanish Glossary

A

a/an un/una [oon/oo-nah]

a little un poco [oon POH-koh]

a lot mucho [MOO-choh]

able, to be poder (ue) (*irreg.*) [poh-DEHR]

about the middle of a mediados de
[ah meh-DYAH-dohs deh]

absent ausente [ah-oo-SEHN-teh]

abuse (physical) el abuso físico
[ehl ah-BOO-soh FEE-see-koh]

abuse (sexual) el abuso sexual
[ehl ah-BOO-soh sehk-SWAHL]

academic prize el premio académico
[ehl PREH-myoh ah-kah-DEH-mee-koh]

accident el accidente
[ehl ahk-see-DEHN-teh]

accountant el contador / la contadora
[ehl kohn-tah-DOHR /
lah kohn-tah-DOH-rah]

acne el acné [ehl ahk-NEH]

acquainted with, to be conocer (*irreg.*)
[koh-noh-SEHR]

actor el actor [ehl ahk-TOHR]

actress la actriz [lah ahk-TREES]

address la dirección
[lah dee-rehk-SYOHN]

administrator el administrador /
la administradora
[ehl ahd-mee-nees-trah-DOHR /
lah ahd-mee-nees-trah-DOH-rah]

admission exam el examen de ingreso
[ehl ehk-SAH-mehn deh een-GREH-soh]

advanced avanzado [ah-bahn-SAH-doh]

advice el consejo [ehl kohn-SEH-hoh]

afraid asustado [ah-soos-TAH-doh]

afraid, to be tener (*irreg.*) miedo
[teh-NEHR MYEH-doh]

afterwards después [dehs-PWEHS]

aide el/la asistente
[ehl/lah ah-sees-TEHN-teh]

AIDS el SIDA [ehl SEE-dah]

air conditioning el aire acondicionado
[ehl AH-ee-reh
ah-kohn-dee-syoh-NAH-doh]

Air Force las fuerzas aéreas
[lahs FWEHR-sahs ah-EH-reh-ahs]

aisle el pasillo [ehl pah-SEE-yoh]

alcoholic alcohólico [ahl-KOH-lee-koh]

alcoholism el alcoholismo
[ehl ahl-koh-LEES-moh]

allergy la alergia [lah ah-LEHR-hyah]

alley el callejón [ehl kah-yeh-HOHN]

alphabet el abecedario
[ehl ah-beh-seh-DAH-ryoh];
el alfabeto [ehl ahl-fah-BEH-toh]

already ya [yah]

also también [tahm-BYEHN]

always siempre [SYEHM-preh]

anger management program
el programa para controlar la cólera
[ehl proh-GRAH-mah PAH-rah
kohn-troh-LAHR lah KOH-leh-rah]

angry enfadado [ehn-fah-DAH-doh];
enojado [eh-noh-HAH-doh]

animal el animal [ehl ah-nee-MAHL]

ankle el tobillo [ehl toh-BEE-yoh]

announce, to anunciar [ah-noon-SYAHR]

announcer (radio/TV) el locutor /
la locutora [ehl loh-koo-TOHR /
lah loh-koo-TOH-rah]

another otro [OH-troh]

answer la respuesta
[lah rrehs-PWEHS-tah]

antacid el antiácido
[ehl ahn-TYAH-see-doh]

antibiotic el antibiótico
[ehl ahn-tee-BYOH-tee-koh]

antihistamine el antihistamínico
[ehl ahn-tees-tah-MEE-nee-koh]

antiseptic el antiséptico
[ehl ahn-tee-SEHP-tee-koh]

anxious ansioso [ahn-SYOH-soh]

anybody alguien [AHL-gyehn]

applaud, to aplaudir [ah-plah-oo-DEER]

application la solicitud
[lah soh-lee-see-TOOD]

appointment la cita [lah SEE-tah]

313

April abril [ah-BREEL]
apron el delantal [ehl deh-lahn-TAHL]
architect el arquitecto / la arquitecta
[ehl ahr-kee-TEHK-toh /
lah ahr-kee-TEHK-tah]
argue, to discutir [dees-koo-TEER]
arm el brazo [ehl BRAH-soh]
Army las fuerzas armadas
[lahs FWEHR-sahs ahr-MAH-dahs];
el ejército [ehl eh-HEHR-see-toh]
around alrededor [ahl-rreh-deh-DOHR]
arrive, to llegar [yeh-GAHR]
arson el incendio premeditado [ehl
een-SEHN-dyoh preh-meh-dee-TAH-doh]
art el arte [ehl AHR-teh]
artistic artístico [ahr-TEES-tee-koh]
ashamed avergonzado
[ah-behr-gohn-SAH-doh]
ask, to preguntar [preh-goon-TAHR]
ask for, to pedir (i) [peh-DEER]
ask for permission, to pedir (i) permiso
[peh-DEER pehr-MEE-soh]
aspirin la aspirina [lah ahs-pee-REE-nah]
assistant principal (vice-principal)
el/la asistente al director / a la directora
[ehl/lah ah-sees-TEHN-teh ahl
dee-rehk-TOHR / ah lah dee-rehk-TOH-rah]
assure, to asegurar [ah-seh-goo-RAHR]
asthma el asma [ehl AHS-mah]
astronaut el/la astronauta
[ehl/lah ahs-troh-NAH-oo-tah]
at once en seguida [ehn seh-GEE-dah]
at the beginning of a principios de
[ah preen-SEE-pyohs deh]
at the end of a fines de [ah FEE-nehs deh]
athletic atlético [ah-TLEH-tee-koh]
attempted murder el intento de
asesinato [ehl een-TEHN-toh deh
ah-seh-see-NAH-toh]
attend, to asistir [ah-sees-TEER]
attendance la asistencia
[lah ah-sees-TEHN-syah]
attention deficit disorder el desorden
deficitario de la atención
[ehl dehs-OHR-dehn deh-fee-see-TAH-ryoh
deh lah ah-tehn-SYOHN]
auditorium el auditorio
[ehl ah-oo-dee-TOH-ryoh];
el salón / la sala de actos
[ehl sah-LOHN / lah SAH-lah deh AHK-tohs]
August agosto [ah-GOHS-toh]
aunt la tía [lah TEE-ah]

author el autor / la autora
[ehl ah-oo-TOHR / lah ah-oo-TOH-rah]
autism el autismo [ehl ah-oo-TEES-moh];
el trastorno generalizado del desarrollo
[ehl trahs-TOHR-noh heh-neh-rah-lee-
SAH-doh dehl deh-sah-RROH-yoh]
autumn el otoño [ehl oh-TOH-nyoh]
avenue la avenida [lah ah-beh-NEE-dah]

B

back la espalda [lah ehs-PAHL-dah]
backache el dolor de espalda
[ehl doh-LOHR deh ehs-PAHL-dah]
backpack la mochila [lah moh-CHEE-lah]
bacon el tocino [ehl toh-SEE-noh]
bad grades, to get sacar malas notas
[sah-KAHR MAH-lahs NOH-tahs]
badly mal [mahl]
bag la bolsa [lah BOHL-sah]
baker el panadero / la panadera
[ehl pah-nah-DEH-roh /
lah pah-nah-DEH-rah]
ball la pelota [lah peh-LOH-tah]; el balón
[ehl bah-LOHN]
balloon el globo [ehl GLOH-boh]
ballpoint pen el bolígrafo
[ehl boh-LEE-grah-foh]
banana el plátano [ehl PLAH-tah-noh]
bandage la venda [lah BEHN-dah]
bandage, to vendar [behn-DAHR]
Band-Aid® la curita® / la tirita®
[lah koo-REE-tah / lah tee-REE-tah]
barber el barbero [ehl bahr-BEH-roh]
basement el sótano [ehl SOH-tah-noh]
bathing suit el traje de baño
[ehl TRAH-heh deh BAH-nyoh]
bathroom el cuarto de baño
[ehl KWAHR-toh deh BAH-nyoh]
bathroom (boy's/girl's) el baño (para
niños/niñas) [ehl BAH-nyoh (PAH-rah
NEE-nyohs/NEE-nyahs)]
battery la batería [lah bah-teh-REE-ah]
battery (physical) el maltrato
[ehl mahl-TRAH-toh]
be, to estar (*irreg.*) [ehs-TAHR]; ser (*irreg.*)
[sehr]
bean el frijol [ehl free-HOHL]
beard la barba [lah BAHR-bah]
bed la cama [lah KAH-mah]
before antes [AHN-tehs]
begin, to comenzar (ie) [koh-mehn-
SAHR]; empezar (ie) [ehm-peh-SAHR]

beginning el principio
[ehl preen-SEE-pyoh]

behave oneself, to portarse bien
[pohr-TAHR-seh byehn]

behavior el comportamiento
[ehl kohm-pohr-tah-MYEHN-toh]

behind detrás de [deh-TRAHS deh]

bell (electric) el timbre [ehl TEEM-breh]

bell (hand) la campana
[lah kahm-PAH-nah]

belt el cinturón [ehl seen-too-ROHN]

bench el banco [ehl BAHN-koh]

better mejor [meh-HOHR]

better, to get mejorarse
[meh-hoh-RAHR-seh]

bicycle la bicicleta
[lah bee-see-KLEH-tah]

birth el nacimiento
[ehl nah-see-MYEHN-toh]

bite, to morder (ue) [mohr-DEHR]

bitter amargado [ah-mahr-GAH-doh]

black negro [NEH-groh]

blackout el apagón [ehl ah-pah-GOHN]

bleed, to sangrar [sahn-GRAHR]

blindness la ceguera [lah seh-GEH-rah]

blister la ampolla [lah ahm-POH-yah]

block (city) la cuadra [lah KWAH-drah]

blocks (wooden) los bloques (de madera)
[lohs BLOH-kehs (deh mah-DEH-rah)]

blood la sangre [lah SAHN-greh]

blood pressure (high/low) la presión
arterial (alta/baja) [lah preh-SYOHN
ahr-teh-RYAHL (AHL-tah/BAH-hah)]

blouse la blusa [lah BLOO-sah]

blue azul [ah-SOOL]

board member el miembro de la junta
directiva [ehl MYEHM-broh deh lah
HOON-tah dee-rehk-TEE-bah]

body el cuerpo [ehl KWEHR-poh]

boiler la caldera [lah kahl-DEH-rah]

bomb explosion el estallido de una
bomba [ehl ehs-tah-YEE-doh deh oo-nah
BOHM-bah]

bomb scare la amenaza de bomba
[lah ah-meh-NAH-sah deh BOHM-bah]

book el libro [ehl LEE-broh]

bookcase la estantería
[lah ehs-tahn-teh-REE-ah]

bored aburrido [ah-boo-RREE-doh]

borrow, to pedir (i) prestado
[peh-DEER prehs-TAH-doh]

both ambos [AHM-bohs]

bottle la botella [lah boh-TEH-yah]

boulevard el paseo [ehl pah-SEH-oh]

bounce (ball), to hacer (*irreg.*) rebotar
(la pelota) [ah-SEHR rreh-boh-TAHR
(lah peh-LOH-tah)]

box la caja [lah KAH-hah]

box office la taquilla [lah tah-KEE-yah]

boy el niño [ehl NEE-nyoh]

boyfriend el novio [ehl NOH-byoh]

bra el sostén [ehl sohs-TEHN]

brace el corrector [ehl koh-rrehk-TOHR]

brain el cerebro [ehl seh-REH-broh]

bread el pan [ehl pahn]

break, to romper [rrohm-PEHR];
romperse [rrohm-PEHR-seh]

breakfast el desayuno
[ehl deh-sah-YOO-noh]

breathe, to respirar [rrehs-pee-RAHR]

breathless sin respiración
[seen rrehs-pee-rah-SYOHN]

bridge el puente [ehl PWEHN-teh]

briefs los calzoncillos
[lohs kahl-sohn-SEE-yohs]

bring, to traer (*irreg.*) [trah-EHR]

broccoli el brécol [ehl BREH-kohl]

broken roto [RROH-toh]

bronchitis la bronquitis
[lah brohn-KEE-tees]

broom la escoba [lah ehs-KOH-bah]

brother el hermano [ehl ehr-MAH-noh]

brother-in-law el cuñado
[ehl koo-NYAH-doh]

brown marrón [mah-RROHN]

bruise el moretón [ehl moh-reh-TOHN]

brush (artist's) el pincel [ehl peen-SEHL]

brush one's hair, to cepillarse el pelo
[seh-pee-YAHR-seh ehl PEH-loh]

brush one's teeth, to cepillarse los
dientes
[seh-pee-YAHR-seh lohs DYEHN-tehs]

bucket el balde [ehl BAHL-deh];
el cubo [ehl KOO-boh]

building el edificio [ehl eh-dee-FEE-syoh]

building site el solar [ehl soh-LAHR]

bullying la intimidación
[lah een-tee-mee-dah-SYOHN]

burn la quemadura
[lah keh-mah-DOO-rah]

burn, to quemar [keh-MAHR]

burn up, to quemarse [keh-MAHR-seh]

burned quemado [keh-MAH-doh]

bus el autobús [ehl ah-oo-toh-BOOS]

bus stop la parada de autobuses
[lah pah-RAH-dah deh ah-oo-toh-BOO-sehs]

businessman el hombre de negocios
[ehl OHM-breh deh neh-GOH-syohs]

businesswoman la mujer de negocios
[lah moo-HEHR deh neh-GOH-syohs]

busy ocupado [oh-koo-PAH-doh]

butcher el carnicero / la carnicera [ehl
kahr-nee-SEH-roh / lah kahr-nee-SEH-rah]

butter la mantequilla
[lah mahn-teh-KEE-yah]

button el botón [ehl boh-TOHN]

button up, to abrocharse
[ah-broh-CHAHR-seh]

C

cafeteria la cafetería
[lah kah-feh-teh-REE-ah]

cake el bizcocho [ehl bees-KOH-choh]

calculator la calculadora
[lah kahl-koo-lah-DOH-rah]

calendar el calendario
[ehl kah-lehn-DAH-ryoh]

call, to llamar [yah-MAHR]

calm tranquilo [trahn-KEE-loh]

calm down, to tranquilizarse
[trahn-kee-lee-SAHR-seh]

cancer el cáncer [ehl KAHN-sehr]

candle la vela [lah BEH-lah]

cane el bastón [ehl bahs-TOHN]

cap la gorra [lah GOH-rrah]

cards (playing) las cartas
[lahs KAHR-tahs]

career la carrera [lah kah-RREH-rah]

careful cuidadoso [kwee-dah-DOH-soh]

carpenter el carpintero / la carpintera
[ehl kahr-peen-TEH-roh /
lah kahr-peen-TEH-rah]

carpet la alfombra [lah ahl-FOHM-brah]

carrot la zanahoria
[lah sah-nah-OH-ryah]

cart (small) el carretón
[ehl kah-rreh-TOHN]

cashier el cajero / la cajera
[ehl kah-HEH-roh / lah kah-HEH-rah]

catalogue el catálogo
[ehl kah-TAH-loh-goh]

ceiling el techo [ehl TEH-choh]

cell phone el celular [ehl seh-loo-LAHR]

cereal el cereal [ehl seh-reh-AHL]

cerebral palsy la parálisis cerebral
[lah pah-RAH-lee-sees seh-reh-BRAHL]

chair la silla [lah SEE-yah]

chairperson (of the _____ department)
el jefe / la jefa (de la cátedra de _____)
[ehl HEH-feh / lah HEH-fah
(deh lah KAH-teh-drah deh)]

chalk la tiza [lah TEE-sah]

chalkboard la pizarra [lah pee-SAH-rrah]

chapter el capítulo [ehl kah-PEE-too-loh]

character el personaje
[ehl pehr-soh-NAH-heh]

checkers las damas [lahs DAH-mahs]

cheek la mejilla [lah meh-HEE-yah]

cheese el queso [ehl KEH-soh]

chess el ajedrez [ehl ah-heh-DREHS]

chest el pecho [ehl PEH-choh]

chew, to masticar [mahs-tee-KAHR]

chicken el pollo [ehl POH-yoh]

chicken pox la varicela
[lah bah-ree-SEH-lah]

child el niño / la niña
[ehl NEE-nyoh / lah NEE-nyah]

child abuse el maltrato de niños
[ehl mahl-TRAH-toh deh NEE-nyohs]

chills los escalofríos
[lohs ehs-kah-loh-FREE-ohs]

chin la barbilla [lah bahr-BEE-yah]

Christmas la Navidad
[lah nah-bee-DAHD]

city la ciudad [lah see-oo-DAHD]

classroom el aula [ehl AH-oo-lah];
el salón de clases
[ehl sah-LOHN deh KLAH-sehs]

clean limpio [LEEM-pyoh]

clean, to limpiar [leem-PYAHR]

clear (weather) despejado
[dehs-peh-HAH-doh]

clerk el/la dependiente
[ehl/lah deh-pehn-DYEHN-teh]

climb, to subir [soo-BEER]

clinic la clínica [lah KLEE-nee-kah]

clock el reloj [ehl rreh-LOH]

close, to cerrar (ie) [seh-RRAHR]

closet el armario [ehl ahr-MAH-ryoh]

clothing la ropa [lah RROH-pah]

clothing style el estilo de ropa
[ehl ehs-TEE-loh deh RROH-pah]

cloudy nublado [noo-BLAH-doh]

coach (sports)   el entrenador /
la entrenadora
[ehl ehn-treh-nah-DOHR /
lah ehn-treh-nah-DOH-rah]

coat   el abrigo   [ehl ah-BREE-goh];
el sobretodo   [ehl soh-breh-TOH-doh]

coffee   el café   [ehl kah-FEH]

cold   frío   [FREE-oh]

cold (common cold)   el catarro
[ehl kah-TAH-rroh];
el resfriado   [ehl rrehs-FRYAH-doh]

cold, to be/feel   tener (*irreg.*) frío
[teh-NEHR FREE-oh]

colic   el cólico   [ehl KOH-lee-koh]

color   el color   [ehl koh-LOHR]

color, to   colorear   [koh-loh-reh-AHR]

coloring book   el libro de colorear
[ehl LEE-broh deh koh-loh-reh-AHR]

Columbus Day   el día de la Raza
[ehl DEE-ah deh lah RRAH-sah]

come, to   venir (*irreg.*)   [beh-NEER]

comfortable   cómodo   [KOH-moh-doh]

compass   el compás   [ehl kohm-PAHS]

computer   la computadora
[lah kohm-poo-tah-DOH-rah]

computer lab   el laboratorio de
computadoras   [ehl lah-boh-rah-TOH-
ryoh deh kohm-poo-tah-DOH-rahs]

concentrate, to   concentrarse
[kohn-sehn-TRAHR-seh]

conflict resolution program
el programa para resolver conflictos
[ehl proh-GRAH-mah PAH-rah
rreh-sohl-BEHR kohn-FLEEK-tohs]

constipation   el estreñimiento
[ehl ehs-treh-nyee-MYEHN-toh]

consultant   el consultor / la consultora
[ehl kohn-sool-TOHR /
lah kohn-sool-TOH-rah];
el asesor / la asesora
[ehl ah-seh-SOHR / lah ah-seh-SOH-rah]

contagious   contagioso
[kohn-tah-HYOH-soh]

cook   el cocinero / la cocinera   [ehl
koh-see-NEH-roh / lah koh-see-NEH-rah]

cookie   la galletita   [lah gah-yeh-TEE-tah]

cool   fresco   [FREHS-koh]

cooperate, to   cooperar
[koh-oh-peh-RAHR]

copy, to   copiar   [koh-PYAHR]

copy machine   la copiadora
[lah koh-pyah-DOH-rah]

copy machine ink   la tinta de copiar
[lah TEEN-tah deh koh-PYAHR]

copy machine room   el cuarto de la
copiadora   [ehl KWAHR-toh deh lah
koh-pyah-DOH-rah]

corn   el maíz   [ehl mah-EES]

corner (inside)   el rincón   [ehl rreen-KOHN]

corner (outside)   la esquina
[lah ehs-KEE-nah]

correspondence   la correspondencia
[lah koh-rrehs-pohn-DEHN-syah]

cost, to   costar (ue)   [kohs-TAHR]

costume   el disfraz   [ehl dees-FRAHS]

cotton   el algodón   [ehl ahl-goh-DOHN]

cough   la tos   [lah tohs]

cough, to   toser   [toh-SEHR]

cough syrup   el jarabe para la tos
[ehl hah-RAH-beh PAH-rah lah tohs]

counseling   el asesoramiento
[ehl ah-seh-soh-rah-MYEHN-toh]

counseling office   la oficina del
consejero / de la consejera
[lah oh-fee-SEE-nah dehl kohn-seh-HEH-
roh / deh lah kohn-seh-HEH-rah]

counselor (advisor)   el consejero /
la consejera   [ehl kohn-seh-HEH-roh /
lah kohn-seh-HEH-rah]

count, to   contar (ue)   [kohn-TAHR]

counter   el mostrador
[ehl mohs-trah-DOHR]

country   el país   [ehl pah-EES]

cousin   el primo / la prima
[ehl PREE-moh / lah PREE-mah]

cramp   el calambre   [ehl kah-LAHM-breh]

crayons   los lápices para pintar
[lohs LAH-pee-sehs PAH-rah peen-TAHR]

cream (ointment)   la pomada
[lah poh-MAH-dah]

cream cheese   el queso crema
[ehl KEH-soh KREH-mah]

creative   creativo   [kreh-ah-TEE-boh]

cross, to   cruzar   [kroo-SAHR]

crossing guard   la persona encargada
de ayudar a los niños a cruzar la calle
[lah pehr-SOH-nah ehn-kahr-GAH-dah
deh ah-yoo-DAHR ah lohs NEE-nyohs
ah kroo-SAHR lah KAH-yeh]

crutches   las muletas   [lahs moo-LEH-tahs]

cry, to   llorar   [yoh-RAHR]

cucumber   el pepino   [ehl peh-PEE-noh]

curb   el contén   [ehl kohn-TEHN]

curriculum   el plan de estudio
[ehl plahn deh ehs-TOO-dyoh]

curse, to   decir (*irreg.*) malas palabras
[deh-SEER MAH-lahs pah-LAH-brahs]

curse words   las malas palabras
[lahs MAH-lahs pah-LAH-brahs]

curtain   el telón   [ehl teh-LOHN]

custodian   el guardián / la guardiana
[ehl gwahr-DYAHN / lah gwahr-DYAH-nah]

cut, to   cortar(se)   [kohr-TAHR(seh)]

D

dad(dy)   el papá   [ehl pah-PAH]

daily   a diario   [ah DYAH-ryoh];
diariamente   [dyah-ryah-MEHN-teh]

danger   el peligro   [ehl peh-LEE-groh]

date (appointment)   la cita   [lah SEE-tah]

date (on calendar)   la fecha
[lah FEH-chah]

daughter   la hija   [lah EE-hah]

daughter-in-law   la nuera   [lah NWEH-rah]

day   el día   [ehl DEE-ah]

day after tomorrow   pasado mañana
[pah-SAH-doh mah-NYAH-nah]

day before yesterday   anteayer
[ahn-teh-ah-YEHR]

deadline   la fecha límite   [lah FEH-chah
LEE-mee-teh]

December   diciembre   [dee-SYEHM-breh]

deeply   profundamente
[proh-foon-dah-MEHN-teh]

defibrillator   el desfibrilador
[ehl dehs-fee-bree-lah-DOHR]

dehydrated   deshidratado
[dehs-ee-drah-TAH-doh]

demanding   exigente   [ehk-see-HEHN-teh]

denim   la mezclilla   [lah mehs-KLEE-yah]

depressed   deprimido
[deh-pree-MEE-doh]

desk   el escritorio   [ehl ehs-kree-TOH-ryoh]

desk (student)   el pupitre
[ehl poo-PEE-treh]

dessert   el postre   [ehl POHS-treh]

detention room   el aula de castigo
[ehl AH-oo-lah deh kahs-TEE-goh]

development   el desarrollo
[ehl dehs-ah-RROH-yoh]

diabetes   la diabetes   [lah dyah-BEH-tehs]

diarrhea   la diarrea   [lah dyah-RREH-ah]

dictionary   el diccionario
[ehl deek-syoh-NAH-ryoh]

die, to   morir (ue)   [moh-REER]

dinner   la cena   [lah SEH-nah]

diphtheria   la difteria   [lah deef-TEH-ryah]

discrimination   la discriminación
[lah dees-kree-mee-nah-SYOHN]

disobey, to   desobedecer (*irreg.*)
[dehs-oh-beh-deh-SEHR]

disrespectful, to be   faltar el respeto
[fahl-TAHR ehl rrehs-PEH-toh]

dizziness   el mareo   [ehl mah-REH-oh]

dizzy   mareado   [mah-reh-AH-doh]

dizzy, to get   marearse
[mah-reh-AHR-seh]

do, to   hacer (*irreg.*)   [ah-SEHR]

doctor   el doctor / la doctora
[ehl dohk-TOHR / lah dohk-TOH-rah];
el médico / la médica
[ehl MEH-dee-koh / lah MEH-dee-kah]

doctor's office   la consulta del médico /
de la médica   [lah kohn-SOOL-tah dehl
MEH-dee-koh / deh lah MEH-dee-kah]

doll   la muñeca   [lah moo-NYEH-kah]

domestic violence   la violencia doméstica
[lah byoh-LEHN-syah doh-MEHS-tee-kah]

door   la puerta   [lah PWEHR-tah]

down the street   calle abajo
[KAH-yeh ah-BAH-hoh]

Down's syndrome   el síndrome de Down
[ehl SEEN-droh-meh deh DAH-oon]

downpour   el aguacero
[ehl ah-gwah-SEH-roh]

draw, to   dibujar   [dee-boo-HAHR]

drawer   el cajón   [ehl kah-HOHN]

dress   el vestido   [ehl behs-TEE-doh]

dress, to   vestir (i)   [behs-TEER]

dressed, to get   vestirse (i)
[behs-TEER-seh]

dressy   vistoso   [bees-TOH-soh]

drink   la bebida   [lah beh-BEE-dah]

drink, to   beber   [beh-BEHR]

driver   el chofer   [ehl choh-FEHR];
el conductor / la conductora
[ehl kohn-dook-TOHR /
lah kohn-dook-TOH-rah]

driver's license   la licencia de conducir
[lah lee-SEHN-syah deh kohn-doo-SEER]

driveway   la entrada (para carros)
[lah ehn-TRAH-dah (PAH-rah KAH-rrohs)]

drizzle, to   lloviznar   [yoh-bees-NAHR]

drug abuse   el abuso de drogas
[ehl ah-BOO-soh deh DROH-gahs]

drug overdose   la sobredosis (de drogas)
[lah soh-breh-DOH-sees (deh DROH-gahs)]

dry your hands, to   secarse las manos
[seh-KAHR-seh lahs MAH-nohs]

dust   el polvo   [ehl POHL-boh]

dust, to   sacudir   [sah-koo-DEER]

dust rag   el trapo   [ehl TRAH-poh]

dustpan   el recogedor de basura
[ehl rreh-koh-heh-DOHR deh bah-SOO-rah]

dyslexia   la dislexia   [lah dees-LEHK-syah]

E

each   cada   [KAH-dah]

each day   cada día   [KAH-dah DEE-ah]

ear   la oreja   [lah oh-REH-hah]

earache   el dolor de oído
[ehl doh-LOHR deh oh-EE-doh]

early   temprano   [tehm-PRAH-noh]

earthquake   el terremoto
[ehl teh-rreh-MOH-toh]

earwax   la cerilla   [lah seh-REE-yah]

Easter   la Pascua de Resurrección
[lah PAHS-kwah deh rreh-soo-rrehk-SYOHN]

easy   fácil   [FAH-seel]

eat, to   comer   [koh-MEHR]

eat breakfast, to   desayunar
[deh-sah-yoo-NAHR]

eat dinner, to   cenar   [seh-NAHR]

eat lunch, to   almorzar (ue)
[ahl-mohr-SAHR]

egg   el huevo   [ehl WEH-boh]

elbow   el codo   [ehl KOH-doh]

electrician   el/la electricista
[ehl/lah eh-lehk-tree-SEES-tah]

electronic organizer   el organizador
electrónico   [ehl ohr-gah-nee-sah-DOHR
eh-lehk-TROH-nee-koh]

elegant   elegante   [eh-leh-GAHN-teh]

elementary school   la escuela primaria
[lah ehs-KWEH-lah pree-MAH-ryah]

elevator   el ascensor   [ehl ah-sehn-SOHR]

e-mail   el correo electrónico
[ehl koh-RREH-oh eh-lehk-TROH-nee-koh]

embarrassed   avergonzado
[ah-behr-gohn-SAH-doh]

emergency room   la sala de emergencia
[lah SAH-lah deh eh-mehr-HEHN-syah]

emotional abuse   el abuso mental
[ehl ah-BOO-soh mehn-TAHL]

emotional instability   la falta de
estabilidad emocional   [lah FAHL-tah deh
ehs-tah-bee-lee-DAHD eh-moh-syoh-NAHL]

emotional problems   los problemas
emocionales   [lohs proh-BLEH-mahs
eh-moh-syoh-NAH-lehs]

encourage, to   animar   [ah-nee-MAHR]

end   el fin   [ehl feen]

engineer   el ingeniero / la ingeniera
[ehl een-heh-NYEH-roh /
lah een-heh-NYEH-rah]

enroll, to   matricular
[mah-tree-koo-LAHR]

entrance   la entrada   [lah ehn-TRAH-dah]

envelope   el sobre   [ehl SOH-breh]

epidemic   la epidemia
[lah eh-pee-DEH-myah]

epilepsy   la epilepsia
[lah eh-pee-LEHP-syah]

erase, to   borrar   [boh-RRAHR]

eraser (chalkboard)   el borrador
(de pizarra)
[ehl boh-rrah-DOHR (deh pee-SAH-rrah)]

eraser (rubber)   la goma de borrar
[lah GOH-mah deh boh-RRAHR]

escalator   la escalera mecánica
[lah ehs-kah-LEH-rah meh-KAH-nee-kah]

essay   el ensayo   [ehl ehn-SAH-yoh]

establish, to   establecer (*irreg.*)
[ehs-tah-bleh-SEHR]

evacuation   la evacuación
[lah eh-bah-kwah-SYOHN]

evaluate, to   evaluar   [eh-bah-LWAHR]

evening   la noche   [lah NOH-cheh]

every day   todos los días
[TOH-dohs lohs DEE-ahs]

exam   la prueba   [lah PRWEH-bah];
el examen   [ehl ehk-SAH-mehn]

examination (medical)
el reconocimiento
[ehl rreh-koh-noh-see-MYEHN-toh]

exhale, to   exhalar   [ehk-sah-LAHR]

exhausted   agotado   [ah-goh-TAH-doh]

exit   la salida   [lah sah-LEE-dah]

expensive   caro   [KAH-roh]

experience   la experiencia
[lah ehs-peh-RYEHN-syah]

explosion   el estallido
[ehl ehs-tah-YEE-doh];
la explosión   [lah ehs-ploh-SYOHN]

extract a tooth, to   sacar una muela
[sah-KAHR OO-nah MWEH-lah]

eye   el ojo   [ehl OH-hoh]

eye doctor   el/la oculista
[ehl/lah oh-koo-LEES-tah]

eyebrow   la ceja   [lah SEH-hah]

eyeglasses   los anteojos
    [lohs ahn-teh-OH-hohs]

F

face   la cara   [lah KAH-rah]

facing   frente a   [FREHN-teh ah]

fail (an exam), to   suspender
    [soos-pehn-DEHR]

fainting spell   el desmayo
    [ehl dehs-MAH-yoh]

fall, to   caerse (*irreg.*)   [kah-EHR-seh]

fall asleep, to   dormirse (ue)
    [dohr-MEER-seh]

family   la familia   [lah fah-MEE-lyah]

far away   lejos   [LEH-hohs]

fast   rápido   [RRAH-pee-doh]

father   el padre   [ehl PAH-dreh]

father-in-law   el suegro   [ehl SWEH-groh]

fax, to   mandar por fax
    [mahn-DAHR pohr fahks]

fax machine   el telefax
    [ehl teh-leh-FAHKS]

February   febrero   [feh-BREH-roh]

fed up   harto   [AHR-toh]

fence   la cerca   [lah SEHR-kah]

fever   la fiebre   [lah FYEH-breh]

fight, to   pelear   [peh-leh-AHR]

file   el archivo   [ehl ahr-CHEE-boh]

file, to   archivar   [ahr-chee-BAHR]

file cabinet   el fichero   [ehl fee-CHEH-roh]

file folder   la carpeta   [lah kahr-PEH-tah]

fill out, to   llenar   [yeh-NAHR]

filling (tooth)   el empaste
    [ehl ehm-PAHS-teh]

financial aid   la ayuda financiera
    [lah ah-YOO-dah fee-nahn-SYEH-rah]

find, to   encontrar (ue)   [ehn-kohn-TRAHR]

fine   la multa   [lah MOOL-tah]

finger   el dedo   [ehl DEH-doh]

fire   el fuego   [ehl FWEH-goh];
    el incendio   [ehl een-SEHN-dyoh]

fire alarm   la alarma de incendios
    [lah ah-LAHR-mah deh een-SEHN-dyohs]

fire door   la puerta contra incendios
    [lah PWEHR-tah KOHN-trah
    een-SEHN-dyohs]

fire drill   el simulacro de incendio
    [ehl see-moo-LAH-kroh deh
    een-SEHN-dyoh]

fire escape   la escalera de emergencia
    [lah ehs-kah-LEH-rah deh
    eh-mehr-HEHN-syah]

fire exit   la salida de emergencia
    [lah sah-LEE-dah deh eh-mehr-HEHN-syah]

fire extinguisher   el extintor
    [ehl ehs-teen-TOHR]

firefighter   el bombero / la bombera
    [ehl bohm-BEH-roh / lah bohm-BEH-rah]

first aid kit   la caja de primeros auxilios
    [lah KAH-hah deh pree-MEH-rohs
    ah-ook-SEE-lyohs]

fish (alive)   el pez   [ehl PEHS]

fish (on a plate)   el pescado
    [ehl pehs-KAH-doh]

fix, to   arreglar   [ah-rreh-GLAHR]

flag   la bandera   [lah bahn-DEH-rah]

flame   la llama   [lah YAH-mah]

flannel   la franela   [lah frah-NEH-lah]

flashlight   la linterna   [lah leen-TEHR-nah]

flight attendant   el/la asistente de vuelo
    [ehl/lah ah-sees-TEHN-teh deh BWEH-loh]

flood   la inundación
    [lah ee-noon-dah-SYOHN]

floor (ground, surface, flooring)   el suelo
    [ehl SWEH-loh]

floor (story)   el piso   [ehl PEE-soh]

flu   la gripe   [lah GREE-peh]

flush (the toilet), to   descargar
    [dehs-kahr-GAHR]

fog   la neblina   [lah neh-BLEE-nah]

fold, to   doblar   [doh-BLAHR]

food   el alimento   [ehl ah-lee-MEHN-toh];
    la comida   [lah koh-MEE-dah]

foodstuff   los comestibles
    [lohs koh-mehs-TEE-blehs]

foot   el pie   [ehl pyeh]

for what   para qué   [PAH-rah keh]

for when   para cuándo
    [PAH-rah KWAHN-doh]

for whom   para quién / para quiénes
    [PAH-rah kyehn / PAH-rah KYEH-nehs]

forbid, to   prohibir   [proh-ee-BEER]

forehead   la frente   [lah FREHN-teh]

form   el formulario
    [ehl fohr-moo-LAH-ryoh]

fountain   la fuente   [lah FWEHN-teh]

fraud   el fraude   [ehl FRAH-oo-deh]

frequently   frecuentemente
    [freh-kwehn-teh-MEHN-teh]

Friday   el viernes   [ehl BYEHR-nehs]

from time to time   de vez en cuando
[deh behs ehn KWAHN-doh]
from where   de dónde [deh DOHN-deh]
front of, in   enfrente de
[ehn-FREHN-teh deh]
fruit   la fruta [lah FROO-tah]
frustrated   frustrado [froos-TRAH-doh]
furious   furioso [foo-RYOH-soh]

G

gang   la pandilla [lah pahn-DEE-yah]
gardener   el jardinero / la jardinera
[ehl hahr-dee-NEH-roh /
lah hahr-dee-NEH-rah]
garlic   el ajo [ehl AH-hoh]
garment   la prenda de vestir
[lah PREHN-dah deh behs-TEER]
gas leak   el escape de gas
[ehl ehs-KAH-peh deh gahs]
gate   la verja [lah BEHR-hah]
get, to   obtener (irreg.) [ohb-teh-NEHR]
get off, to   bajar de [bah-HAHR deh]
get on, to   subir a [SOO-BEER ah]
get up, to   levantarse
[leh-bahn-TAHR-seh]
girl   la niña [lah NEE-nyah]
girlfriend   la novia [lah NOH-byah]
give, to   dar (irreg.) [dahr]
give a shot (injection), to   inyectar
[een-yehk-TAHR];
ponerle (irreg.) una inyección
[poh-NEHR-leh oo-nah een-yehk-SYOHN]
give advice, to   aconsejar
[ah-kohn-seh-HAHR]
give back, to   devolver (ue)
[deh-bohl-BEHR]
glove   el guante [ehl GWAHN-teh]
glue   la cola [lah KOH-lah]
go, to   ir (irreg.) [eer]
go down, to   bajar [bah-HAHR]
go out, to   salir (irreg.) [sah-LEER]
go to (a place), to   ir (irreg.) a (+ place)
[eer ah]
go to bed, to   acostarse (ue)
[ah-kohs-TAHR-seh]
go to sleep, to   dormirse (ue)
[dohr-MEER-seh]
go up, to   subir [SOO-BEER]
goddaughter   la ahijada
[lah ah-ee-HAH-dah]
godfather   el compadre [ehl kohm-PAH-
dreh]; el padrino [ehl pah-DREE-noh]

godmother   la comadre [lah koh-MAH-
dreh]; la madrina [lah mah-DREE-nah]
godson   el ahijado [ehl ah-ee-HAH-doh]
good grades, to get   sacar buenas notas
[sah-KAHR BWEH-nahs NOH-tahs]
good-bye   adiós [ah-DYOHS]
grab, to   agarrar [ah-gah-RRAHR]
grade (level)   el grado [ehl GRAH-doh]
grade (mark)   la nota [lah NOH-tah]
grade, to   calificar [kah-lee-fee-KAHR]
graduation   la graduación
[lah grah-dwah-SYOHN]
granddaughter   la nieta [lah NYEH-tah]
grandfather   el abuelo [ehl ah-BWEH-loh]
grandmother   la abuela
[lah ah-BWEH-lah]
grandson   el nieto [ehl NYEH-toh]
grape   la uva [lah OO-bah]
grass   la hierba [lah YEHR-bah]
grateful   agradecido
[ah-grah-deh-SEE-doh]
gray   gris [grees]
green   verde [BEHR-deh]
green pea   el guisante [ehl gee-SAHN-teh]
guide dog   el perro guía
[ehl PEH-rroh GEE-ah]
gymnasium   el gimnasio
[ehl heem-NAH-syoh]

H

hail   el granizo [ehl grah-NEE-soh]
hailstorm   la granizada
[lah grah-nee-SAH-dah]
hair   el cabello [ehl kah-BEH-yoh];
el pelo [ehl PEH-loh]
hairdresser   el peluquero / la peluquera
[ehl peh-loo-KEH-roh /
lah peh-loo-KEH-rah]
Halloween   la Víspera de Todos los Santos
[lah BEES-peh-rah deh TOH-dohs lohs
SAHN-tohs]
hallway   el pasillo [ehl pah-SEE-yoh]
ham   el jamón [ehl hah-MOHN]
hamburger   la hamburguesa
[lah ahm-boor-GEH-sah]
hand   la mano [lah MAH-noh]
handkerchief   el pañuelo
[ehl pah-NYWEH-loh]
handwriting   la caligrafía
[lah kah-lee-grah-FEE-ah];
la escritura [lah ehs-kree-TOO-rah]

Hanukkah la Fiesta de las Luces
[lah FYEHS-tah deh lahs LOO-sehs]
happy contento [kohn-TEHN-toh]
harassment el acoso [ehl ah-KOH-soh]
hardworking trabajador/trabajadora
[trah-bah-hah-DOHR/
trah-bah-hah-DOH-rah]
hat el sombrero [ehl sohm-BREH-roh]
have, to tener (*irreg.*) [teh-NEHR]
head la cabeza [lah kah-BEH-sah]
headache el dolor de cabeza
[ehl doh-LOHR deh kah-BEH-sah]
headmaster/headmistress el director /
la directora [ehl dee-rehk-TOHR /
lah dee-rehk-TOH-rah]
headscarf el pañuelo
[ehl pah-NYWEH-loh]
health la salud [lah sah-LOOD]
healthy saludable [sah-loo-DAH-bleh]
hear, to oír (*irreg.*) [oh-EER]
hearing aid el audífono
[ehl ah-oo-DEE-foh-noh];
el aparato de oído
[ehl ah-pah-RAH-toh deh oh-EE-doh]
hearing problems la sordera
[lah sohr-DEH-rah];
la pérdida de capacidad auditiva
[lah PEHR-dee-dah deh kah-pah-see-DAHD
ah-oo-dee-TEE-bah]
heart el corazón [ehl koh-rah-SOHN]
heart attack el ataque cardíaco
[ehl ah-TAH-keh kahr-DEE-ah-koh]
heat (weather, warmth) el calor
[ehl kah-LOHR]
heat(ing) la calefacción
[lah kah-leh-fahk-SYOHN]
height la estatura
[lah ehs-tah-TOO-rah]
hello hola [OH-lah]
help el auxilio [ehl ah-ook-SEE-lyoh];
el socorro [ehl soh-KOH-rroh]
hepatitis la hepatitis
[lah eh-pah-TEE-tees]
her su [SOO]
here aquí [ah-KEE]
hiccup(s) el hipo [ehl EE-poh]
high school la escuela secundaria
[lah ehs-KWEH-lah seh-koon-DAH-ryah]
highlighter el marcador
[ehl mahr-kah-DOHR]
hip la cadera [lah kah-DEH-rah]
his su [SOO]

hit, to golpear [gohl-peh-AHR];
pegar [peh-GAHR]
hobby el pasatiempo favorito
[ehl pah-sah-TYEHM-poh fah-boh-REE-toh]
holiday el día feriado
[ehl DEE-ah feh-RYAH-doh]
home el hogar [ehl oh-GAHR]
homeless, to be estar (*irreg.*) sin hogar/
vivienda [ehs-TAHR seen oh-GAHR/
bee-BYEHN-dah]
homelessness la falta de hogar/vivienda
[lah FAHL-tah deh oh-GAHR/
bee-BYEHN-dah]
homework la tarea [lah tah-REH-ah]
honest honesto [oh-NEHS-toh]
hope, to esperar [ehs-peh-RAHR]
hot dog el perro caliente
[ehl PEH-rroh kah-LYEHN-teh]
house la casa [lah KAH-sah]
how cómo [KOH-moh]
how many cuántos/cuántas
[KWAHN-tohs/KWAHN-tahs]
how much cuánto/cuánta
[KWAHN-toh/KWAHN-tah]
hunger el hambre [ehl AHM-breh]
hungry, to be tener (*irreg.*) hambre
[teh-NEHR AHM-breh]
hurricane el huracán [ehl oo-rah-KAHN]
hurry, to be in a tener (*irreg.*) prisa
[teh-NEHR PREE-sah]
hurry up, to darse (*irreg.*) prisa
[DAHR-seh PREE-sah]
hurt, to doler (ue) [doh-LEHR]
husband el esposo [ehl ehs-POH-soh]

I

I yo [yoh]
illness la enfermedad
[lah ehn-fehr-meh-DAHD]
immediately inmediatamente
[een-meh-dyah-tah-MEHN-teh]
improve, to mejorarse
[meh-hoh-RAHR-seh]
in the middle of a mediados de
[ah meh-DYAH-dohs deh]
incest el incesto [ehl een-SEHS-toh]
income el ingreso [ehl een-GREH-soh]
independent independiente
[een-deh-pehn-DYEHN-teh]
indigestion la indigestión
[lah een-dee-hehs-TYOHN]
inexpensive barato [bah-RAH-toh]

infected infectado [een-fehk-TAH-doh]

infection la infección
[lah een-fehk-SYOHN]

infectious disease la enfermedad
infecciosa [lah ehn-fehr-meh-DAHD
een-fehk-SYOH-sah]

inhale, to inhalar [ee-nah-LAHR]

ink la tinta [lah TEEN-tah]

ink jet printer la impresora de chorro
de tinta [lah eem-preh-SOH-rah deh
CHOH-rroh deh TEEN-tah]

inner ear (hearing) el oído
[ehl oh-EE-doh]

inquisitive curioso [koo-RYOH-soh]

insect bite la picadura
[lah pee-kah-DOO-rah]

insecure inseguro [een-seh-GOO-roh]

inside adentro [ah-DEHN-troh]

inside of dentro de [DEHN-troh deh]

instructor el instructor / la instructora
[ehl eens-trook-TOHR /
lah eens-trook-TOH-rah]

insurance el seguro [ehl seh-GOO-roh]

intelligent inteligente
[een-teh-lee-HEHN-teh]

interpreter el/la intérprete
[ehl/lah een-TEHR-preh-teh]

intersection la bocacalle
[lah boh-kah-KAH-yeh]

interview la entrevista
[lah ehn-treh-BEES-tah]

iodine el yodo [ehl YOH-doh]

itch la picazón [lah pee-kah-SOHN]

J

jacket el saco [ehl SAH-koh]; la chaqueta
[lah chah-KEH-tah]

janitor el/la conserje
[ehl/lah kohn-SEHR-heh]

January enero [eh-NEH-roh]

jealous celoso [seh-LOH-soh]

jeans los blue jeans [lohs bloo yeens];
los vaqueros [lohs bah-KEH-rohs]

job application la solicitud de empleo
[lah soh-lee-see-TOOD deh ehm-PLEH-oh]

journalist el reportero / la reportera
[ehl rreh-pohr-TEH-roh /
lah rreh-pohr-TEH-rah]

juice el jugo [ehl HOO-goh]

July julio [HOO-lyoh]

jump, to saltar [sahl-TAHR]

jump rope la cuerda de saltar
[lah KWEHR-dah deh sahl-TAHR]

June junio [HOO-nyoh]

juvenile delinquency la delincuencia
juvenil
[lah deh-leen-KWEHN-syah hoo-beh-NEEL]

K

keep silent, to guardar silencio
[gwahr-DAHR see-LEHN-syoh]

kick, to dar (*irreg.*) patadas
[dahr pah-TAH-dahs];
patear [pah-teh-AHR]

kidnapping el secuestro
[ehl seh-KWEHS-troh]

kindergarten el jardín de infancia
[ehl hahr-DEEN deh een-FAHN-syah];
el kinder [ehl KEEN-dehr]

kite la cometa [lah koh-MEH-tah]

knee la rodilla [lah rroh-DEE-yah]

know (facts), to saber (*irreg.*) [sah-BEHR]

know (person, place), to conocer (*irreg.*)
[koh-noh-SEHR]

L

Labor Day el día del Trabajador
[ehl DEE-ah dehl trah-bah-hah-DOHR]

labor union el sindicato
[ehl seen-dee-KAH-toh]

laboratory el laboratorio
[ehl lah-boh-rah-TOH-ryoh]

landslide el desprendimiento de tierra
[ehl dehs-prehn-dee-MYEHN-toh deh
TYEH-rrah]

language el lenguaje
[ehl lehn-GWAH-heh]

last, to durar [doo-RAHR]

last night anoche [ah-NOH-cheh]

late atrasado [ah-trah-SAH-doh]

later luego [LWEH-goh]; más tarde
[mahs TAHR-deh]

laugh, to reír(se) (*irreg.*) [rreh-EER(seh)]

lawyer el abogado / la abogada
[ehl ah-boh-GAH-doh /
lah ah-boh-GAH-dah]

lead el plomo [ehl PLOH-moh]

learn, to aprender [ah-prehn-DEHR]

learning disability la discapacidad de
aprendizaje [lah dees-kah-pah-see-DAHD
deh ah-prehn-dee-SAH-heh]

leather el cuero [ehl KWEH-roh]

leave, to salir (*irreg.*) [sah-LEER]

left izquierda [ees-KYEHR-dah]
leg pierna [lah PYEHR-nah]
lemonade la limonada
  [lah lee-moh-NAH-dah]
less (fewer) menos [MEH-nohs]
lesson la lección [lah lehk-SYOHN]
letter la carta [lah KAHR-tah]
letter of recommendation la carta
  de recomendación [lah KAHR-tah
  deh rreh-koh-mehn-dah-SYOHN]
lettuce la lechuga [lah leh-CHOO-gah]
leukemia la leucemia
  [lah leh-oo-SEH-myah]
librarian el bibliotecario / la bibliotecaria
  [ehl bee-blyoh-teh-KAH-ryoh /
  lah bee-blyoh-teh-KAH-ryah]
library la biblioteca
  [lah bee-blyoh-TEH-kah]
library card la tarjeta de biblioteca
  [lah tahr-HEH-tah deh bee-blyoh-TEH-kah]
lice los piojos [lohs PYOH-hohs]
lie down, to acostarse (ue)
  [ah-kohs-TAHR-seh]
light la luz [lah loos]
lighting las luces [lahs LOO-sehs]
lightning el relámpago
  [ehl rreh-LAHM-pah-goh]
like, to gustar [goos-TAHR]
liniment el linimento
  [ehl lee-nee-MEHN-toh]
lip el labio [ehl LAH-byoh]
listen, to escuchar [ehs-koo-CHAHR]
little (not much) poco [POH-koh]
loan el préstamo [ehl PREHS-tah-moh]
lobby el vestíbulo [ehl behs-TEE-boo-loh]
lock el candado [ehl kahn-DAH-doh]
locker el cajón con llave
  [ehl kah-HOHN kohn YAH-beh]
locker room el vestuario
  [ehl behs-TWAH-ryoh]
long largo [LAHR-goh]
look bad, to lucir (*irreg.*) mal
  [loo-SEER mahl]
look for, to buscar [boos-KAHR]
look good, to lucir (*irreg.*) bien
  [loo-SEER byehn]
lose, to perder (ie) [pehr-DEHR]
lost perdido [pehr-DEE-doh]
lotion la loción [lah loh-SYOHN]
loudspeaker el altavoz
  [ehl ahl-tah-BOHS]

lucky, to be tener (*irreg.*) suerte
  [teh-NEHR SWEHR-teh]
lunch el almuerzo [ehl ahl-MWEHR-soh]
lung el pulmón [ehl pool-MOHN]

M

magazine la revista [lah rreh-BEES-tah]
mail room el cuarto de correo
  [ehl KWAHR-toh deh koh-RREH-oh]
make, to hacer (*irreg.*) [ah-SEHR]
make an appointment, to hacer (*irreg.*)
  una cita [ah-SEHR OO-nah SEE-tah]
make better, to mejorar
  [meh-hoh-RAHR]
make fun, to burlarse [boor-LAHR-seh]
man el hombre [ehl OHM-breh]
mandatory obligatorio
  [oh-blee-gah-TOH-ryoh]
manslaughter el homicidio involuntario
  [ehl oh-mee-SEE-dyoh
  een-boh-loon-TAH-ryoh]
many times muchas veces
  [MOO-chahs BEH-sehs]
marble (toy) la canica [lah kah-NEE-kah]
March marzo [MAHR-soh]
margarine la margarina
  [lah mahr-gah-REE-nah]
marvelous maravilloso
  [mah-rah-bee-YOH-soh]
match el fósforo [ehl FOHS-foh-roh]
match (game) el partido
  [ehl pahr-TEE-doh]
match, to hacer (*irreg.*) juego con
  [ah-SEHR HWEH-goh kohn]
mathematics las matemáticas
  [lahs mah-teh-MAH-tee-kahs]
May mayo [MAH-yoh]
measles el sarampión
  [ehl sah-rahm-PYOHN]
meat la carne [lah KAHR-neh]
mechanic el mecánico / la mecánica
  [ehl meh-KAH-nee-koh /
  lah meh-KAH-nee-kah]
medicine la medicina
  [lah meh-dee-SEE-nah]
medicine (drug) el medicamento
  [ehl meh-dee-kah-MEHN-toh]
meeting la reunión [lah rreh-oo-NYOHN]
melon el melón [ehl meh-LOHN]
meningitis la meningitis
  [lah meh-neen-HEE-tees]

menstrual period
  la regla [lah RREH-glah];
  el período [ehl peh-REE-oh-doh]
mental retardation   el retraso mental
  [ehl rreh-TRAH-soh mehn-TAHL]
merry-go-round   el tiovivo
  [ehl tee-oh-BEE-boh]
microphone   el micrófono
  [ehl mee-KROH-foh-noh]
middle (center)   el medio [ehl MEH-dyoh]
middle (half)   medio [MEH-dyoh]
migraine   la jaqueca [lah hah-KEH-kah]
milk   la leche [lah LEH-cheh]
mineral water   el agua mineral
  [ehl AH-gwah mee-neh-RAHL]
minus (sign)   menos [MEH-nohs]
mirror   el espejo [ehl ehs-PEH-hoh]
misbehave, to   portarse mal
  [pohr-TAHR-seh mahl]
Miss   la señorita [lah seh-nyoh-REE-tah]
modeling clay   la plasticina
  [lah plahs-tee-SEE-nah]
molestation   el asalto sexual
  [ehl ah-SAHL-toh sehk-SWAHL]
Monday   el lunes [ehl LOO-nehs]
money   el dinero [ehl dee-NEH-roh]
mononucleosis   la mononucleosis
  [lah moh-noh-noo-kleh-OH-sees]
month   el mes [ehl mehs]
mop   el trapeador [ehl trah-peh-ah-DOHR]
mop, to   trapear [trah-peh-AHR]
more   más [mahs]
morning   la mañana [lah mah-NYAH-nah]
mother   la madre [lah MAH-dreh]
mother-in-law   la suegra [lah SWEH-grah]
moustache   el bigote [ehl bee-GOH-teh]
mouth   la boca [lah BOH-kah]
Mr./mister/sir   el señor [ehl seh-NYOHR]
Mrs./madam   la señora
  [lah seh-NYOH-rah]
mucus   la flema [lah FLEH-mah]
multiple sclerosis   la esclerosis múltiple
  [lah ehs-kleh-ROH-sees MOOL-tee-pleh]
mumps   las paperas [lahs pah-PEH-rahs]
murder   el homicidio
  [ehl oh-mee-SEE-dyoh]
muscular dystrophy   la distrofia
  muscular [lah dees-TROH-fyah
  moos-koo-LAHR]
music   la música [lah MOO-see-kah]
my   mi [mee]

N

nail   la uña [lah OO-nyah]
nap   la siesta [lah SYEHS-tah]
nap, to   dormir (ue) la siesta
  [dohr-MEER lah SYEHS-tah]
nausea   la náusea [lah NAH-oo-seh-ah]
nauseous   mareado [mah-reh-AH-doh]
Navy   la marina de guerra
  [lah mah-REE-nah deh GEH-rrah]
navy blue   azul marino
  [ah-SOOL mah-REE-noh]
nearby   cerca [SEHR-kah]
neck   el cuello [ehl KWEH-yoh]
neighborhood   el barrio [ehl BAH-rryoh]
neither   tampoco [tahm-POH-koh]
nephew   el sobrino [ehl soh-BREE-noh]
nervous   nervioso [nehr-BYOH-soh]
never   nunca [NOON-kah]
New Year's Day   el día de Año Nuevo
  [ehl DEE-ah deh AH-nyoh NWEH-boh]
newspaper   el periódico
  [ehl peh-RYOH-dee-koh]
next   próximo [PROHK-see-moh]
next to   al lado de [ahl LAH-doh deh]
niece   la sobrina [lah soh-BREE-nah]
night   la noche [lah NOH-cheh]
night before last   anteanoche
  [ahn-teh-ah-NOH-cheh]
no   no [noh]
no one   nadie [NAH-dyeh];
  ninguno/ninguna
  [neen-GOO-noh/neen-GOO-nah]
nobody   nadie [NAH-dyeh];
  ninguno/ninguna
  [neen-GOO-noh/neen-GOO-nah]
none   ninguno/ninguna
  [neen-GOO-noh/neen-GOO-nah]
noon   el mediodía
  [ehl meh-dyoh-DEE-ah]
nose   la nariz [lah nah-REES]
not yet   todavía no [toh-dah-BEE-ah noh]
notebook   el cuaderno
  [ehl kwah-DEHR-noh]
nothing   nada [NAH-dah]
November   noviembre
  [noh-BYEHM-breh]
now   ahora [ah-OH-rah]
nurse   el enfermero / la enfermera
  [ehl ehn-fehr-MEH-roh /
  lah ehn-fehr-MEH-rah]

nurse's office   la oficina del enfermero /
de la enfermera [lah oh-fee-SEE-nah
dehl ehn-fehr-MEH-roh /
deh lah ehn-fehr-MEH-rah]

nursery   la guardería
[lah gwahr-deh-REE-ah]

O

oatmeal   la avena [lah ah-BEH-nah]

obedient   obediente [oh-beh-DYEHN-teh]

obesity   la obesidad
[lah oh-beh-see-DAHD]

obey, to   obedecer (*irreg.*)
[oh-beh-deh-SEHR]

obscene phone call   la llamada
telefónica indecente/obscena
[lah yah-MAH-dah teh-leh-FOH-nee-kah
een-deh-SEHN-teh/ohb-SEH-nah]

obtain, to   obtener (*irreg.*) [ohb-teh-NEHR]

occupation   la profesión
[lah proh-feh-SYOHN]

October   octubre [ohk-TOO-breh]

often   a menudo [ah meh-NOO-doh]

omelet   la tortilla [lah tohr-TEE-yah]

once   una vez [OO-nah behs]

one   un/uno/una [oon/oo-noh/oo-nah]

one-way street   la calle de dirección
única [lah KAH-yeh deh dee-rehk-SYOHN
OO-nee-kah]

onion   la cebolla [lah seh-BOH-yah]

open, to   abrir [ah-BREER]

orange (color)   anaranjado
[ah-nah-rahn-HAH-doh]

orange (fruit)   la naranja
[lah nah-RAHN-hah]

organized   organizado
[ohr-gah-nee-SAH-doh]

orthodontist   el/la ortodontista
[ehl/lah ohr-toh-dohn-TEES-tah]

our   nuestro [NWEHS-troh]

outdoors   al aire libre
[ahl AH-ee-reh LEE-breh]

outside   afuera [ah-FWEH-rah]

outside of   fuera de [FWEH-rah deh]

over there   allá [ah-YAH]

overalls   el overol [ehl oh-beh-ROHL]

overhead projector   el retroproyector
[ehl rreh-troh-proh-yehk-TOHR]

P

page   la página [lah PAH-hee-nah]

paint, to   pintar [peen-TAHR]

painter   el pintor / la pintora
[ehl peen-TOHR / lah peen-TOH-rah]

painting   el cuadro [ehl KWAH-droh];
la pintura [lah peen-TOO-rah]

pajamas   la piyama
[lah pee-YAH-mah]

panties   las bragas
[lahs BRAH-gahs]

pants   los pantalones
[lohs pahn-tah-LOH-nehs]

pantyhose   las pantimedias
[lahs pahn-tee-MEH-dyahs];
los pantis [lohs PAHN-tees]

paper   el papel [ehl pah-PEHL]

paper (colored)   el papel (de colores)
[ehl pah-PEHL (deh koh-LOH-rehs)]

paper clip   el sujetapapeles
[ehl soo-heh-tah-pah-PEH-lehs]

paper towel   la toalla de papel
[lah toh-AH-yah deh pah-PEHL]

paralysis   la parálisis
[lah pah-RAH-lee-sees]

parents   los padres
[lohs PAH-drehs]

park   el parque [ehl PAHR-keh]

parking lot   el estacionamiento
[ehl ehs-tah-syoh-nah-MYEHN-toh]

part-time   a tiempo parcial
[ah TYEHM-poh pahr-SYAHL]

pass (permission)   el pase [ehl PAH-seh];
el permiso [ehl pehr-MEE-soh]

pass (a class), to   aprobar (ue)
[ah-proh-BAHR]

Passover   la Pascua (de los judíos)
[lah PAHS-kwah (deh lohs hoo-DEE-ohs)]

paste, to   pegar [peh-GAHR]

pay, to   pagar [pah-GAHR]

pay attention, to   prestar atención
[prehs-TAHR ah-tehn-SYOHN]

pay the fine, to   pagar la multa
[pah-GAHR lah MOOL-tah]

peach   el melocotón
[ehl meh-loh-koh-TOHN]

peanut   el cacahuete
[ehl kah-kah-WEH-teh];
el maní [ehl mah-NEE]

pear   la pera [lah PEH-rah]

pedestrian crossing   el paso de peatones
[ehl PAH-soh deh peh-ah-TOH-nehs]

peer mediation program el programa que usa a otros jóvenes como intermediarios en conflictos [ehl proh-GRAH-mah keh OO-sah ah OH-trohs HOH-beh-nehs KOH-moh een-tehr-meh-DYAH-ryohs ehn kohn-FLEEK-tohs]

pen la pluma [lah PLOO-mah]

pencil el lápiz [ehl LAH-pees]

pencil sharpener el sacapuntas [ehl sah-kah-POON-tahs]

penicillin la penicilina [lah peh-nee-see-LEE-nah]

people la gente [lah HEHN-teh]; las personas [lahs pehr-SOH-nahs]

pepper la pimienta [lah pee-MYEHN-tah]

pet el animal doméstico [ehl ah-nee-MAHL doh-MEHS-tee-koh]

photocopy, to fotocopiar [foh-toh-koh-PYAHR]

photographer el fotógrafo / la fotógrafa [ehl foh-TOH-grah-foh / lah foh-TOH-grah-fah]

physical education la educación física [lah eh-doo-kah-SYOHN FEE-see-kah]

pick up, to recoger (*irreg.*) [rreh-koh-HEHR]

picture el cuadro [ehl KWAH-droh]; la pintura [lah peen-TOO-rah]

pineapple la piña [lah PEE-nyah]

pink rosado [rroh-SAH-doh]

place, to poner (*irreg.*) [poh-NEHR]

play, to jugar (ue) [hoo-GAHR]

play (a game), to jugar (ue) a (+ *game*) [hoo-GAHR ah]

play (a musical instrument), to tocar [toh-KAHR]

play "dress up," to jugar (ue) a disfrazarse [hoo-GAHR ah dees-frah-SAHR-seh]

play hide-and-seek, to jugar (ue) al escondite [hoo-GAHR ahl ehs-kohn-DEE-teh]

play "house," to jugar (ue) a la casita [hoo-GAHR ah lah kah-SEE-tah]

playground el patio de recreo [ehl PAH-tyoh deh rreh-KREH-oh]

plumber el plomero / la plomera [ehl ploh-MEH-roh / lah ploh-MEH-rah]

pneumonia la pulmonía [lah pool-moh-NEE-ah]

pocket el bolsillo [ehl bohl-SEE-yoh]

pocketbook el bolso [ehl BOHL-soh]

poisoning el envenenamiento [ehl ehn-beh-neh-nah-MYEHN-toh]

police la policía [lah poh-lee-SEE-ah]

police custody la custodia policial [lah koos-TOH-dyah poh-lee-SYAHL]

police force el cuerpo de policía [ehl KWEHR-poh deh poh-lee-SEE-ah]

police officer el policía / la mujer policía [ehl poh-lee-SEE-ah / lah moo-HEHR poh-lee-SEE-ah]

police record los antecedentes penales [lohs ahn-teh-seh-DEHN-tehs peh-NAH-lehs]

police station la comisaría [lah koh-mee-sah-REE-ah]

polyester el poliéster [ehl poh-LYEHS-tehr]

poster el cartel [ehl kahr-TEHL]

potato la papa [lah PAH-pah]; la patata [lah pah-TAH-tah]

poverty la pobreza [lah poh-BREH-sah]

powder el polvo [ehl POHL-boh]

pregnancy (unwanted) el embarazo (no deseado) [ehl ehm-bah-RAH-soh (noh deh-seh-AH-doh)]

President's Day el día de los Presidentes [ehl DEE-ah deh lohs preh-see-DEHN-tehs]

pretty bonito [boh-NEE-toh]; lindo [LEEN-doh]

principal el director / la directora [ehl dee-rehk-TOHR / lah dee-rehk-TOH-rah]

print, to imprimir [eem-pree-MEER]

print (write in block letters), to escribir en letra de molde [ehs-kree-BEER ehn LEH-trah deh MOHL-deh]

printer la impresora [lah eem-preh-SOH-rah]

problem el problema [ehl proh-BLEH-mah]

programmer el programador / la programadora [ehl proh-grah-mah-DOHR / lah proh-grah-mah-DOH-rah]

prohibit, to prohibir [proh-ee-BEER]

pronunciation la pronunciación [lah proh-noon-syah-SYOHN]

proud orgulloso [ohr-goo-YOH-soh]

psychologist el psicólogo / la psicóloga [ehl see-KOH-loh-goh / lah see-KOH-loh-gah]

pull, to jalar [hah-LAHR]; tirar de [tee-RAHR deh]

punctual puntual [poon-TWAHL]
puppet el títere [ehl TEE-teh-reh]
purple morado [moh-RAH-doh]
purse el monedero
[ehl moh-neh-DEH-roh];
el portamonedas
[ehl pohr-tah-moh-NEH-dahs]
push, to empujar [ehm-poo-HAHR]
put, to poner (*irreg.*) [poh-NEHR]
put a cast on, to enyesar [ehn-yeh-SAHR]
put away, to guardar [gwahr-DAHR]
put on, to ponerse (*irreg.*) [poh-NEHR-seh]
put puzzles together, to armar
rompecabezas
[ahr-MAHR rrohm-peh-kah-BEH-sahs]
puzzle (jigsaw) el rompecabezas
[ehl rrohm-peh-kah-BEH-sahs]

Q

quarter (one-fourth part) un cuarto
[oon KWAHR-toh]
question la pregunta
[lah preh-GOON-tah]
quickly de prisa [deh PREE-sah];
rápidamente [RRAH-pee-dah-MEHN-teh]

R

racism el racismo [ehl rrah-SEES-moh]
radio (battery-powered) el radio
(de baterías)
[ehl RRAH-dyoh (deh bah-teh-REE-ahs)]
railroad crossing el cruce de ferrocarril
[ehl KROO-seh deh feh-rroh-kah-RREEL]
railroad track la vía de ferrocarril
[lah BEE-ah deh feh-rroh-kah-RREEL]
rain la lluvia [lah YOO-byah]
rain, to llover (ue) [yoh-BEHR]
raincoat el impermeable
[ehl eem-pehr-meh-AH-bleh];
la gabardina [lah gah-bahr-DEE-nah]
rainy lluvioso [yoo-BYOH-soh]
Ramadan Ramadán [rrah-mah-DAHN]
rape la violación [lah byoh-lah-SYOHN]
rarely rara vez [RRAH-rah behs]
rash la erupción [lah eh-roop-SYOHN]
read, to leer (*irreg.*) [leh-EHR]
reading la lectura [lah lehk-TOO-rah]
receive, to recibir [rreh-see-BEER]
receptionist el/la recepcionista
[ehl/lah rreh-sehp-syoh-NEES-tah]
recess el recreo [ehl rreh-KREH-oh]

recommend, to recomendar (ie)
[rreh-koh-mehn-DAHR]
recruiting station la oficina de
reclutamiento [lah oh-fee-SEE-nah deh
rreh-kloo-tah-MYEHN-toh]
red rojo [RROH-hoh]
reference la referencia
[lah rreh-feh-REHN-syah]
registration la matrícula
[lah mah-TREE-koo-lah]
relative el/la pariente
[ehl/lah pah-RYEHN-teh]
relax, to relajarse [rreh-lah-HAHR-seh]
relaxed relajado [rreh-lah-HAH-doh]
remember, to recordar (ue)
[rreh-kohr-DAHR]
repeat, to repetir (i) [rreh-peh-TEER]
report el informe [ehl een-FOHR-meh]
report card el boletín
[ehl boh-leh-TEEN]
request, to pedir (i) [peh-DEER]
require, to requerir (ie) [rreh-keh-REER]
requirement el requisito
[ehl rreh-kee-SEE-toh]
rescue el rescate [ehl rrehs-KAH-teh]
research, to investigar
[een-behs-tee-GAHR]
resentful resentido [rreh-sehn-TEE-doh]
respectful respetuoso
[rrehs-peh-TWOH-soh]
rest, to descansar [dehs-kahn-SAHR]
restless inquieto [een-KYEH-toh]
return (give back), to devolver (ue)
[deh-bohl-BEHR]
return (go back), to regresar
[rreh-greh-SAHR]; volver (ue) [bohl-BEHR]
return date la fecha de devolución
[lah FEH-chah deh deh-boh-loo-SYOHN]
review, to repasar [rreh-pah-SAHR]
rheumatism el reumatismo
[ehl rreh-oo-mah-TEES-moh]
rice el arroz [ehl ah-RROHS]
ride, to montar [mohn-TAHR]
right now ahora mismo
[ah-OH-rah MEES-moh]
right of way sign la señal de preferencia
[lah seh-NYAHL deh preh-feh-REHN-syah]
riot el motín [ehl moh-TEEN]
roll el panecillo [ehl pah-neh-SEE-yoh]
roof el techo [ehl TEH-choh]
room el cuarto [ehl KWAHR-toh]

Rosh Hashanah el día de Año Nuevo
  Judío [ehl DEE-ah deh AH-nyoh
  NWEH-boh hoo-DEE-oh]

row la fila [lah FEE-lah]

rubella la rubéola [lah rroo-BEH-oh-lah]

rug la alfombra [lah ahl-FOHM-brah]

rule la regla [lah RREH-glah]

ruler (instrument) la regla
  [lah RREH-glah]

run, to correr [koh-RREHR]

runaway child el niño / la niña que huyó
  de casa [ehl NEE-nyoh / lah NEE-nyah
  keh oo-YOH deh KAH-sah]

S

sad triste [TREES-teh]

salad la ensalada [lah ehn-sah-LAH-dah]

salesperson el vendedor / la vendedora
  [ehl behn-deh-DOHR /
  lah behn-deh-DOH-rah]

salt la sal [lah sahl]

same mismo [MEES-moh]

sandbox el cajón de arena
  [ehl kah-HOHN deh ah-REH-nah]

sandwich el emparedado
  [ehl ehm-pah-reh-DAH-doh];
  el sándwich [ehl SAHND-weech]

Saturday el sábado [ehl SAH-bah-doh]

sausage la salchicha
  [lah sahl-CHEE-chah]

scarf la bufanda [lah boo-FAHN-dah]

scarlet fever la escarlatina
  [lah ehs-kahr-lah-TEE-nah]

schedule el horario [ehl oh-RAH-ryoh]

scholarship la beca [lah BEH-kah]

school la escuela [lah ehs-KWEH-lah]

school crossing el cruce escolar
  [ehl KROO-seh ehs-koh-LAHR]

school supplies los materiales para la
  clase [lohs mah-teh-RYAH-lehs PAH-rah
  lah KLAH-seh]

school year el año escolar
  [ehl AH-nyoh ehs-koh-LAHR]

science la ciencia [lah SYEHN-syah]

scissors (plastic) las tijeras (de plástico)
  [lahs tee-HEH-rahs (deh PLAHS-tee-koh)]

scratch (scrape) el arañazo
  [ehl ah-rah-NYAH-soh]

season (of the year) la estación
  [lah ehs-tah-SYOHN]

seat (theater) la butaca
  [lah boo-TAH-kah]

secretary el secretario / la secretaria
  [ehl seh-kreh-TAH-ryoh /
  lah seh-kreh-TAH-ryah]

security guard el/la guardia de seguridad
  [ehl/lah GWAHR-dyah deh
  seh-goo-ree-DAHD]

security personnel el personal de
  seguridad [ehl pehr-soh-NAHL deh
  seh-goo-ree-DAHD]

see, to ver (*irreg.*) [behr]

seesaw el subibaja [ehl soo-bee-BAH-hah]

seizure la convulsión
  [lah kohn-bool-SYOHN]

semester el semestre
  [ehl seh-MEHS-treh]

sensitive sensible [sehn-SEE-bleh]

sentence la oración [lah oh-rah-SYOHN]

September septiembre
  [sehp-TYEHM-breh]

serve, to servir (i) [sehr-BEER]

several varios [BAH-ryohs]

sexual harassment el acoso sexual
  [ehl ah-KOH-soh sehk-SWAHL]

sexual relations las relaciones sexuales
  [lahs rreh-lah-SYOH-nehs sehk-SWAH-lehs]

shake, to sacudir [sah-koo-DEER]

share, to compartir [kohm-pahr-TEER]

sheet of paper la hoja de papel
  [lah OH-hah deh pah-PEHL]

shelf el estante [ehl ehs-TAHN-teh]

shellfish el marisco [ehl mah-REES-koh]

shelter el refugio [ehl rreh-FOO-hyoh]

shirt la camisa [lah kah-MEE-sah]

shoemaker el zapatero / la zapatera
  [ehl sah-pah-TEH-roh /
  lah sah-pah-TEH-rah]

shooting el tiroteo [ehl tee-roh-TEH-oh]

short corto [KOHR-toh]

shorts los pantalones cortos
  [lohs pahn-tah-LOH-nehs KOHR-tohs]

shoulder el hombro [ehl OHM-broh]

shout, to gritar [gree-TAHR]

show, to demostrar (ue)
  [deh-mohs-TRAHR];
  mostrar (ue) [mohs-TRAHR]

sick enfermo [ehn-FEHR-moh]

sick, to get enfermarse
  [ehn-fehr-MAHR-seh]

sidewalk la acera [lah ah-SEH-rah]

sign (notice) el letrero [ehl leh-TREH-roh]

sign (road) la señal [lah seh-NYAHL]

sign, to firmar [feer-MAHR]

signal la señal [lah seh-NYAHL]

singer el/la cantante
  [ehl/lah kahn-TAHN-teh]

sink el lavamanos
  [ehl lah-bah-MAH-nohs]

siren la sirena [lah see-REH-nah]

sister la hermana [lah ehr-MAH-nah]

sister-in-law la cuñada
  [lah koo-NYAH-dah]

sit (down), to sentarse (ie)
  [sehn-TAHR-seh]

skates los patines [lohs pah-TEE-nehs]

skim milk la leche desnatada
  [lah LEH-cheh dehs-nah-TAH-dah]

skin la piel [lah pyehl]

skirt la falda [lah FAHL-dah]

skyscraper el rascacielos
  [ehl rrahs-kah-SYEH-lohs]

sled el trineo [ehl tree-NEH-oh]

sleep, to dormir (ue) [dohr-MEER]

sleepy, to be tener (*irreg.*) sueño
  [teh-NEHR SWEH-nyoh]

sleeve la manga [lah MAHN-gah]

slide el tobogán [ehl toh-boh-GAHN]

slowly despacio [dehs-PAH-syoh]

smoke el humo [ehl oo-moh]

smoke, to fumar [foo-MAHR]

smoke detector el detector de humo
  [ehl deh-tehk-TOHR deh oo-moh]

snack la merienda [lah meh-RYEHN-dah]

snake la culebra [lah koo-LEH-brah]

sneeze, to estornudar
  [ehs-tohr-noo-DAHR]

snow la nieve [lah NYEH-beh]

snow, to nevar (ie) [neh-BAHR]

snowstorm la nevada [lah neh-BAH-dah]

soap el jabón [ehl hah-BOHN]

social studies los estudios sociales
  [lohs ehs-TOO-dyohs soh-SYAH-lehs]

socks los calcetines
  [lohs kahl-seh-TEE-nehs]

soft drink el refresco
  [ehl rreh-FREHS-koh]

some alguno [ahl-GOO-noh]

somebody alguien [AHL-gyehn]

someone alguien [AHL-gyehn]

something algo [AHL-goh]

sometimes a veces [ah BEH-sehs]

son el hijo [ehl EE-hoh]

son-in-law el yerno [ehl YEHR-noh]

soon pronto [PROHN-toh]

sore throat el dolor de garganta
  [ehl doh-LOHR deh gahr-GAHN-tah]

so-so regular [rreh-goo-LAHR]

sound el sonido [ehl soh-NEE-doh]

soup la sopa [lah SOH-pah]

spaghetti los espaguetis
  [lohs ehs-pah-GEH-tees]

speaking problems los trastornos
  del habla y el lenguaje
  [lohs trahs-TOHR-nohs dehl AH-blah
  ee ehl lehn-GWAH-heh]

spell, to deletrear [deh-leh-treh-AHR]

spelling la ortografía
  [lah ohr-toh-grah-FEE-ah];
  el deletreo [ehl deh-leh-TREH-oh]

spelling book el abecedario
  [ehl ah-beh-seh-DAH-ryoh]

spina bifida la espina bífida
  [lah ehs-PEE-nah BEE-fee-dah]

spinach la espinaca
  [lah ehs-pee-NAH-kah]

spit, to escupir [ehs-koo-PEER]

sponge la esponja [lah ehs-POHN-hah]

sport el deporte [ehl deh-POHR-teh]

sprain la torcedura
  [lah tohr-seh-DOO-rah]

spring (season) la primavera
  [lah pree-mah-BEH-rah]

square (city) la plaza [lah PLAH-sah]

staff room la sala de maestros
  [lah SAH-lah deh mah-EHS-trohs]

stage el escenario [ehl eh-seh-NAH-ryoh]

staircase la escalera
  [lah ehs-kah-LEH-rah]

stamp el sello [ehl SEH-yoh]

standardized test la prueba uniforme
  [lah PRWEH-bah oo-nee-FOHR-meh]

staple la grapa [lah GRAH-pah]

staple, to sujetar con grapas
  [soo-heh-TAHR kohn GRAH-pahs]

stapler la grapadora
  [lah grah-pah-DOH-rah]

starting from _____ on a partir de
  [ah pahr-TEER deh]

station la estación [lah ehs-tah-SYOHN]

statue la estatua [lah ehs-TAH-twah]

stay in bed, to guardar cama
  [gwahr-DAHR KAH-mah]

stepbrother el hermanastro
  [ehl ehr-mah-NAHS-troh]

stepdaughter la hijastra
  [lah ee-HAHS-trah]

stepfather el padrastro
[ehl pah-DRAHS-troh]

stepmother la madrastra
[lah mah-DRAHS-trah]

stepsister la hermanastra
[lah ehr-mah-NAHS-trah]

stepson el hijastro [ehl ee-HAHS-troh]

sting la mordedura
[lah mohr-deh-DOO-rah]

stitch el punto [ehl POON-toh]

stockings (hose) las medias
[lahs MEH-dyahs]

stomach el estómago
[ehl ehs-TOH-mah-goh]

stomachache el dolor de estómago
[ehl doh-LOHR deh ehs-TOH-mah-goh]

stop la parada [lah pah-RAH-dah]

stop sign la señal de parar
[lah seh-NYAHL deh pah-RAHR]

store window la vitrina
[lah bee-TREE-nah]

story el cuento [ehl KWEHN-toh]

straight derecho [deh-REH-choh]

stranger desconocido
[dehs-koh-noh-SEE-doh]

strawberry la fresa [lah FREH-sah]

street la calle [lah KAH-yeh]

streetlight el farol [ehl fah-ROHL]

strike la huelga [lah WEHL-gah]

strong fuerte [FWEHR-teh]

student el/la estudiante
[ehl/lah ehs-too-DYAHN-teh];
el alumno / la alumna
[ehl ah-LOOM-noh / lah ah-LOOM-nah]

studious aplicado [ah-plee-KAH-doh];
estudioso [ehs-too-DYOH-soh]

study, to estudiar [ehs-too-DYAHR]

stuffed animal el animal de peluche
[ehl ah-nee-MAHL deh peh-LOO-cheh]

style, to be in estar (*irreg.*) de moda
[ehs-TAHR deh MOH-dah]

style, to be out of estar (*irreg.*) pasado
de moda
[ehs-TAHR pah-SAH-doh deh MOH-dah]

subject (school) la asignatura
[lah ah-seeg-nah-TOO-rah];
la materia [lah mah-TEH-ryah]

subscription la suscripción
[lah soos-kreep-SYOHN]

subway station la estación de metro
[lah ehs-tah-SYOHN deh MEH-troh]

success el éxito [ehl EHK-see-toh]

successful, to be tener (*irreg.*) éxito
[teh-NEHR EHK-see-toh]

suicide el suicidio [ehl swee-SEE-dyoh]

suit el traje [ehl TRAH-heh]

summary el resumen
[ehl rreh-SOO-mehn]

summer el verano [ehl beh-RAH-noh]

sun el sol [ehl sohl]

Sunday el domingo
[ehl doh-MEEN-goh]

sunny soleado [soh-leh-AH-doh]

superintendent el/la superintendente
[ehl/lah soo-pehr-een-tehn-DEHN-teh]

supervisor el supervisor / la supervisora
[ehl soo-pehr-bee-SOHR /
lah soo-pehr-bee-SOH-rah]

surgeon el cirujano / la cirujana
[ehl see-roo-HAH-noh /
lah see-roo-HAH-nah]

surprised sorprendido
[sohr-prehn-DEE-doh]

suspenders los tirantes
[lohs tee-RAHN-tehs]

swallow, to tragar [trah-GAHR]

sweater el suéter [ehl SWEH-tehr]

sweatshirt la sudadera
[lah soo-dah-DEH-rah]

sweep, to barrer [bah-RREHR]

swimming pool la piscina
[lah pee-SEE-nah]

swing el columpio [ehl koh-LOOM-pyoh]

swollen hinchado [een-CHAH-doh]

T

table la mesa [lah MEH-sah]

table game el juego de mesa
[ehl HWEH-goh deh MEH-sah]

tablet (lozenge) la pastilla
[lah pahs-TEE-yah]

take care of yourself, to cuidarse
[kwee-DAHR-seh]

take notes, to hacer (*irreg.*) apuntes
[ah-SEHR ah-POON-tehs]

take off, to quitarse [kee-TAHR-seh]

take (one's) blood pressure, to tomarle
la presión arterial [toh-MAHR-leh
lah preh-SYOHN ahr-teh-RYAHL]

take (one's) pulse, to tomarle el pulso
[toh-MAHR-leh ehl POOL-soh]

take (one's) temperature, to tomarle
la temperatura [toh-MAHR-leh
lah tehm-peh-rah-TOO-rah]

take pictures, to   sacar fotos
   [sah-KAHR FOH-tohs]

tea   el té   [ehl teh]

teacher   el maestro / la maestra
   [ehl mah-EHS-troh / lah mah-EHS-trah]

teacher's aide   el/la asistente de
   maestro / de maestra
   [ehl/lah ah-sees-TEHN-teh deh
   mah-EHS-troh / deh mah-EHS-trah]

tee shirt   la camiseta
   [lah kah-mee-SEH-tah]

telephone   el teléfono
   [ehl teh-LEH-foh-noh]

tell, to   contar (ue)   [kohn-TAHR];
   decir (*irreg.*)   [deh-SEER]

tell stories, to   contar (ue) cuentos
   [kohn-TAHR KWEHN-tohs]

tense   tenso   [TEHN-soh]

test   la prueba   [lah PRWEH-bah];
   el examen   [ehl ehk-SAH-mehn]

tetanus   el tétano   [ehl TEH-tah-noh]

Thanksgiving   el día de Acción de Gracias
   [ehl DEE-ah deh ahk-SYOHN deh
   GRAH-syahs]

that   aquel/aquella   [ah-KEHL/ah-KEH-yah];
   ese/esa   [EH-seh/EH-sah]

the   el/la   [ehl/lah]

theft   el robo   [ehl RROH-boh]

their   su   [soo]

theme   el tema   [ehl TEH-mah]

then   entonces   [ehn-TOHN-sehs]

therapist   el/la terapista
   [ehl/lah teh-rah-PEES-tah]

there   allí   [ah-YEE]

there is / there are   hay   [AH-ee]

thermometer   el termómetro
   [ehl tehr-MOH-meh-troh]

these   estos/estas   [EHS-tohs/EHS-tahs]

thigh   el muslo   [ehl MOOS-loh]

think, to   pensar (ie)   [pehn-SAHR]

thirsty, to be   tener (*irreg.*) sed
   [teh-NEHR sehd]

this   este/esta   [EHS-teh/EHS-tah]

those   aquellos/aquellas
   [ah-KEH-yohs/ah-KEH-yahs];
   esos/esas   [EH-sohs/EH-sahs]

threat   la amenaza
   [lah ah-meh-NAH-sah]

throat   la garganta   [lah gahr-GAHN-tah]

throw, to   lanzar   [lahn-SAHR];
   tirar   [tee-RAHR]

throw away, to   botar   [boh-TAHR];
   tirar   [tee-RAHR]

thunder   el trueno   [ehl TRWEH-noh]

thunderstorm   la tormenta
   [lah tohr-MEHN-tah]

Thursday   el jueves   [ehl HWEH-behs]

tie   la corbata   [lah kohr-BAH-tah]

tie, to   amarrar   [ah-mah-RRAHR]

tie one's shoes, to   abrocharse los
   zapatos
   [ah-broh-CHAHR-seh lohs sah-PAH-tohs]

tights   los leotardos
   [lohs leh-oh-TAHR-dohs]

time   el tiempo   [ehl TYEHM-poh]

time (clock)   la hora   [lah OH-rah]

time, on   a tiempo   [ah TYEHM-poh]

tired   cansado   [kahn-SAH-doh]

title   el título   [ehl TEE-too-loh]

toast   el pan tostado
   [ehl pahn tohs-TAH-doh]

today   hoy   [OH-ee]

toe   el dedo del pie
   [ehl DEH-doh dehl pyeh]

together, to get   juntarse   [hoon-TAHR-seh]

toilet   el servicio   [ehl sehr-BEE-syoh]

toilet paper   el papel higiénico
   [ehl pah-PEHL ee-HYEH-nee-koh]

tomato   el tomate   [ehl toh-MAH-teh]

tomorrow   mañana   [mah-NYAH-nah]

tomorrow afternoon   mañana por la
   tarde
   [mah-NYAH-nah pohr lah TAHR-deh]

tomorrow morning   mañana por la
   mañana
   [mah-NYAH-nah pohr lah mah-NYAH-nah]

tomorrow night   mañana por la noche
   [mah-NYAH-nah pohr lah NOH-cheh]

tongue   la lengua   [lah LEHN-gwah]

tonight   esta noche   [EHS-tah NOH-cheh]

too (much)   demasiado
   [deh-mah-SYAH-doh]

tooth   el diente   [ehl DYEHN-teh]

toothache   el dolor de muelas
   [ehl doh-LOHR deh MWEH-lahs]

top (spinning)   el trompo
   [ehl TROHM-poh]

tornado   el tornado   [ehl tohr-NAH-doh]

toward   hacia   [AH-syah]

towel   la toalla   [lah toh-AH-yah]

town   el pueblo   [ehl PWEH-bloh]

toy   el juguete   [ehl hoo-GEH-teh]

traffic el tránsito [ehl TRAHN-see-toh]

traffic accident el accidente de tráfico
[ehl ahk-see-DEHN-teh deh TRAH-fee-koh]

traffic light el semáforo
[ehl seh-MAH-foh-roh]

train el tren [ehl trehn]

trainer el entrenador / la entrenadora
[ehl ehn-treh-nah-DOHR /
lah ehn-treh-nah-DOH-rah]

training el entrenamiento
[ehl ehn-treh-nah-MYEHN-toh]

transcript la relación de notas
[lah rreh-lah-SYOHN deh NOH-tahs]

transfer la transferencia
[lah trahns-feh-REHN-syah]

transfer, to trasladar(se)
[trahs-lah-dahr(seh)]

translate, to traducir (*irreg.*)
[trah-doo-SEER]

translator el traductor / la traductora
[ehl trah-dook-TOHR /
lah trah-dook-TOH-rah]

transportation el transporte
[ehl trahns-POHR-teh]

trash can el cubo de basura
[ehl KOO-boh deh bah-SOO-rah];
el basurero [ehl bah-soo-REH-roh]

tricycle el triciclo [ehl tree-SEE-kloh]

truck el camión [ehl kah-MYOHN]

true la verdad [lah behr-DAHD]

try on, to probarse (ue) [proh-BAHR-seh]

tsunami el maremoto
[ehl mah-reh-MOH-toh]

tuberculosis la tuberculosis
[lah too-behr-koo-LOH-sees]

Tuesday el martes [ehl MAHR-tehs]

tunnel el túnel [ehl TOO-nehl]

turn in, to entregar [ehn-treh-GAHR]

twice dos veces [dohs BEH-sehs]

twisted torcido [tohr-SEE-doh]

two-way street la calle de doble sentido
[lah KAH-yeh deh DOH-bleh sehn-TEE-doh]

U

ugly feo [FEH-oh]

uncle el tío [ehl TEE-oh]

uncomfortable incómodo
[een-KOH-moh-doh]

under debajo (de) [deh-BAH-hoh (deh)]

understand, to comprender
[kohm-prehn-DEHR];
entender (ie) [ehn-tehn-DEHR]

undress, to desvestirse (i)
[dehs-behs-TEER-seh]

unemployment el desempleo
[ehl deh-sehm-PLEH-oh]

unhappy descontento
[dehs-kohn-TEHN-toh];
infeliz [een-feh-LEES]

uniform el uniforme
[ehl oo-nee-FOHR-meh]

until hasta [AHS-tah]

unwanted no deseado
[noh deh-seh-AH-doh]

upstairs arriba [ah-RREE-bah]

urinal el orinal [ehl oh-ree-NAHL]

V

vacation las vacaciones
[lahs bah-kah-SYOH-nehs]

vaccinated, to get vacunarse
[bah-koo-NAHR-seh]

vaccination la vacuna [lah bah-KOO-nah]

Valentine's Day el día de los
Enamorados [ehl DEE-ah deh lohs
eh-nah-moh-RAH-dohs]

vandalism el vandalismo
[ehl bahn-dah-LEES-moh]

vegetables los vegetales
[lohs beh-heh-TAH-lehs]

venereal disease la enfermedad venérea
[lah ehn-fehr-meh-DAHD beh-NEH-reh-ah]

violence la violencia
[lah byoh-LEHN-syah]

violent violento [byoh-LEHN-toh]

violet morado [moh-RAH-doh]

visual impediments los impedimentos
visuales [lohs eem-peh-dee-MEHN-tohs
bee-SWAH-lehs]

vitamin la vitamina
[lah bee-tah-MEE-nah]

voice la voz [lah bohs]

volume (book) el tomo [ehl TOH-moh]

volunteer el voluntario / la voluntaria
[ehl boh-loon-TAH-ryoh /
lah boh-loon-TAH-ryah]

vomit, to vomitar [boh-mee-TAHR]

W

waist la cintura [lah seen-TOO-rah]

wait for, to esperar [ehs-peh-RAHR]

wake up, to despertarse (ie)
[dehs-pehr-TAHR-seh]

walk, to caminar [kah-mee-NAHR]

wall la pared [lah pah-REHD]
wallet la billetera [lah bee-yeh-TEH-rah];
  la cartera [lah kahr-TEH-rah]
want, to querer (ie) (*irreg.*) [keh-REHR]
warning la advertencia
  [lah ahd-behr-TEHN-syah]
wash, to lavar [lah-BAHR]
wash (a part of one's body), to lavarse
  (+ *part of body*) [lah-BAHR-seh]
wash up, to lavarse [lah-BAHR-seh]
wastepaper basket la papelera
  [lah pah-peh-LEH-rah]
watch, to mirar [mee-RAHR]
water el agua [ehl AH-gwah]
water fountain la fuente de agua potable
  [lah FWEHN-teh deh AH-gwah
  poh-TAH-bleh]
watermelon la sandía [lah sahn-DEE-ah]
weak débil [DEH-beel]
wear, to llevar [yeh-BAHR]
weather el tiempo [ehl TYEHM-poh]
weather forecast el pronóstico del
  tiempo
  [ehl proh-NOHS-tee-koh dehl TYEHM-poh]
Wednesday el miércoles
  [ehl MYEHR-koh-lehs]
week la semana [lah seh-MAH-nah]
weight el peso [ehl PEH-soh]
welfare la asistencia social
  [lah ah-sees-TEHN-syah soh-SYAHL]
well bien [byehn]
what qué [keh]
wheelchair la silla de ruedas
  [lah SEE-yah deh RRWEH-dahs]
when cuándo [KWAHN-doh]
where dónde [DOHN-deh]
where (to) adónde [ah-DOHN-deh]
which cuál [kwahl]
white blanco [BLAHN-koh]
who quién/quiénes [kyehn/KYEH-nehs]
whooping cough la tos ferina
  [lah tohs feh-REE-nah]
whose de quién / de quiénes
  [deh kyehn / deh KYEH-nehs]
why por qué [pohr keh]

wife la esposa [lah ehs-POH-sah]
wind el viento [ehl BYEHN-toh]
window la ventana [lah behn-TAH-nah]
window shade/blind la persiana
  [lah pehr-SYAH-nah]
winter el invierno [ehl een-BYEHR-noh]
wish, to desear [deh-seh-AHR]
with me conmigo [kohn-MEE-goh]
with what con qué [kohn keh]
with whom con quién / con quiénes
  [kohn kyehn / kohn KYEH-nehs]
with you (*familiar*) contigo
  [kohn-TEE-goh]
woman la mujer [lah moo-HEHR]
wool la lana [lah LAH-nah]
word la palabra [lah pah-LAH-brah]
work el trabajo [ehl trah-BAH-hoh]
worried preocupado
  [preh-oh-koo-PAH-doh]
worry, to preocuparse
  [preh-oh-koo-PAHR-seh]
worse peor [peh-OHR]
wound (cut) la herida [lah eh-REE-dah]
wound, to herir (ie) [eh-REER]
write, to escribir [ehs-kree-BEER]
write in longhand, to escribir a mano
  [ehs-kree-BEER ah MAH-noh];
  escribir en cursiva
  [ehs-kree-BEER ehn koor-SEE-bah]
writer el escritor / la escritora
  [ehl ehs-kree-TOHR /
  lah ehs-kree-TOH-rah]

Y

year el año [ehl AH-nyoh]
yell, to gritar [gree-TAHR]
yellow amarillo [ah-mah-REE-yoh]
yesterday ayer [ah-YEHR]
yesterday afternoon ayer por la tarde
  [ah-YEHR pohr lah TAHR-deh]
yesterday morning ayer por la mañana
  [ah-YEHR pohr lah mah-NYAH-nah]
yogurt el yogurt [ehl yoh-GOOR]
your (*familiar*) tu [too]
your (*formal*) su [soo]